The Plot to Kill God

The Plot to Kill God

Findings from the Soviet Experiment in Secularization

Paul Froese

UNIVERSITY OF CALIFORNIA PRESS
Berkeley · Los Angeles · London

University of California Press, one of the most
distinguished university presses in the United States,
enriches lives around the world by advancing scholarship in the humanities, social sciences, and natural
sciences. Its activities are supported by the UC Press
Foundation and by philanthropic contributions from
individuals and institutions. For more information, visit
www.ucpress.edu.

University of California Press
Berkeley and Los Angeles, California

University of California Press, Ltd.
London, England

Library of Congress Cataloging-in-Publication Data

Froese, Paul.
   The plot to kill God : findings from the Soviet experi-
ment in secularization / Paul Froese.
       p.   cm.
   Includes bibliographical references and index.
   ISBN: 978-0-520-25528-9 (cloth : alk. paper)
   ISBN: 978-0-520-25529-6 (pbk. : alk. paper)
   1. Secularization — Soviet Union.   2. Church and
state — Soviet Union.   3. Communism and religion —
Soviet Union.   I. Title.

BR936.F76   2008
211'.809470904 — dc22   2007052238

Manufactured in the United States of America

17   16   15   14   13   12   11   10   09   08
10   9   8   7   6   5   4   3   2   1

The paper used in this publication meets the minimum
requirements of ANSI/NISO Z39.48−1992 (R 1997)
(Permanence of Paper).

For Jana

Contents

Illustrations

Tables

Acknowledgments

As social scientists often demonstrate, we are largely the product of our environment. With that in mind, it saddens and humbles me that so many must traverse their lives without a fraction of the assistance and nurturing I have received.

I am grateful for my many teachers and colleagues who have knowingly and sometimes unwittingly encouraged me through the years. Daniel Chirot and Rodney Stark, my main advisors, have my sincerest thanks for their boundless wisdom and humanity. I am also deeply indebted to my good friends Steven Pfaff and Edward Blum, who have helped me immensely in the writing of this manuscript. In addition, I greatly value the continuing support and inspiration of my academic comrades Christopher Bader, Carson Mencken, Laurence Iannaccone, Roger Finke, Anthony Gill, Chuck North, Margarita Mooney, and Byron Johnson. I also thank my many superb professors, who include John Mohan, Edgar Kiser, Paul Burstein, and Julius Sensat. Finally, I want to express my appreciation to Reed Malcolm, Kalicia Pivirotto, Suzanne Knott, and Steven Hanson for their assistance in this project.

My loving parents, Margaret and Menno (a fellow sociologist) Froese, fostered my interest in intellectual life, and they have my deepest gratitude and love. Also, I am blessed by my in-laws, Danie and Jack Carr, who have shown me nothing but love and support since our first meeting.

And to Jana, thanks for putting up with the drama and drudgery it took to get this book finished. You are my best friend and my most reliable critic.

I end with a shout out to Milo and Sasha.

Introduction

The Great Secularization Experiment

I would reverse Voltaire's remark, and say that if God
really exists, it will be necessary to get rid of Him.

— Mikhail Bakunin

It is easier to invoke God than to get rid of him. This is one simple yet important conclusion that we can draw from the prolonged and often vicious experiment to eradicate religion from Soviet society. Communist leaders in the Soviet Union attempted something never considered by earlier rulers, be they emancipators or tyrants. For the first time in history, rulers of a modern state hoped to expunge not only the existence of religious institutions but also daily expressions of spirituality and, most dauntingly, belief in a supernatural realm. Religion has often been used by political rulers to justify their self-interests or to validate the status quo. Religion has also been used by social activists to motivate protest movements and inspire passions for social change. Throughout history, social and civic leaders have often, and many times quite successfully, attempted to show that God was on their side; in other words, politicians naturally tended to use preestablished religious traditions to bolster their political legitimacy. But never before had political authorities attempted to justify their rule and motivate their citizens through an appeal to atheism. The results of this massive Soviet "Secularization Experiment" demonstrated that although the idea of God often provides political legitimation, earthly powers can do little to unseat the idea of an otherworldly sovereign, and, in future, they may be best advised to seek God's allegiance rather than challenge his authority.

This is not to say that atheism is a false philosophy or that some individuals do not rationally come to the conclusion that all religion is myth.

In fact, even in the religiously fervent United States there is a recent spate of best-selling books that glorify the value of atheism while decrying the hypocrisy and detriment of religious belief.[1] But the best available international data on religion reveals that atheism is quite rare in even the most modern societies and that religious faith is currently thriving in countless different forms.[2] In other words, the idea of the supernatural and, more specifically, the idea of God is a fundamental cultural element common to all modern societies, so common as to make it a core belief from which a multitude of radically divergent worldviews spring.

The Soviet Secularization Experiment sought to undermine this basic fact with an emerging plot to kill God. In doing so, Marxist-Leninists were forced to consider deep philosophical questions concerning human nature, the necessity of religious faith to the human condition, and the social sources of religiosity. Their dynamic experiment in secularization provides us with central insights into the universality of belief in the supernatural and how religion and politics, even in conflict, closely inform one another. Although Communist rulers correctly realized that the demand for religious comfort is certainly elastic, the religious urge is elastic only to a point. And that point is crossed when one attacks the very idea of God. This book tells the epic story of secularization in the Soviet Union and uncovers key sociological findings from this unique endeavor to systematically alter the human spirit.

A QUESTION OF FAITH

In 1938, two very different men sat in prison cells, in different regions of the Soviet Union, for different reasons. One was the high-ranking Communist official Nikolai Bukharin, who was charged with undermining the society he dedicated his life to create. The other was a devout Christian, one of thousands of forgotten Soviet citizens imprisoned for the ideological crime of religious belief. Each contemplated his commitment to the faith that had guided his life.

"Can God possibly exist?" thought the nameless religious prisoner as he was taunted by his prison mate, a man who laughed at the idea of God within the walls of their earthly hell.[3] And Bukharin, sentenced to death, asked himself, "If you must die, what are you dying for?" He wrote that he felt an "absolute black vacuity" in which "there was nothing to die for."[4] His commitment to the cause of the Russian Revolution and his hopes for an earthly utopia were weakened, perhaps beyond repair. Similarly, the convicted religious believer admitted his troubling doubts to his indifferent companion. The Communist and the Christian were both momentarily robbed of their faith through circumstance and castigation.

How do you weaken a person's faith? The religious prisoner faced a harsh confinement in which God's grace and attention appeared lost, and the career Communist realized that he had been deceived and abandoned by his comrades. Whereas their dire circumstances explain their creeping doubts, many people throughout history have suffered dishonor and even death for their faiths. In fact, both Bukharin and the religious prisoner eventually overcame their misgivings to reassert their former convictions with greater devotion. Bukharin wrote that his life had not been wasted in pursuit of the Communist ideal, and the religious prisoner again felt a divine presence in the midst of his lonely cell. Their stories indicate that faith, while often in peril, can be difficult to fully dislodge.

Marxist-Leninists grappled with the malleability of the human spirit as they actively sought to dispel widespread belief in the supernatural and replace it with an antireligious ideology. The utopian goals of the Soviet project required nothing less than instilling a new faith among the citizenry. Although Soviet religious policies would change dramatically over the years due to shifts in leadership and reactions to current events, a basic assumption concerning the plasticity of the human spirit guided the Soviet regime's persisting conviction that religion was an unnecessary and even detrimental aspect of society. With the proper incentives and instruction, be they persuasive or coercive, Soviet leaders for most of the Soviet era firmly believed that religious faith could be purged from the human psyche. An American psychologist studying the policies of the Soviet regime in the 1950s aptly summarized the Soviet project as premised on "a belief that Communist morality can be instilled more or less universally. [Communist leaders] bolster this belief with the assumption that there are no important internal forces for personal development that they need to worry about or respect, hence relieving themselves of any limitations on the extent to which transformation can occur."[5]

In other words, Marxist-Leninists, quite naturally, had an extensively socialized vision of human nature. This initially led them to expect that the secularization of society would be an easy task; as their economic and social policies took root, early Bolsheviks imagined that religion would simply evaporate in response to the demise of the old political and economic system. In this, they were badly mistaken, and as religious belief and activity persisted, Communist leaders began a lengthy and tortuous battle against religion to uncover the hidden sources of enduring faith.

EXPERIMENTAL PHASES

In the beginning, the problem of religion was certainly secondary to the Bolsheviks, who first had to contend with the political authority and strength of their opponents both within the czarist regime and among other radical political movements. In fact, Bolsheviks initially played with the idea of recruiting revolutionaries through religious channels. The ideals of the renovationist movement within the Russian Orthodox Church initially appeared compatible with the goals of the burgeoning Communist Party; renovationists were seeking to revitalize the church and expressed more progressive views concerning both religious and political change. After the 1917 Revolution, Leon Trotsky, the first of many Soviet officials to oversee religious matters, viewed the renovationist movement as an indication that the "proletarian revolution had finally reached the Church."[6] But to the chagrin of the Bolshevik elite, the renovationist movement failed to gain widespread support from Orthodox parishioners, who felt that the movement inappropriately questioned many of the sacred traditions and rituals of the church.[7] As the Communist movement collapsed within the Orthodox Church, early Bolsheviks settled into a position of growing antagonism toward religion in general.

Even while Lenin continued to toy with the idea of using religious radicals to bolster the Bolsheviks' weak grasp on power, he wrote a telegram on April 2, 1919, to a prominent cardinal, explaining the current antireligious position of the Communist Party: "The aim of the Party is finally to destroy the ties between the exploiting classes and the organization of religious propaganda, at the same time helping the toiling masses actually to liberate their minds from religious superstitions, and organizing on a wide scale scientific-educational and antireligious propaganda."[8]

Lenin is quite clear that his new government will not be sympathetic to religious concerns. But Lenin's stated position can also be read more specifically as an attack on the cultural dominance of the Russian Orthodox Church. Many religious minorities, such as small Protestants sects and non-Christian groups, believed the new Soviet leaders would emancipate them from the religious tyranny of the Russian Orthodox Church and celebrated the prospect of gaining equal status under the Communist regime. And by 1923, the Communist Party solidified its antagonistic stance toward the Russian Orthodox Church, officially stating, "The Church is dead . . . for the vanguard of the world proletariat there can be no neutrality or indifference in the question of religion. The brain and hearts of the working class are here at stake; the struggle must be waged, of course, by modern methods, by methods of exhortation, by opposing the results of scientific research to the phantasmagoria of superstition. But this fight must go on — on to the ultimate victory."[9]

Although the Orthodox Church ultimately suffered the brunt of religious regulation in the early years of Soviet rule, it soon became clear that the antireligious mission of the new Soviet empire would not be limited to attacking the Russian Church. In addition to seizing Orthodox Church resources, arresting church leaders, and destroying church buildings, the Soviet government began to view all religious organizations as potential threats to the new Soviet order.

Still, the religious restrictions and regulations of the early 1920s were mild by comparison to what was to come during the Stalinist purges of the 1930s. Nevertheless, Russian Orthodox patriarch Tikhon, who had officially denounced the Bolsheviks in 1918, declared loyalty to the Soviet regime in 1923 to retain his position of leadership within the church.[10] The early 1920s also marked the beginning of a campaign to lure individuals away from religious organizations by atheist conversion. Through educational programs, propaganda campaigns, and the creation of atheist ceremonies and rituals, Soviet officials hoped to demonstrate clearly the falsity and vacuity of religious belief so that citizens would logically come to the conclusion, with appropriate prodding, that they were better off without religion in their lives.

An Atheist Alternative Emerges

Probably the most fascinating aspect of the great Secularization Experiment was the unprecedented creation of an atheist alternative to religion. The 1917 Revolution did not immediately wash away religious faith, leading Soviet elites to realize that their naive assumptions concerning the frailty of religion needed reconsideration. By the late 1920s, the Soviet regime established the Standing Commission on Religious Questions to study and oversee religious activities, the League of Militant Atheists to spread the message that religion was scientifically falsifiable, and a number of atheist universities to educate a new generation of antireligious intellectuals. In hopes of undermining religion, the Soviet regime made itself into a kind of antichurch, with atheist schools and meetinghouses, antireligious proselytizers, and a clearly defined atheist moral worldview called "scientific atheism."

The League of Militant Atheist was the organization that most closely mimicked the activities of a religious organization. The league functioned from 1925 to 1941 and represented a shift in Communist Party power and thought concerning religion.[11] Leon Trotsky was replaced as head of religious matters by Emelian Yaroslavsky, an aide to Josef Stalin. Yaroslavsky viewed religion as a cultural phenomenon and promoted the idea that secularization could only occur once religious cultural expressions were abandoned.[12] Initially, this was to be accomplished through reeducation. Yaroslavsky's League of Militant Atheists hoped to bring antireligious education to the masses through propaganda campaigns, which began to resemble religious crusades. For instance, the league set up meetinghouses to replace local parishes and established league memberships as an alternative to religious affiliation. Atheist propagandists would preach antireligious sermons and try to persuade attendees to spread the atheist message to their friends, neighbors, and coworkers.

The creation of the League of Militant Atheists indicated that Communist Party elites in the 1920s and 1930s did not view secularization as the absence of religious commitment but instead as the conversion of the population to a new faith: scientific atheism. In tandem with these quasi-proselytizing efforts, Marxist-Leninists began to create secular ceremonies and rituals to replace religious ones. Again, these ceremonies indicate a movement to replace religion with something new.

After the 1917 Revolution, some celebrations naturally evolved to mark the creation of a new society. But under Josef Stalin, a vast and intricate ceremonial system began to take shape that would continue to grow through the entire Soviet era.[13] Stalin, and later Khrushchev, oversaw the creation of Soviet alternatives to baptisms, confirmations, religious marriages, funerals, and many other religious life cycle rituals and celebrations. Although secular alternatives to religious marriage ceremonies, for example, have always existed because nonreligious people want to marry for reasons other than affirming a covenant with God, religious rituals that have no clear secular purpose tend to be abandoned by the nonreligious. Nonetheless, Communist Party elites established atheist alternatives to religious ceremonies with no clear secular meaning, such as ritual baptisms and religious confirmations.

Baptisms, for instance, tend to serve as religious blessings; there is no alternative reason for nonreligious families to participate in this activity. In a sample text from a Soviet baptism, parents and members of the gathering first pledge to raise the child in the proper moral (meaning antireligious) environment. Then a Soviet official recites a series of invocations over the baby, such as the following:

Life becomes much brighter and more beautiful
Much quicker is its wonderful course
Suddenly here in our Soviet family
A small person is born.
Today we are celebrating in honor of him to whom
Belongs the future, and we are saying to him
"Hail, new citizen of our great Soviet state."[14]

This Soviet, or "Red," baptism was intended to retain the solemnity and sentiment of a religious baptism while omitting references to God. And Soviet leaders fully expected that atheist alternatives to religious rituals would naturally fulfill any innate or culturally established desire for ritual celebrations and eventually make religious ritual expression obsolete. In essence, Soviet officials hoped to replace the spirit and symbol of God with that of the Soviet state.

Clearly, the Soviet mimicry of certain cultural aspects of religion is somewhat ironic and was often viewed by outsiders as a new kind of religion. But in the beginning stages of Soviet rule, officials felt that they were not creating a new religion but simply undermining the traditional religious culture of the past thousand years. The Secularization Experiment began as an attempt to prove to Soviet citizens through atheist rituals and antireligious propaganda that the idea of God was wholly unnecessary to living a happy and fulfilled life.

Forcing the Issue

In 1937, the Soviet regime administered a nationwide census containing a question on religion. Once the results had been tabulated, the Kremlin issued this statement in *Pionerskaya Pravda*: "In view of the fact that the All-Union census of the population of January 6, 1937 was carried out by the Central Administration of the National Economic Registry of the USSR Gosplan with gross violation of the elementary fundamentals of statistical science, and also in violation of government-approved instructions, the Council of People's Commissars of the USSR has recognized the organization of the census to be unsatisfactory and the very results of the census to be defective."[15] Behind the scenes, Soviet social scientists had discovered that data from the 1937 census indicated that religious belief and activity was still quite pervasive throughout the Soviet empire. This came as an unwelcome finding to Stalin and officials in charge of antireligious propaganda, who immediately attempted to discredit the census report and suppress the true results of the data.[16]

Beyond the 1937 census, there were other indicators that reeducation, atheist proselytizing, and Soviet rituals were making little progress in the ever-expanding campaign to secularize society. As Glennys Young puts it, religious persistence "helped to convince Stalin and his supporters of the need for a profound and violent restructuring of the cultural, economic, and political life of the Soviet countryside."[17] Under the iron fist of Stalin, the drive to pull citizens away from religion with atheist alternatives soon became a full-on push to force a resistant population finally to give up religion. Before the 1930s, many religious leaders and activists had been either imprisoned or executed, but this persecution had been relatively intermittent and haphazard. By the mid-1930s, the attack on religious figures became systematic and widespread.

The violence waged against religious leaders, activists, and followers during the 1930s cannot be overstated. Tens of thousands of clergy and religious adherents were sent into the horrific prison camp system of the Stalinist era, never to be heard from again.[18] The Gulag prison camp system is now infamous for its brutality, and the indescribable wretchedness of Gulag life is most notably evoked by Alexander Solzhenitsyn in *Gulag Archipelago*. One religious prisoner of the system later described some of his experience as follows:

> Camp regime has become so totalitarian, so hostile towards the idea of the individual, that in its practical application it is in the process of creating a new anthropological type. The main objects of the regime's hatred are God, the spirit, the word, and man's need to live in a cultural context. . . . Since it cannot actually rule over consciousness and yet thirsts for our souls, camp regime struggles to prevent any objective embodiment of thought, stretching forth its heavy hand to snatch up anything written, seeking by relentless confiscations to wean us away from the fundamentally human urge to put thoughts into words. . . . [I have become] only a pitiful little lump of flesh, tortured by hunger and cold.[19]

While tens of thousands of religious prisoners faced such a fate, thousands of clergy were officially executed for committing ideological crimes against the state. The year 1938 marked the height of these formal executions when, for instance, 192 priests were put to death in the southern Russian region of Ulyanovsk alone.[20] These brutal tactics sought to scare individuals out of their religious convictions, and by many measures it worked, as believers left their churches in droves and publicly denied their religious faiths.

This was especially true of the Russian Orthodox Church, which suffered enormous losses of adherents, clergy, and resources. By 1940, approximately 97 percent of the Russian Orthodox Churches that had been functioning in 1916 were closed.[21] But as the Russian Orthodox Church was collapsing, Communist Party elites realized that the Orthodox Church was only one aspect, albeit an important one, of the religious traditions and cultures of the Soviet people. People from different regions of the Soviet Union differed dramatically in their ethnic identities and religious histories. Russia, the Ukraine, Moldavia, Belarus, Georgia, and Armenia were all predominantly Christian Orthodox but had distinct ethnic identities (see map 1). In general, the Orthodox Church is divided into ethnic categories, and these divisions represent different church traditions.[22] The regions of Central Asia were overwhelmingly Muslim and economically undeveloped. They were incorporated fully into the Soviet Union in the 1920s. Both Sunni and Shiite groups were active across Central Asia, but the majority of the population was Sunni of the Hanafi school. During World War II, Estonia, Latvia, and Lithuania were absorbed into the Soviet Union. Lithuania was predominantly Roman Catholic and closely tied to the Roman Catholic tradition of Poland. Estonia and Latvia were religiously more diverse, with large populations of both Protestants and Roman Catholics. In constructing a new Communist culture, Stalin faced centuries of ethnic and religious divisions within the Soviet population.

As Communist Party leaders turned their attentions to non-Orthodox groups, they had to rethink their antireligious policies. In dealing with the Russian Orthodox Church, the Soviet regime attacked it head-on by arresting clergy and closing parishes. But Protestant sects and other religious minorities presented different problems because they could hide more easily and, in fact, were accustomed to persecution under the czarist regime. While violent Soviet repression continued to focus on the Orthodox Church, some covert religious minorities slipped through their fingers. And there is scattered evidence that some small religious sects actually grew under Soviet rule.

One of the most daunting issues in the ever-expanding secularization campaign was how to deal with the massive number of Muslims in Central Asia. When Soviet leaders gained control over Central Asia, they encountered millions of Muslims with deeply held religious-ethnic identities. Centuries of foreign invaders and Christian missionaries had taught Central Asian Muslims that religion was one of their defining and unifying characteristics as an embattled people. In 1922, early Bolshevik sympathizer and Tartar Communist leader Sultan-Galiev, who was later executed by the Stalinist regime, warned the Soviet leadership of the del-

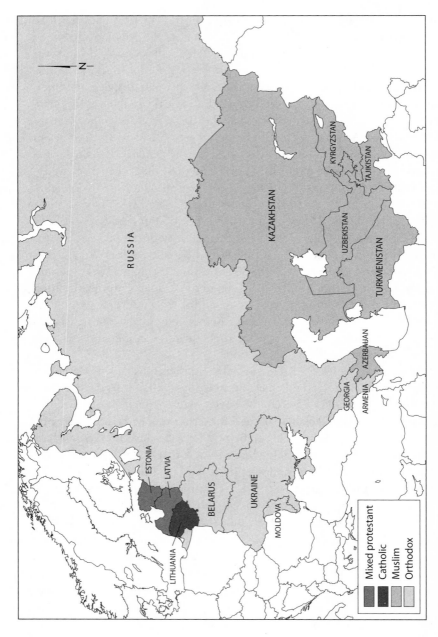

Map 1. Majority Religions by Soviet Republic. Source: compiled from Barrett, Kurian, and Johnson 1980.

icate nature of approaching the topic of atheism in Central Asia; he argued that "Islam is even today, in the eyes of the Moslem peoples, a religion which is oppressed and which must be defended. Hence the difficulty of antireligious propaganda among Moslems. . . . Speaking of obstacles to antireligious propaganda among the Moslems, we must also mention that these people are very backward. . . . As long as we do not break these chains of political backwardness, as long as we do not make these peoples truly free and equal citizens of the Soviet Republic, no antireligious propaganda can be successful."[23] This sensitive situation made it impossible to directly attack Islam with tactics similar to those used on the Russian Orthodox Church, although with time Stalin certainly subjected Central Asian Muslims to extreme acts of violence. Ultimately, the Soviet treatment of Muslims is one of the most convoluted and paradoxical stories of religious repression under Communism. A central problem for the Soviet leadership was that many Muslim Jadids in Central Asia supported the ethic of Communism as part of their religious worldview. For the most part, Muslims were accepting of the economic and political innovations of Soviet Communism yet resistant to relinquishing their traditional religious culture. In the end, the Soviet bureaucracy in Central Asia became entangled with Muslim culture, producing a Communist secular hierarchy based on the institutional structure of the Communist Party superimposed on preexisting Islamic tribal structures. The result was a bizarre blend of antireligious policy sporadically enforced by a local leadership of self-proclaimed Muslims.

In total, the 1930s were marked by massive and violent campaigns to force the religious issue into the past. This stage in the Secularization Experiment employed all the resources available to forcefully shut down religious institutions and activities. By the end of the 1930s, most Russian Orthodox churches, Roman Catholic parishes, Jewish synagogues, Protestant houses of worship, and Muslim institutions, such as Islamic courts and schools, were no longer in existence.

The Concordat

And then something unexpected happened. Stalin embraced the Orthodox Church or at least granted it some surprising concessions beginning in 1941. The church was declared an official part of Soviet culture, and in 1943, Stalin even agreed to meet with church leaders to discuss its future. There are many reasons historians give for this dramatic turn of events. Most obviously, World War II was sapping Soviet resources, and

Stalin could ill afford to continue his violent campaign against the church while invaders threatened the very stability of his empire. However, as Soviet historian Anna Dickinson notes, it is important to realize that "the meeting [between Stalin and the Orthodox hierarchy] was not an act of goodwill on Stalin's part, nor was it indicative of his essential religiosity as folklore has suggested; it was the calculated elimination of a potential enemy—or, at best, a source of uncontrolled and independent values—by the cooptation of apparently trustworthy elements of the church in order to control believers and eliminate counterrevolutionary threats from religious communities."[24]

The success of Stalin's plan to co-opt the church is difficult to calculate because the church concordant was short-lived, and by 1948, the Soviet regime again officially denounced the church. Nevertheless, this period of reprieve for the Russian Orthodox Church had two clear outcomes. First, the church took advantage of the opportunity by opening hundreds of new churches and attracting thousands of attendees. Second, collaboration with Soviet officials would become a topic of painful sensitivity for the Russian Orthodox Church in years to come.

A Return to the Basics

The death of Stalin in 1953 opened the door to many potential shifts in policy and ideology within the Soviet state. But from the beginning of his rule, Nikita Khrushchev was quite clear about his commitment to atheism and the antireligious propaganda of his predecessor. Khrushchev continued the policy of banning religious believers from Communist Party membership, arguing, "We are atheists. Certainly we use the name of God, as in 'God's truth.' But it is only a habit. . . . We are atheists, but we have a tolerant attitude toward all people. But if the acceptance of religion in intermingled with political activity that works against the Communist Party, that is different.[25] Although the extreme violence toward religious adherents during the 1930s had subsided, Khrushchev renewed the antireligious propaganda campaign with new vigor. In particular, Khrushchev greatly expanded the Soviet system of rituals and ceremonies by adding dozens of new holidays to the Soviet calendar and creating more life cycle rituals. Also, schools and universities amplified their antireligious curriculum.

By the 1950s, visitors to the Soviet Union commented on the clear lack of religiosity among Soviet youth. Perhaps decades of violence and reeducation had been successful. An American scholar traveling in the

Soviet Union in the late 1950s systematically questioned youth about their religious beliefs and found little to report; he explained that a typical answer to his inquiries was summarized by the reaction of a young man he met on the streets of Leningrad who asserted, "Religion is false. Communism is true. Of course, Communism satisfies me. What more do I need? What more is there? We have it all."[26] From the perspective of this young Leningrader, the Soviet alternative to religion was quite sufficient for his personal and existential needs.

Even though many Soviet youth appeared to have abandoned any interest in religious matters, stories of covert religious activities from imprisoned and embattled religious activists became common. Many religious proselytizers in the 1950s and 1960s saw themselves as secret agents infiltrating the Iron Curtain. In one example of Bible smuggling, an activist describes his ingenuity in alluding authorities when visiting Christians in prison:

> But as I entered the jail building again the chief passed by me and ordered the guard to search me all the way to my skin! He had gotten wind of something! Well, I went into the searching chamber with him and started to take off my clothes. All the while I was speculating about what I could do with the little Bible. So when the guard turned around for a second, I stuffed the Bible into his coat pocket! He went through all my stuff, looked into my mouth and my ears, then ordered me to get dressed again. Then the guard headed for the door. I nearly screamed, "Stop! My Bible!" But I contained myself and with two fingers snatched that thing out of his pocket and stuffed it into my own.[27]

The ongoing covert activities of this religious "spy" evoke the atmosphere of the cold war years, when interaction between the Soviet Union and the West increased but with heightened suspicion and active distain. And both sides had radically different perspectives about life behind the Iron Curtain. Stories of underground religious activists juxtaposed against the secular veneer of Soviet society produce two conflicting assessments of the success of the Soviet Secularization Experiment.[28] One depicts a society that has grown beyond the puerile concepts of God and salvation. The other describes a culture seething for spiritual nourishment but too afraid to openly express these urges.

The Great Unraveling

A Communist Party leader during the end of Khrushchev era cautioned the Soviet central committee: "You Communists have become as passive

as the Western Christians. Therefore despite all our persecutions the
Christians have found fertile ground in Russia for their evangelizing."[29]
This warning became reality during the coming Brezhnev era. In the
1970s, Soviet officials either became tired of persecuting religious adherents or simply became disillusioned with their own ideological commitments, as many scholars have argued.[30] As a result, religious activists
attempted to foster a religious revival on Soviet soil more boldly.

The ideological disillusionment of the Brezhnev era left the door open
for Gorbachev to implement the most radical policy changes in Soviet history, which would, in turn, lead to the eventual collapse of the Soviet system. In fact, the era of glasnost and perestroika is seen as an attempt
to reclaim the original ideals of the Russian Revolution by offering Soviet
citizens new freedoms; it produced the most relaxed and open policy
toward religion since the first days of Bolshevik rule but ironically
revealed the extent to which the population yearned for ideological and
religious alternatives to Marxist-Leninism.[31] Glasnost marked the end of
the Soviet Secularization Experiment and a recognition that it was no
longer defensible to deny individuals the right to think and worship freely.

THE ASSESSMENT

The history of the Soviet Union is in a constant state of reassessment.
Part of the difficulty in creating an accurate picture of Soviet society
occurs because Soviet life was premised on a series of deep internal paradoxes. The historian Alexei Yurchak has written a brilliant assessment of
these paradoxes in his book *Everything Was Forever, until It Was No
More,* in which he demonstrates how the final generation of Soviet citizens existed within a culture of dullness yet persistent optimism and how
Soviet institutions demanded full submission while also expecting cre-
ativity. These paradoxes make Soviet culture an enigma that is still in the
process of being unraveled and evaluated by historians, who continue to
delve into the endless files and archives of the Soviet system and produce
books with ever-greater detail.

My assessment of the Soviet Secularization Experiment is not a
detailed history of religion in the Soviet Union. Specifically, I do not provide previously undocumented descriptions of the actions of particular
religious and political leaders or closely chronicle the story of individual
religious groups. And a wealth of data exists from research and testimonials only available in the dozens of languages of the former Soviet
Union, to which I have no access. Therefore, readers are cautioned that

my sources are limited to the English-language testimonials, histories, and translated documents.[32] Overall, I am not attempting to rewrite an established history with new revelations that will surprise those already intimately knowledgeable of Soviet religious history.

Instead, I have culled many historical and quantitative data sources that explicitly address a set of important sociological questions. Scholarship on the Soviet era is growing as more official documents become accessible to the general public. This book is an attempt to take what historians and area specialists currently know about the Soviet Union and apply it to theoretical debates in the social scientific study of religion. Although these two areas of scholarship are immense, they are rarely linked, despite an obvious connection. Soviet policies directly tested widespread sociological assertions about religion and ideology on millions of people.

At the heart of my assessment of the Soviet Secularization Experiment is the question of belief. What determines the faith of individuals, and how do large-scale structural changes impact the ideologies and religious worldviews of a population? The Soviet experience tests some of the most basic social scientific expectations concerning ideological commitment and religious faith. The following summary of the next six chapters provides an overview of how the Secularization Experiment informs broad topics in the social scientific study of religion, ideology, and faith.

Hypotheses

Soviet elites toyed with many antireligious policies and techniques. They explored the possibility that secularization is a response to economic and political structural shifts. This is a core conviction in many contemporary theories of secularization. In fact, the ideas of Marxist-Leninists fit firmly within an ongoing movement within the sociology of religion which asserts that modern economies, technologies, and cultures naturally dispel public religiosity. Communist Party leaders also experimented with ideas and theories in contemporary sociology which hold that religious activity is a rational calculation in response to the perceived costs and benefits of individual decisions. And finally, Marxist-Leninists probed the cultural and existential sources of religious faith. In the end, the Soviet Secularization Experiment, by design or by chance, grappled with vastly divergent yet core theories in the contemporary sociological study of religion.

Chapter 1 explicates six basic sociological assertions concerning the sources of religion that were directly tested by various Soviet antireligious policies throughout the different periods of religious repression. In general, these assertions can be classified in two ways: religious persistence is mainly a product of cultural indoctrination or religious believers come to faith through a process of rational calculation. While these perspectives are not mutually exclusive, they tend to be pitted against one another in sociological research and lead to different predictions about how religious believers will respond to cultural and social change. The remaining chapters are dedicated to parsing out the theoretical import of the Soviet Union's great experiment in secularization.

What Is Marxist-Leninism?

Soviets consciously hoped to replace religious belief with atheism, which has led some scholars to call Marxist-Leninism a religion.[33] But the discussion concerning whether Soviet Communism was its own religion is really about the definition of religion. Clearly, Marx, Lenin, Stalin, and various antireligious propagandists of the Soviet era saw themselves as nonreligious and were, in fact, ardently atheistic. Their disgust for religion motivated the massive campaign to replace it during the Soviet era. That Soviet Communism is often heralded as a religion is extremely ironic.

   Chapter 2 explicates the characteristics of Soviet Communism that have led so many to think of it as an alternative religion and outlines the elements of Soviet ideology that are opposed to religion. Some theorists have attempted to reconcile the tension between the religious and secular elements of Soviet society by labeling official Soviet culture a form of civil religion.[34] Certainly, Soviet Communism had sacred symbols, a sense of myth, and a system of rituals, but unlike any other civil religion, it did not infuse national culture with supernatural meaning.[35] Instead, it sought to undermine the spiritual significance of religious symbolism and ritual by directly denying the existence of God. This point becomes crucial to understanding the limitations of the Soviet civil religion and how it differs from other forms of civil religion. What made Soviet Communism an alternative to religion rather than a competing religion was its underlying plot to kill God.

Coercion

Can you force someone into believing almost anything? Some observers of religious cults view cult members essentially as victims who have been brainwashed into spouting convictions that appear ridiculous to nonmembers.[36] And even devout Communists have been depicted as brainwashed followers of a radical political ideology. The 1962 film *The Manchurian Candidate* established the quintessential depiction of Communist brainwashing. In this tale, American soldiers are subjected to a series of psychological tortures that render them pawns of their Communist masters. But this popular notion of brainwashing stands in opposition to more scientifically rigorous studies that show how social incentives and networks lead reasonable people to accept with full consciousness the teachings of highly deviant religious or political groups.[37] This means that, in general, individuals cannot be forced to believe in ideas, concepts, or leaders against their will. Instead, changing social and personal circumstances lead rational individuals to believe in things that may appear irrational to others not in those circumstances.[38]

Soviet antireligious policy, especially in the 1920s and 1930s, altered the social and personal circumstances of hundreds of millions of people. Stalin and other brutal Communist Party officials hoped to convince their citizens that the religious path was unwise. In sociological language, they drastically shifted social incentives concerning religious decision making. Before Soviet rule, cultural norms dictated that everyone hold some nominal religious identity. Consequently, even individuals who never attended church or practiced religious rituals could say they were Orthodox or Muslim or had some other religious identity. But the Communist Party changed that. Under Soviet Communism, citizens had powerful incentives to not go to church and had fewer opportunities to interact with religious communities. Soviet policies that destroyed religious institutions and eliminated religious leaders followed the basic logic of sociological theories, which state that religious persistence is simply a process of socialization. In theory, without churches and religious activists, religion would go away.

Chapter 3 explores the use of coercion in the ongoing experiment to secularize society. While antireligious policies successfully scared many citizens away from religion and produced a great deal of religious ignorance, it never produced the Communist zombies of fiction. While coercion can effectively curb behavior, its impact on belief is erratic. By limiting choices and creating massive incentives to lie about one's beliefs, the Soviet system did not brainwash its citizenry but rather produced a population teeming with halfhearted loyalists and silent malcontents.

Conversion

Although the pre–World War II years were marked by extreme violence toward religious adherents, most of the Soviet Secularization Experiment consisted of massive campaigns to reeducate the population with propaganda. Schoolchildren were taught that religious belief was just plain stupid, and Soviet citizens encountered daily statements about the falsity and dangers of religion in the media and their places of work. These propaganda tactics were intended to not only alter behavior but also to convert the population into convinced atheists.

But how attractive is Marxist-Leninism as an alternative to religion? Chapter 4 analyzes the various strategies used to convert the Soviet population: education, propaganda, and atheistic ritual. By comparing the tactics employed by Soviet propagandists to the approaches of successful religious proselytizers, one can see some clear differences in how both groups approached the challenges of conversion. Most important, Soviet officials used their centralized authority and extensive resources to coordinate a blanket effort to convert millions in a relatively short period of time. While their considerable resources and strict hierarchy certainly appeared to provide powerful advantages for atheist proselytizers, these apparent benefits robbed the atheist campaign of any real passion or vitality.

In the conversion trade, bigger is not always better. As any successful missionary knows, souls are saved one at a time. And the Soviet Secularization Experiment arrogantly presumed to covert millions all at once.

Religious Revivals?

Did Communist Party elites secularize their society? Some scholars point to the separation of church and state and a massive amount of religious ignorance as evidence that post-Soviet lands are currently secularized.[39] Others observe that many individuals who had expressed no interest in religion during the Communist era are now experimenting with religion, evidence that the Secularization Experiment failed in its mission.[40] Again, these divergent attitudes come down to differing definitions of secularization.

The fifteen successor states of the Soviet Union have all established governments that are not ruled by religious leaders and contain fully secularized schools, universities, and courts. In this sense, these countries are secularized and have inherited a division of church and state from the

Soviet era. Nevertheless, certain religious-national identities have arisen throughout these regions that have been quickly exploited for political ends by emerging national leaders. The result is that certain religious traditions have achieved favored status in most of the former Soviet states.

In the 1990s, the former Soviet population was grappling with the spiritual aimlessness of the post-Communist era. As the *Encyclopedia of Religious Life in Russia Today (2001)* states, "There is plenty of spirituality, but it is impressionistic, spontaneous and unformed."[41] Many former Soviet citizens are actively exploring their religious histories and also experimenting with new Western religious movements. A young Russian intellectual explains a common path to spirituality experienced by himself and his friends as they struggled with the vacuity of post-Soviet life. "My friends and I grew up in atheist families. Each of us has come along a complicated, sometimes agonizing path of spiritual searching. From Marxist convictions, through nihilism and through the total rejection of any ideology at all, through an attraction to the 'hippy' lifestyle, we have come to the Church."[42] The return of millions of former Soviet citizens to religious affiliation and spiritual experimentation can be properly called a religious revival of epic proportions.

Chapter 5 looks at religious change since the fall of Communism and describes how the reemergence of traditional religious monopolies through the favoritism of post-Soviet states has attempted to harness an emerging curiosity and interest in all things religious. The results follow the predictions of some established theories of religious change and strongly demonstrate that confidence in atheism was quick to evaporate with the coming of intellectual freedom.

THE POLITICS OF GOD

In actively seeking to secularize society, the Soviet regime took on something much bigger than any of the early Bolsheviks could imagine. By the 1940s, Communist Party leaders had eliminated most of the houses of worship in the Soviet Union and gotten rid of tens of thousands of religious activists and followers. But while this massive twenty-year campaign shattered the foundations of institutionalized religion, it failed to dislodge popular religious belief. As Soviet religion scholar Michael Bourdeaux eloquently puts it, "Beneath the surface, the elimination of religion had not proceeded as smoothly as the propagandists never tired of reporting in the Soviet press. Indeed, there was something frenetic and despairing in the tone of the constant assertions in the press that religion was of course dying out, 'but . . .' After the qualifying conjunction, the reader would find diversified accounts illustrating the ways in which survivals of religion persisted long after the destruction of the institutions."[43] This fact confused not only Marxist-Leninists but also might confuse many contemporary sociologists of religion.

How can religion survive without religious institutions? Marxist-Leninists assumed, to use the language of economics, that the demand for religion was a product of religious supply. In other words, the suppliers of religious ideology, such as leaders of churches, mosques, synagogues, and other religious organizations, created a cultural system and social structure to perpetuate the religious socialization of individuals. Within this context, individuals were taught to believe in religious concepts, which, in turn, became a source of meaning, purpose, and identity. Consistent with this commonly held perspective in contemporary social science, the Soviet Secularization Experiment sought to sever the link between supply-side religious organizations and the responding demand for spirituality and religious meaning. Nonetheless, in the absence of religious supply, religious demand did not disappear.

Perhaps the demand for religion is an essential aspect of the human condition.[44] This is really at heart a philosophical question, but empirical evidence indicates that humans universally are drawn to religious explanations of world. As Christian Smith argues, "Individual humans only, always, and can ever enjoy life, identity, and significance by locating themselves within stories and cultural orders outside and beyond themselves, in terms of which their lives have place and purpose. This is an elementary sociological insight. But the same is true for life, history, and the world. They are not self-interpreting. They need a transcendent horizon or framework of understanding derived from above and beyond themselves to be given significance."[45] Perhaps historically established world religions provide this framework better than any existing secular ideology, at least for the vast majority of humanity. In fact, organized religions are sustainable only to the extent that humans are attracted to the transcendent explanations and meanings they offer. Without the human need for transcendental meaning and purpose, religious organizations would simply fold for lack of interest.

But in the reverse instance, of which the Soviet Union is a unique example, religious demand can be sustained without religious supply. As Soviet leaders recognized that they could force individuals to stop going to church but could not stop them from believing in God, they tinkered with an atheist alternative to religion that they felt could satisfy the lingering need for religious meaning and practice without the harmful concept of God. This atheist alternative failed to establish the same level of commitment and confidence that successful religious worldviews enjoy. While certain social structural conditions point to weaknesses in how the atheist campaign was conducted, the most glaring difference between the Soviet experiment and traditional religions is the absence of God.

Chapter 6 explains why it is easier to invoke God than to kill him by reviewing the general empirical findings of the book and presenting a final comparison of the religious and political cultures of the Soviet Union, Western Europe, the United States, and Communist China. These four cases reveal four distinct religious cultures and four distinct political strategies for how to tame religion for political ends. The religious and political effects of church-state relationships in each of these cultures provide further evidence that beliefs about God are something to be taken seriously in the realm of politics.

The idea of God is currently a fundamental aspect of human culture and shows no signs of fading, even in some of the most secularized regions of the globe. While quite malleable to divergent political and cultural environments, beliefs about God lie at the core of human understanding. The Soviet Secularization Experiment wanted to reject this basic thesis but ultimately found it to be undeniable.

CHAPTER I

Dreams of Secularization

We have not the right to close the doors of [the Socialist Party]
to a man who is infected with religious belief; but we are
obliged to do all that depends on us in order to destroy that
faith in him.

> — George Plekhanov,
> "Notes to Engels' Ludwig Feuerbach," 1892

Nineteenth- and early-twentieth-century Marxists imagined a world without religion. What they pictured was a society free from the negative influences of religious institutions that had become the lapdogs of the European
power elite. Before the Russian Revolution, Russian Marxists saw the
Russian Orthodox Church as defending and blessing a tyrannical political
leadership and supporting a morally unjustified war effort. Revolutionaries viewed religious institutions as the source of the twisted moral ideology that defended an inherently immoral social and political system. Their
dreams of secularization were premised on a desire to rid the world of all
that was harmful to the struggling and exploited masses of humanity.

By the end of the Russian Revolution, Bolshevik leaders had achieved
something astonishing. For the first time in history, Marxist theorists
gained control over millions of people and found themselves finally able
to implement their dreams. Karl Marx had initially raised the battle cry
for a new brand of social activism, urging intellectuals to turn their
thoughts into action. Radical members of the Russian intelligentsia fer-
vently took up the cause, and after decades of fomenting rebellion, formerly marginal, exiled, and basement-dwelling revolutionaries took
charge of one of the largest countries on earth. Their plans were vast, and
with the collapse of the czarist regime, Bolsheviks fortified their utopian
dream to alter every aspect of society. They now debated about how they
would eliminate private property, restructure the economy, and produce
a Communist culture with a new set of values, beliefs, and identities.

The importance of the cultural aspect of the Soviet project cannot be overestimated. As Khrushchev reaffirmed nearly four decades after the revolution, "It is the function of all ideological work of our Party and State to develop new traits in Soviet people, to train them in collectivism and love of work, in proletarian internationalism and patriotism, in lofty ethical principles of the new society, Marxism-Leninism."[1] Central to this utopian goal of the new Soviet culture was the elimination of former ideological and religious loyalties. Religion proved one of the most challenging rivals because it existed at every level of society, from nationwide church hierarchies to local clerics with personal ties to their congregations, and from nationally celebrated religious festivals to daily rituals performed in the privacy of one's home. The complete secularization of society was a daunting task, but Bolshevik leaders were confident that they would succeed.

According to the early Marxist-Leninist secularization dream, religion was a castle made of sand. As the waves of social and political change washed across its base, Bolsheviks believed that religion would collapse under its own weight and be washed away without a trace. But this secularization dream was much more ambitious than most scholarly conceptions of secularization stipulate. Secularization, in contemporary social science literature, normally refers to a number of distinct events relating to a general weakening of religious institutions. David Martin, in his work *A General Theory of Secularization,* indicates that secularization tendencies include (1) the deterioration of religious institutions, (2) the decline of religious practices, (3) the erosion of stable religious communities, and (4) the differentiation of churches from other institutional spheres.[2] Clearly, the tendencies toward secularization make no direct reference to religious faith, but Marxist-Leninists assumed that religious belief would naturally disappear with the process of institutional secularization. And this general assumption continues to confound contemporary debates about secularization, in which some scholars point to the decline of religious organizations as confirmation of religious decline while others note the persistence of religious belief as evidence to the contrary.[3]

But as the Soviet Union systematically enacted new religious policies, Communist Party leaders discovered that the banning of religious activities along with the forced destruction of religious institutions could actually inspire religious belief through opposition to a perceived injustice. Consequently, the deterioration of religious institutions, the decline of religious practices, the erosion of religious communities, and the differentiation of religious and secular spheres did *not* produce widespread religious disbelief. As Yaroslavsky, head of the League of Militant Atheists, noted to Stalin in the early 1930s, "Religion is like a nail, the harder you hit it the deeper it goes."[4] Yaroslavsky's quip advanced the idea that religion was not merely a collection of institutions or rituals but instead an ideological conviction embedded within a larger culture.

The creation of the League of Militant Atheists, a churchlike atheist propaganda organization, marked the beginning of an emerging Soviet theory of religion. Communist Party theorists, especially Yaroslavsky, argued that religion constituted a worldview or set of moral beliefs that lie in the hearts of individuals but are propagated by religious institutions and instilled through religious practices. From this perspective, secularization was nothing less than the eradication of religious faith. In the 1920s and 1930s, Yaroslavsky was given the daunting task of secularizing all of Soviet culture. And because Yaroslavsky and his colleagues were committed Marxist-Leninists, they were careful to lay out the philosophical assertions that guided their plans.

Even though the theories of Yaroslavsky and the atheist propagandists who would follow him were broad in their scope and certainly single-minded in their intent, much of their content reflects hypotheses that are still popular in the social sciences today. Consequently, the secularization strategies of the Soviet era produced a rich laboratory full of data from which to test a wide range of pertinent sociological hypotheses. Overall, the Soviet Secularization Experiment employed and tested six key theoretical assertions concerning the substance and persistence of religion. Not all of these assertions are logically derived from the ideology of Marxist-Leninism, but, nonetheless, Soviet policies addressed their validity.

In sum, the Secularization Experiment tested the extent to which religious vitality or decline are a product of ignorance, ritual activity, social institutions, social rewards, salvation incentives, and church-state relationships. The following chapter investigates the substance of these six assertions in greater depth.

SECULARIZATION ASSERTIONS

Assertion 1

Religion is but the false sun which revolves around man
while he is not yet fully self-aware.

— Karl Marx

In 1549, Lelio Sozzini wrote to John Calvin that "most of my friends are so well educated they can scarcely believe God exists."[5] The idea that enlightened minds are naturally adverse to religious belief is not a new one. Antireligious intellectual movements have a lengthy history that most clearly dates back to ancient Greek philosophers, who questioned the existence of the gods. In the fifth century, Xenophanes, as translated by George Henry Lewes, concluded, "God, the infinite, could not be infinite, neither could He be finite."[6] Sharing his discovery, Xenophanes toured cities and the countryside explaining to spectators how logic proves that the supernatural is meaningless.

Although skeptics throughout the ages certainly applied logic, science, and common sense to question the tenets of religious belief, progress in science and the rise of liberal thought in the modern era did little to bolster empirical claims for atheism. For instance, Newton's theory of gravity was initially understood as support for the existence of an active God because "it involved the rejection of all purely mechanical explanations of the movement of the heavens."[7] And even though many modern revolutionaries proclaimed an active tension between liberalism and religious faith, Rousseau, the intellectual guru of the French Revolution, was an active theist and in fact believed that social change required the assistance of God. Intellectual traditions that posited that science and liberalism are at war with religion have always existed alongside scientists and revolutionaries who were religious. Therefore, the empowerment of antireligious ideology requires a sociological explanation because it was by no means a philosophically necessary outcome of modern worldviews.

The sociologist Auguste Comte believed that religion would slowly erode as technology and modern thinking penetrated popular culture; in fact, he argued that sociology would replace religion as a way to not only understand society but to also determine common moral attitudes concerning behavior and the social order.[8] Although contemporary sociologists of religion no longer make this claim, the argument that the process of modernization itself diminishes religion remains. But what is it about modernization that is so incompatible with religion?

The history of Western Europe indicates that modernizing countries are more likely to develop distinct religious and secular spheres — in other words, they become societies in which the church is formally separated from the state. Both Max Weber and Emile Durkheim believed this was the result of a natural division of labor as societies got more complex and bureaucratic. Nevertheless, if modernization erodes religious belief, aspects of modernization such as urbanization, industrialization and scientific advancement must also undermine religious views of the world.

The separation of church and state by itself does not logically lead to non-belief. Therefore, modernization can only affect religious faith if modern political and scientific worldviews are inherently antireligious or atheistic.

Following Marx, early Communist Party leaders subscribed to this belief and assumed that modernizing the regions of the Soviet Union and educating the population in the basic tenets of science would speed up the inevitable process of secularization. From their perspective, technology and science were wholly incompatible with beliefs in the supernatural — Marxist-Leninists assumed that individuals would have to choose one in the final analysis. And as the advantages of modernization and the logic of science became apparent, they supposed that all rational individuals would abandon religion.

Industrial and urban growth followed quickly from the implementation of Soviet economic plans. And after World War II, the space and arms races between the United States and the Soviet Union demonstrated that the Soviet system enjoyed a high level of technological advancement and industrial might. In addition, Soviet officials successfully put into practice a massive educational effort that brought schools, books, and educational materials to tens of millions of children for the first time. As a professor from Moscow State University explained, "Soviet education aims at creating human beings, grounded in a scientific, materialistic outlook, people who endeavor to make life happy in this world rather than in some world to come."[9] This educational program explicitly communicated that technological and scientific advancements disproved religious systems of belief. A curriculum of "scientific atheism" became central in the education of youth, scientists, and scholars. Soviet citizens learned that religious belief was tantamount to scientific ignorance. If the Soviet people were to enter a modern age of Communism, they were told that they needed to abandon their antiquated ideas. With the weapons of modern science, technology, and industrialization, early Communist Party leaders fully expected to eliminate all traces of religious belief from society.

The Secularization Experiment represents the first time in history that the belief that science and modernity undermine religion became official state ideology. As such, Soviet policy tested Marx's assertion that education and self-awareness will ultimately extinguish the false sun of religion. Subsequent chapters will uncover the extent to which Soviet citizens were persuaded to discard their religious sentiments as antireligious philosophy came to dominate their intellectual, academic, and professional lives.

Assertion 2

There are rites without gods, and indeed rites from
which gods derive.

> — Emile Durkheim,
> *The Elementary Forms of Religious Life*

Emile Durkheim maintained, "Religious beliefs rest upon a specific experience whose demonstrative value is, in one sense, not one bit inferior to that of scientific experiments, though different from them."[10] The experience to which Durkheim refers is the feeling of "collective effervescence," an intense emotional response to ritualistic interaction. Through participation in ritual, individuals feed off the fervor of other participants to create a general enthusiasm that an individual could not attain in isolation. The intensity of this collectively generated emotion can produce a wide of range of thoughts and perceptions, from strident senses of nationalism and group solidarity to, in the case of religious rituals, firm convictions of religious devotion. For Durkheim, ritual activities produce religious faith as individuals elicit from one another powerful feelings that later get ascribed to some external force. In sum, Durkheim believed that social ecstasy is misperceived by the individual as mystical experience.

Communist Party officials became increasingly concerned with religious ritual activity as religious practices persisted, even as many religious organizations dissolved. While Soviet elites were certainly not Durkheimian in their philosophical worldview, they began to view ritual as a key aspect of religious perseverance and concluded that public and private religious rituals must be ended. Nonetheless, Communist Party leaders sensed that ritualistic activity was a necessary and potentially productive aspect of human expression. So instead of attempting to eliminate all ritual activity, they sought to replace religious rituals with Soviet ones.

In their blatant attempt to manufacture new rituals, Soviet officials revealed certain Durkheimian assumptions concerning the substance of rituals. Durkheim supposed that the beliefs that explain the meaning and purpose of rituals are secondary. Specifically, religious beliefs are simply an explanatory system that provided a framework from which the individual describes her experience after the fact. William James noted how religious experiences, while physiologically and emotionally very similar, are explained in the language of the individual's cultural environment. For instance, Muslims will attribute their experience to Allah, while Christians might believe that Jesus spoke to them. If beliefs about a religious experience were transposed onto a universal feeling of social solidarity, Soviets could retain the social and emotional element of religious practices while replacing the symbolic and ideological elements of the ritual. Individuals would continue to experience the emotional power of religious rituals but reattribute their feelings to the effects of Communism.

Simply put, Communist Party leaders hoped to connect Communist symbols and ideology to experiences of "collective effervescence." The end result would be a population that no longer worshiped God but instead revered the Soviet system with religiouslike devotion. In actuality, Soviet elites hoped to realize something that Durkheim only believed to be true. Namely, they were going to replace the false object of ritual activity, God, with the true object, Society. In this way, rituals would continue to promote social solidarity but no longer under the guise of a false ideology.

Actual Communist rituals reveal the simplicity of this plan. Soviet officials quite consciously mimicked many aspects of common religious ceremonies and plainly replaced certain phrases and symbols with Communist alternatives. For instance, "God" is replaced by "the proletariat" in texts, and the hammer and sickle stand in for the cross as emblems of the sacred. Soviet weddings, funerals, confirmations, baptisms, festivals, and national holidays were intended to create a new faith — a faith in Soviet Communism. This is why many scholars of the Soviet Union observe that Soviet Communism was its own religion. But in the minds of Communist Party leaders, Soviet rituals were the antithesis of religion because they removed God from the explanatory scheme.

The Secularization Experiment tested Durkheim's assertion that rituals inspire social solidarity through a collective focus on God but, alternatively, do not require God. Subsequent chapters investigate the extent to which Soviet ritual activities inspired citizens to abandon centuries-old religious rites and traditions.

Assertion 3

Bishops and archbishops enjoy authority merely as
deputies of the temporal power.
   — Leon Trotsky, *The History of the Russian Revolution*

Religious institutions — churches, mosques, temples, synagogues, spiritual organizations, religious schools, and religious courts — provide an organizational structure to perpetuate religious belief and commitment. These institutions strive to attract and retain members and maintain loyalty to their religious message and mission. Individuals are committed to religious organizations for a number of reasons. A common view of religious commitment holds that individuals are mainly socialized into a religious community. They learn as children to attend church or participate in an accepted religious practice. Through this socialization, individuals may internalize religious ideas or simply continue religious behavior out of habit. Alternatively, people may also accept religious institutions out of fear of sanctions from religious authorities.

From a Marxist-Leninist perspective, religious institutions ultimately justify current power relations and provide an otherworldly object at which to direct individual problems and personal requests. In return, political structures support and bolster the influence of religious institutions. Marxist-Leninists viewed the institution of religion within this mutually beneficial relationship as merely one propaganda arm of the larger political structure. As such, they expected that religion would die without the continued support and favoritism of the power elite.

In Russia, Marxist-Leninists argued, the Russian Orthodox Church only legitimated czarist rule and offered little material assistance to the population. By destroying the Russian Orthodox Church, Soviet leaders felt they could break the cycle of religious socialization that had survived through official state propagation. Emelian Yaroslavsky, the Soviet minister of antireligious propaganda, explained, "The Party strives for the complete dissolution of the ties between the exploiting classes and the organizations of religious propaganda."[11] Marxist-Leninists assumed that without state support, religious institutions would collapse and individuals would naturally drift toward nonbelief. They also assumed that the ideological dominance of Roman Catholicism in Lithuania, Christian Orthodoxy in the territories around Russia, and Islam in Central Asia would fade as the religious institutions in these regions buckled under state regulation.

The campaign to annihilate religious institutions was massive and quite brutal. Within a mere decade, Soviet forces had destroyed or overtaken most of the property holdings and buildings of the dominant religions throughout the Soviet Union. In addition, Soviet officials closed Orthodox, Roman Catholic, and Islamic schools and completely shut down the Islamic court system throughout Central Asia. Before Soviet rule, dominant religious groups in the various regions of the Russian empire enjoyed governmental support and protection. They ran state-funded institutions, oversaw most cultural events, and provided national ceremonies and political legitimation. Consequently, citizens became accustomed to a society in which religion was a recognized feature of their daily experiences. Soviet rule changed this dramatically. No longer did dominant religious institutions bask in the favoritism of political elites; now, they were forced to fight for their very existence.

According to Trotsky's assertion, bishops and archbishops would lose sway without the continued support of the temporal authority. The Secularization Experiment tested the mettle of religious organizations across the Soviet Union, and, as we will see, some proved more resilient than others.

Assertion 4

Religious or magical behavior or thinking must not be
set apart from the range of everyday purposive conduct,
particularly since even the ends of the religious and
magical actions are predominantly economic.
                              — Max Weber, *Economy and Society*

In contrast to theories of religious persistence that stress the cultural, ritual, and institutional socialization of individuals toward a religious worldview, contemporary social theorists have explored the role of rational calculations in religious decision making. While individuals are certainly socialized into particular beliefs and worldviews, they may also ponder ideas presented to them, weighing explanations of the world against personal experiences and desires. Individuals may alter their political opinions and religious beliefs as they learn more about the world or develop different social ties through interaction with new friends, neighbors, and coworkers. Within the boundaries of our cultural environment, we are exploratory beings. As such, Max Weber, along with more contemporary economic and social theorists, posited that individuals will make decisions in their own interests; this is often referred to as the assumption of rational choice. For instance, a person is unlikely to espouse a belief system that condemns an activity in which she is repeatedly engaged. While the instance of an individual directly undermining her own goals is not impossible, it is certainly an anomaly and more suitably the topic of abnormal psychology. Therefore, rational choice theorists expect individuals, en masse, to behave and state beliefs in ways that are personally advantageous.

From this perspective, individuals openly ponder the advantages to religious behavior and belief. In cost-benefit terms, social rewards are a clear and common advantage to religious participation. As an active member of a religious community, one reaps a number of valuable social rewards — companionship, access to social networks, and social status, to name a few. Churchgoers often find spouses, employment, and sources of important information through their church community, have support from other church members if they fall ill or find themselves in need of assistance, and are generally perceived as respectable members of society. Therefore, religious participation can be quite rewarding socially and economically.

While social rewards might explain why individuals participate in religious organizations, they say little about religious belief. Namely, one can participate and reap rewards without actually believing in religious ideas. These types of religious participants are referred to as *free riders* — like bus riders who have not bought a ticket and attempt to ride for free — because they seek the social rewards of religious participation while shirking true commitment to the group and the belief system. In times of need or when religious membership becomes detrimental, free riders will abandon their group because they have no deep investment in the ideas or members of the group. Before Soviet rule, it is difficult to know how many fervent religious believers existed in the regions that would make up the Soviet Union. Most individuals were affiliated with a certain religious tradition, but because state-supported religions were culturally ubiquitous in Russia and the surrounding areas, it is unclear whether religious identities were simply ethnic and national labels or indicative of a deep devotion to religious concepts. In the nineteenth century, Russian intellectuals debated the extent to which the Russian people were comprised mainly of religious free riders or faithful believers who would fight and die for their convictions. In one heated debate, the author Nikolai Gogol asserted that the Russian population was deeply spiritual while the literary critic Vissarion Belinsky objected. Belinsky wrote Gogol, "In your opinion, the Russian people are the most religious in the world. This is a lie! The basis of religiousness is pietism, reverence, fear of God. But the Russian pronounces the name of God while scratching. . . . Look closer and you will see that it is by nature a profoundly atheist people."[12] According to Belinsky, Russian religiosity was a meaningless facade that would fall away when religious habits became social liabilities. Community Party elites would test this idea.

The Secularization Experiment radically altered the social rewards of religious participation. In a complete reversal of past expectations, religious believers could be denied career promotion, could be harassed at work or school, and, in the most extreme cases, could be imprisoned in labor camps or psychiatric wards and sometimes executed for their faith. Under these circumstances, religious free riders would be expected to jump ship because religious organizations could no longer offer any benefits for membership and social expectations would no longer urge religious participation. Antireligious repression, at the very least, rid religious groups of free riders. Anyone who remained openly religious in the Soviet system demonstrated that their commitment to their faith did not depend on social rewards. Soviets expected that few religious adherents would turn out to be true believers once social incentives no longer existed.

To augment the harsh costs of religious commitment, Soviet society offered social incentives to adopt the official ideology of the Soviet state and become atheist. For this reason, individuals had many reasons to falsify their religious beliefs and fake commitment to the Communist project: to avoid discrimination, to seek favoritism, and to protect their well-being. Ironically, while Soviet rule rid society of religious free riders, it may have produced a population of Communist free riders. And in the end, free riders will rob any system or group of vitality because they always attempt to take more than they give.

Subsequent chapters probe the extent to which expressions of pre-Soviet-era religiosity were mere facades and to which atheist identities were embraced by social and political opportunists.

Assertion 5

Religion is concerned with the supernatural; everything
else is secondary.
                    —Rodney Stark and Roger Finke, *Acts of Faith*

Because religious communities rely heavily on the active contribution of members, they are extremely vulnerable to individuals who exploit group resources. Religious organizations tend to solve this free rider problem by placing high costs on religious membership.[13] Costs can include tithing requirements, expectations of time commitment, and behavioral restrictions that may increase social stigma and social isolation from the larger society. These kinds of costs insure that individuals are not simply exploiting a group for personal gain; their personal sacrifices become evidence of their good faith. Nevertheless, many outside observers of strict religious groups feel that the costs of religious participation far outweigh the benefits and question whether the faithful closely consider the costs involved in their religion. Why would someone give away their earthly belongings, deny themselves certain pleasures in life, or risk their lives for a religious group if they are calculating their self-interest? Religious believers do these things because they *believe* that they are commanded by some higher power.

Sociologists Rodney Stark and Roger Finke argue that belief should be considered an integral part of an individual's calculations in making any decision. If one believes she will go to hell if she does not give away her possessions, then the idea of hell becomes a perceived cost of religious inaction.[14] Certainly, the eternal pleasures of heaven are worth the temporary pains of worldly deprivation. For this reason, Stark and Finke indicate that compensations of the afterlife, or *otherworldly rewards*, are perhaps more important than social rewards in making religious decisions. Belief in otherworldly rewards often explains action that appears wholly irrational; suicide bombers and religious martyrs are not necessarily depressed or hopeless but are instead idealists who expect to receive compensation in the afterlife for their earthly sacrifice. Within this mindset, death does not appear final but is instead a doorway into a preferable existence. In the final analysis, true religious faith profoundly influences decision making and can lead to astonishing actions.

Soviet officials certainly understood the power of religious belief to motivate extraordinary behavior. Yaroslavsky warned Stalin that Soviet policy should "carefully avoid giving offense to the religious sentiments of believers, which only leads to the strengthening of religious fanaticism."[15] Even though they would offend religious believers all over the world, Soviet officials remained conscious of the need to convert individuals from their religious faith and win the population's ideological loyalty.

Consequently, Communist Party leaders created a massive missionary effort intended to spread the gospel of atheism. The League of Militant Atheists, a propaganda arm of the Community Party, served as a kind of a church of Communism in the 1920s and 1930s, with atheist proselytizers and atheist meetinghouses standing in for clerics and churches. The league distributed atheist newspapers, gave atheist lectures, and preached the message of scientific atheism to anyone who would listen (many of whom were compelled to do so). They hoped to transfer people's faith in God to a belief in historical materialism and scientific atheism. Soviet officials felt that atheist conversion was the only way individuals would abandon fanatical behavior aimed at improving one's standing in a nonexistent afterlife. In the language of Stark and Finke, atheist propagandists wanted to convince the Soviet population that otherworldly rewards were illusory.

The way to replace religion was clear. Soviet rituals mimicked religious rites, Soviet theoretical texts were treated like sacred scripture, and Soviet leaders were hailed as saintlike and deserving of holy reverence. Did Soviet leaders also attempt to offer individuals a Communist alternative to otherworldly rewards? Perhaps the promise of Communism was itself an otherworldly reward. A society devoid of injustice, inequality, or alienation sounds similar to many descriptions of heaven. The doctrine of historical materialism explained that this earthly paradise was inevitable but could only be achieved with the eradication of all religion. Therefore, a high cost of the Communist dream was the relinquishing of heavenly dreams — trading one otherworldly reward for another.

But heavenly dreams offer something that Communism could not: Religious believers were to experience heaven for themselves, while faithful Communists could only revel in the *thought* that their dreams would be attained by some future generation. Soviet leaders attempted to resolve this obvious problem in two ways. First, they promised that the Communist ideal was within reach and therefore a likely reward in the near future. This strategy was empirically problematic because Soviet citizens continued to encounter social problems that were, in theory, nearing their end. Second, Soviet officials maintained that future generations would always remember the pioneers in the struggle against oppression; in this way, the faithful would live forever in the collective memory of humanity at the "end of history." In tandem with this effort was a bizarre reconceptualization of time in which linear conceptions of time were eschewed in favor of a more "sacred" or "charismatic," to quote the political theorist Stephen Hanson, sense of Soviet time.[16] But promises of remembrance and new conceptions of earthly time fall short of an eternal life in heaven surrounded by one's friends and loved ones. Nevertheless, an attempt was made to convince Soviet citizens that their personal sacrifices would not go unrewarded. And in many instances, committed Communists laid down their lives for the dream of a Soviet utopia.

The importance of otherworldly rewards becomes central to understanding the inability of Soviet officials to convert individuals to scientific atheism. One wonders what might draw individuals to hold atheist beliefs. The idea that the supernatural is a sham appears to offer no comfort or delight. But by tying atheism to historical materialism and scientific progress, Soviet rulers hoped to demonstrate that atheism had its own benefits. In the end, they argued that atheism was about liberation from false belief and salvation from earthly oppression. The attractiveness of "this-worldly" salvation reveals much about the primary importance of the supernatural in religion.

The desire for salvation is difficult to measure. Nevertheless, the Secularization Experiment pitted religious and Communist salvation against one another, and the following chapters investigate the extent to which the Soviet population favored one over the other.

Assertion 6

Market forces constrain churches just as they constrain
secular firms.

> —Adam Smith, *An Inquiry into the Nature*
> *and Causes of the Wealth of Nations*

As a result of their strategies to secularize society, Soviet leaders dramatically altered the composition of religious markets across the Soviet Union. *Religious market* is a phrase used to describe all the religious activity going on in any society comprised mainly of one or more organizations seeking to attract or maintain adherents.[17] The market analogy is applied to religion because it is expected that religious groups will compete for members. Few religious groups want members to divide their time and commitment between multiple groups; therefore, groups tend to stress exclusive commitment. Because there are a finite number of people, religious groups must contend for adherents just like sellers of wares compete for buyers in a market setting. The winners are religious groups that can attract and sustain members.

Religious markets, like economic markets, are greatly influenced by how much the state controls them. The Soviet economy was a state-controlled economy; likewise, Soviet religious culture was state controlled. When the Bolsheviks initially took power, they dramatically altered the control of existing religious markets. Before the Russian Revolution, Russians were mostly Orthodox, Lithuanians were mostly Roman Catholic, and Uzbeks were mostly Muslim. When a population is overwhelmingly affiliated with one religious tradition, this group has a *religious monopoly:* they have successfully cornered the religious market. While large numbers of Jews, Old Believers, and Sufis populated the various regions of the Soviet empire, the Russian Orthodox Church, the Lithuanian Catholic Church, and Islam all held monopoly control of their respective republics.

Social theorists posit that religious monopolies can only exist when a religious group is favored by the state. In other words, the government must actively suppress religious groups that hope to compete with a favored religion for that religion to maintain its dominance. Studies of religious deregulation in Europe, Latin America, and the United States show that reductions in state regulatory policies will lead to the introduction of new religious doctrines and the growth of minority religions.[18] Without religious regulation or in circumstances of complete religious freedom, a religious market will be more pluralistic because it allows for the promotion of multiple religious doctrines.[19]

Up until the Secularization Experiment, there was no test of what happens to monopoly religions that encounter antireligious policies. One prediction is that strong opposition to atheism would appear in regions with a historically dominant majority religion. Wouldn't members of a dominant church rally in large numbers to either secure some religious freedom or at least successfully withstand religious repression once the state enacted antireligious policies? This actually seems unlikely when one considers that religious monopolies require the support of a state to sustain their dominance. In fact, while the majority of the population may be affiliated with a monopoly religion, they tend to rarely participate in religious activities.[20] This means that although monopoly churches enjoy high membership rates, members tend to have low levels of commitment. Therefore, uncommitted members of a dominant church may easily acquiesce to atheistic policies because they are unwilling to risk personal harm for a religion that they very rarely practice. In other words, most members of a religious monopoly should turn out to be free riders.

Nevertheless, individuals may still retain a religious perspective of the world, even if they are attached halfheartedly to the dominant religious tradition of their region. Namely, it is one thing to be a "Christmas Catholic" — someone who only attends church on special occasions — and quite another to be a convinced atheist. Therefore, Soviet leaders wanted to do more than just drive individuals away from their religious traditions; they wanted to drive the population *toward* something. Their systematic attempts to convert individuals to atheism introduced something unique into the religious market: an atheist competitor!

Atheism has probably existed as long as there have been religious worldviews. But never before had atheism been promoted so systematically and on such a large scale. Practically overnight, formerly accepted, mainstream religious perspectives became viewed officially as radical and antiestablishment. With state support, institutional promotion, the full force of the media, and atheist proselytizers, the doctrine of scientific atheism became the new ideological monopoly. While Soviets criticized the religious monopolies of the past, they actually replicated czarist attempts to establish devotion and loyalty from the top down.

Soviets understood conversion in terms consistent with the story of Russia's Christianization in 988. Legend has it that Prince Vladimir sent envoys out to investigate the world's religions. After carefully considering their reports, Vladimir chose Greek Orthodoxy as the state religion, and his decree marked the conversion of Russia to Christianity. Nearly one thousand years later, Soviet leaders would decree atheism the state ideology to mark the secularization of society.

In actuality, Christian ideas mixed with indigenous pagan beliefs over many centuries to result in the Russian Orthodox tradition we know today. While Vladimir certainly played a key role in altering the religious landscape of his kingdom by creating a state-supported religion, the Christianization of Russia was a slow and arduous process that ultimately depended on the success of thousands of Christian messengers over hundreds of years. Scientific atheists attempted to absorb and alter many Christian rituals in ways similar to how early Christians infused pagan practices with Christian messages. Nevertheless, it remained to be seen if scientific atheism could inspire a popular movement that would ultimately spread the faith of Communism. Perhaps Soviets would require a thousand years to secularize the population. But Soviet leaders had high expectations and, in the end, mistakenly believed that if Vladimir could Christianize Russia overnight, they could secularize in similar fashion.

Soviet officials assumed the success of the Secularization Experiment depended on the elimination of religious monopolies. Ironically, this goal was celebrated by religious sects throughout the Soviet Union. These groups had previously suffered intense religious repression under policies that favored dominant religious monopolies. Therefore, many religious sects viewed the Soviet assault on the Russian Orthodox Church and other dominant groups as an overdue comeuppance. In fact, as Soviet leaders concentrated their antireligious policies on dominant religions, many of these formerly marginalized religious groups formed new bonds with the Soviet population. As a result, some small religious groups actually increased in size under Communism. In the end, the Secularization Experiment would have a lasting impact on levels of religious pluralism.

Religious pluralism's effect on religious vitality is a much-debated topic in the social sciences.[21] The market model of religion holds that religious pluralism increases religiosity because, as in any market, competition is good for business. The fall of the Soviet Union provides a perfect test case for this idea. Before Soviet rule, dominant religious groups enjoyed state favoritism, and during the Soviet era, scientific atheism became the new ideological monopoly. The collapse of Soviet Communism left a religious market with no clear monopoly.

Which religious groups succeeded and which failed in the post-Communist world reveals much about the role of religious competition and the importance of state regulation in the composition and vitality of religious markets. Using the market analogy, the Secularization Experiment offers something rarely observed — a marginal philosophical tradition that achieved massive state support almost overnight and subsequently lost its political and social advantages just as quickly. The effects of this bizarre phenomenon greatly inform our understanding of how changing church-state relationships alters beliefs in a relatively short span of time.

MAKING DREAMS A REALITY

Early Bolsheviks certainly had their work cut out for them. Not only were their revolutionary dreams big, they had no prior examples of successful Communist revolutions from which to model their plans. Consequently, early revolutionaries relied on theory. Unlike natural scientists, it is rare that a social theorist gets the opportunity to implement his or her hypotheses to test how they will work in the environment studied. I expect this is a welcome blessing for most of the population. But in the Soviet Union's case, a social experiment was conducted on the most massive scale imaginable. The religious arm of this experiment was guided by a series of distinct hypotheses concerning the function, structure, and purpose of religion and also by some innovative responses to changing events.

Borrowing from the language of the economics, the multiple theoretical assertions tested by the Secularization Experiment can be loosely grouped into *demand-side* and *supply-side hypotheses*. Demand-side hypotheses of religious growth and decline focus on how the elements of religion that are attractive to people change over time. For instance, if one hypothesizes that individuals seek out religious meaning and explanation in times of personal crisis, she would expect that natural disasters and social upheavals would send large portions of the population running to seek guidance from religious organizations. In contrast, supply-side hypotheses of religious growth and decline focus on how the supply of religious goods changes over time. A popular supply-side assertion is the controversial religious pluralism hypothesis developed by Stark and Finke that states, "To the degree that religious economies are unregulated and competitive, overall levels of religious commitment will be high."[22] This hypothesis indicates that religiosity changes to the extent that churches are allowed to and attempt to actively recruit new members. In simple terms, demand-side explanations analyze why individuals seek out religion, and supply-side explanations study how churches seek out members.

Contemporary theorists of religion tend to pit these two explanatory perspectives against one another. But Soviet officials experimented with both supply-side and demand-side models of religious change. At first, the Soviet regime assumed that religiosity was wholly a product of religious supply. Their altering of church-state relationships and attempts to shut down religious institutions represent tactics to cut off religious supply. The successes and failures of this supply-side strategy are investigated in chapter 3, "Shutting Off Religious Supply."

But Soviet theorists also hypothesized that the demand for religion was the product of economic woes, simple ignorance, and an innate need for ritual expression. The campaign to modernize and reeducate the Soviet population and provide them with atheist rituals was a demand-side strategy to redirect what theorists posited were the sources of religious need. The successes and failures of this strategy are investigated in chapter 4, "Hunting for Religious Demand."

Finally, chapter 6 revisits the six assertions presented above to clarify how findings from the Soviet Secularization Experiment support or undermine these basic theoretical perspectives. Ultimately, the secularization dreams of the early Bolsheviks never became a reality, but their attempts to make their dreams real drastically altered the religious lives of Soviet citizens and have a lasting influence across the post-Soviet regions of Eastern Europe and Central Asia. And their application of social theories of religion still have much to teach theorists and researchers today.

CHAPTER 2

The Atheist Crusade

Atheistic philosophies which culminate in the cult of the State
or of Man, are only theological insurrections.
                                        — Albert Camus, *The Rebel*

Most visitors to Moscow during the Soviet era made a requisite stop at
Lenin's mausoleum. Those who visited in the 1980s will probably share
my recollection of lining up outside the marble entrance and solemnly
entering the tomb. Inside, Lenin lay in an open coffin looking exactly as
he appeared in the numerous pictures and posters of him that covered the
buildings, offices, and homes of Soviet citizens. One would not have
guessed that he died more than fifty years earlier. Those accompanying
me in line, mainly elderly Soviet women, bowed in reverence as they
shuffled past a man who clearly held their heartfelt devotion. My experience was nearly identical to that of Yugoslavian vice president Milovan
Djilas, who recorded his visit to Lenin's tomb forty years earlier. Djilas
observed, "As we descended into the Mausoleum, I saw how simple
women in shawls were crossing themselves as though approaching the
reliquary of a saint."[1] A saint who sought to put an end to all saints.

Although performing a religious blessing over a man who called for
the destruction of religion is certainly a curiosity, the symbolism and
aura of Lenin's mausoleum actually provokes such a response. By placing
Lenin in a state of suspended animation, Soviet officials intentionally imi-
tated how the bodies of saints were displayed in monasteries throughout
Russia. Lenin's embalming derived its significance and meaning from the
Russian Orthodox belief that the bodies of saints decompose at a slower
rate.[2] Within this cultural tradition, Lenin's perfectly preserved body sent
a powerful symbolic message that he had transcended and supplanted all

previous saints. Following Lenin's death, the Communist Party Central Committee drove home the sacred significance of Lenin's embalmment with the following official proclamation: "Lenin lives on in the soul of every member of our Party. Every member of our Party is a particle of Lenin. Our entire Communist family is a collective embodiment of Lenin."[3]

The consecration of Lenin's body stands in stark contrast to Soviet treatment of the remains of religious saints. Soviet officials opposed the display of Orthodox saints and argued that their bodies were not actually preserved but were, in fact, frauds made of wax. To prove their point, Soviets exhumed the bodies of saints and performed tests to determine their true consistency.[4] Meanwhile, the waxy corpse of Lenin served as a genuine replacement, another example of how Communism could harness the forces of nature. The religious symbolism surrounding the presentation of Lenin's body communicated that science, materialism, and socialist ethics were the authentic objects of adoration and devotion. Mausoleum visitors' reverence and awe were therefore appropriate and expected. As the poet Vladimir Maiakovsky famously wrote:

'Lenin' and 'Death' — these words are enemies.
'Lenin' and 'Life' — are comrades . . .
Lenin — lived.
Lenin — lives.
Lenin — will live.[5]

That adoration for a militant atheist could be expressed through the sign of the cross and claims of immortality reveals the deep contradictions within Soviet culture and ideology. Leon Trotsky was one of the first to point out the absurdity of Lenin's suspended animation and surrounding ritual, demanding to "know who these comrades are who, according to the words of Stalin, propose that with the help of modern science the remains of Lenin should be embalmed, transformed into a relic. I would tell them that they have absolutely nothing to do with the science of Marxism."[6]

Nonetheless, the "science of Marxism" was about to delve completely into the realm of the mystical, with Soviet Communists claiming to have scientifically proven that religion was a main source of depravity and oppression in the world. Evoking Marxist rhetoric, Communist Party theorists explained that science undeniably validates that the supernatural is illusory, explicitly invented for to delude the general population into a false perception of the world. And Communist Party elites felt it was their moral duty to educate the population, by force if necessary, to the harms and evils of religious ideologies. In fact, the total destruction of religion became ideologically crucial to the utopian goals of the socialist state, and the persistence of religion was often blamed for failures to meet precise economic and political goals.

Specifically, Soviets believed the socialist state depended upon the creation of a "Soviet Man," an individual who acted instinctively according to the dictates of a new socialist morality and with an unquestioned faith in the prophecies of historical materialism. Moreover, the ideology of Soviet Communism recast religious believers as "disbelievers" and, during eras of extreme violence, justified their extermination or forced conversion as a necessary part of the coming earthly paradise. According to this uniquely Soviet eschatology, only a society filled with devout Communists could realize the "end of history" and enjoy the fantastic rewards of an earthly community free from conflict, oppression, or uncertainty.

Creating the Soviet Man proved more difficult than Communists originally expected. Faced with a population that continued to celebrate religious holidays and make use of religious symbols, Communist Party elites decided that their citizens required more than just atheistic instruction to relinquish their religious habits; they also needed atheistic rituals. As discussed in the previous chapter, the Communist Party created weddings, baptisms, confirmations, funerals, and holidays all mired in atheistic symbolism and language. They even constructed atheist "cells" to replicate the role of local church parishes. The style and solemnity of religious rituals were retained to produce a near-religious reverence for atheist concepts. Soviet texts and ceremonies acquired sacred status, and Soviet heroes such as Marx, Lenin, and Stalin were depicted as saintlike, deserving of everlasting adoration and faithful devotion.

Never before in history had an antireligious philosophy come to so closely resemble a religion. As Ernest Gellner observed, the Communist Party attempted to "turn the profane into the sacred," with the Marxist-Leninist philosophy of historical materialism serving as its sacred scripture.[7] Accordingly, Soviet elites depicted religious concepts, beliefs, and practices as profane. Through this fascinating reversal of sacred and profane, the Communist Party created an antireligious faith in which the faithful were atheists and the religiously devout, blasphemers. The Secularization Experiment is ultimately a story of how a political movement grew into an antireligious crusade in which a powerful government created and imposed a very different kind of state church.

THE SIGNIFICANCE OF RELIGION

If Bolshevik strategists were only concerned with their political authority, the brutality of their attacks on religion appears somewhat irrational. Couldn't Communist Party officials simply pay off religious leaders or halfheartedly fund traditional religious organizations to avoid the possibility of a religious war? Much of this book indicates why, for many reasons, this may have been a more effective strategy if the Soviet government simply wanted to diminish the importance of religion. But regardless of the many instances in which Communist Party leaders acted in conceited self-interest without real concern for their stated ideals, Marxist-Leninists were, at heart, committed ideologues. And the ends they pursued to destroy religion reveal the strength of their ideological convictions.

The Soviet project rested on twin pillars — one economic and the other ideological. According to this vision, complete state control of the economic system and the absence of a free market could produce a more efficient, productive, and contented society. The errors of this economic plan have been demonstrated in numerous historical and social critiques of the fall of the Soviet Union.[8] Generally, these analyses indicate that a controlled economy fails to provide incentives to innovate technology, work hard, and produce desirable products. In other words, the Soviet ideal of a classless society failed to take advantage of people's natural hunger for wealth and status and, therefore, was unable to inspire individual initiative.

But the Communist vision of a working economy posited a very different view of human nature. According to Marxist-Leninism, human nature could be altered by ideological and material conditions. Although workers in more industrialized countries certainly toiled for their wages, Communist Party planners believed that work could ultimately be a reward itself, and that in the proper environment, workers would come to enjoy the intrinsic value of their labor without concern for monetary or status incentives. Scholar of Soviet history Tim McDaniel explains that the road to Soviet Communism "could be interpreted as a painful transition period on the way to an ethically higher form of society. In this context, the personal sacrifices necessary for industrialization had a moral meaning. They were part of the struggle for a higher form of society and so could be connected to belief, not just interest. . . . In this regard, it has been frequently and correctly pointed out that Communist ideology provided a socialist substitute for the Protestant ethic of the West."[9]

Max Weber famously argued that ordinary laborers were able to accumulate wealth in Calvinist societies because they had developed a Protestant work ethic. According to Weber's theory, Calvinists labored to demonstrate their godliness and, as an important side effect, generated investment capital. As such, wealth and status were not the main reasons to work hard and be diligent. Instead, a religious work ethic motivated individuals to be productive members of society. Marxist-Leninists similarly posited that individuals could be motivated by a very different kind of moral calling.

The moral core of Marxist-Leninism is its assertion that economic relationships are inherently exploitive. From this perspective, wealth and status inequalities are unfair, and any ideology that justifies them is immoral. Furthermore, Marxist-Leninists believed that religion tended to validate manipulative power relations and taught oppressed people a demented view of justice — one that relied on a final judgment in the afterlife. Marx forcefully argued, "The abolition of religion as the *illusory* happiness of the people is required for their *real* happiness."[10] The moral conclusion of Marx's critique is that religion is innately corrupt.

Vladimir Lenin was greatly influenced by Marx's moral fervor. Lenin asserted, "Everything that contributes to the building of a Communist society is moral, everything that hinders it is immoral."[11] Logically, the ethic of Soviet Communism followed from its conception of a classless society. As Lenin stated, "Our morality is entirely subordinate to the interests of the class struggle of the proletariat."[12] Lenin's outrage at the horrible conditions suffered by industrial workers produced an intense hatred not only for the Russian power structure but also for the religious traditions of the Russian people. Lenin equated religious traditions with social oppression because he believed that religious concepts tricked workers into accepting their fate. Lenin clearly asserted his disgust for religion: "Every religious idea, every idea of God, even flirting with the idea of God, is unutterable vileness . . . vileness of the most dangerous kind, 'contagion' of the most abominable kind. Millions of sins, filthy deeds, acts of violence and physical contagions . . . are far less dangerous than the subtle, spiritual idea of a God decked out in the smartest 'ideological' costumes. . . . Every defense or justification of the idea of God, even the most refined, the best intentioned, is a justification of reaction."[13] While Marx provided the philosophical and ethical justification for the demise of religion, Lenin additionally argued that enlightened individuals were morally obliged to destroy religion.

Within the Soviet Union, virtue became synonymous with sacrifice to

Communist Party dictates. Ivan Kairov, a prominent Soviet intellectual, explained that Soviet virtues included "proclaiming the principles of solidarity, mutual aid, devotion to the general welfare, and faithfulness to duty."[14] In workplaces, schools, and the media, Soviet citizens were urged to only consider the needs of the Communist Party. Summarizing the commitment necessary from loyal Communists, the novelist Alexander Ostrowski wrote that a Communist citizen should to be able to say on her deathbed, "My whole life, my whole strength I gave to the most wonderful thing in the world — the battle for the liberation of humanity."[15] And in her comprehensive study of daily life under Stalinism, Sheila Fitzpatrick argues Soviet citizens came to internalize much of this moral propaganda, which was presented in the form of dramatic stories. She writes, "One of the stories which was most widely disseminated in the 1930s may be called 'The Radiant Future,' after Alexandr Zinoviev's book by that name. In the story, the present was the time when the future, socialism, was being built. For the time being, there must be sacrifice and hardship. The rewards would come later."[16]

Whether the fall of the Soviet Union can be attributed to flaws in its economic system or to its continued dependency on creating a new Soviet Man who tirelessly worked toward a "radiant future" is difficult to ascertain because the two became intricately linked. Marxist-Leninists believed that economic and social problems were predominantly rooted in the ideological backwardness of their population. From the start, Lenin demanded that Communist propaganda stress "militancy and irreconcilability towards all forms of idealism and religion. And that means that materialism organically reaches that consequence and perfection which in the language of philosophy is called — militant atheism."[17] When militant atheism did not spread like wildfire, Communist Party ideologues began to blame religion for all social and economic problems. In turn, successes were attributed to the power of atheist ideology. As Emelian Yaroslavsky asserted, "There can be no doubt that the fact that the new state of the USSR led by the Communist Party, with a program permeated by the spirit of militant atheism, gives the reason why this state is successfully surmounting the great difficulties that stand in its way — that neither 'heavenly powers' not the exhortations of all the priests in all the world can prevent its attaining its aims it has set itself."[18] The fact that Communist Party officials paid so much attention to religion reveals a deep-seated incongruity — Marxist-Leninists thought religious ideology was an obvious sham but also believed deeply in the power of religious concepts. Although their conviction that the persistence of religious belief would lead to economic and social failure remained unquestioned, Soviet officials began to more deeply investigate how religion could be effectively extinguished. And this proved as big a goal as any they would tackle.

RELIGIOUS SUPPLY AND DEMAND

Marxist-Leninists initially equated secularization with the elimination of religious supply.[19] Although the process to cut off religious supply proved quite brutal and destructive, it was straightforward and compatible with Marxist theory. Marx viewed religion as a form of ideological domination. Therefore, if the state could destroy the institutional means of domination — in this case, religious organizations — the ideology advanced by these institutions would naturally disappear. Of course, this strategy assumes that individuals' demand for religious concepts and meanings is mainly a product of supply. In other words, individuals' belief in God, worship in churches and mosques, and performance of religious rituals are explained by the power of religious institutions to indoctrinate the population. Trotsky asserted that as religious authorities lost their "temporal power," their religious followers would abandon them. According to this scheme, individuals would find that they had no need for religious concepts or meaning when they ceased to be promoted through official avenues of socialization. In theory, religious ideology would reveal itself to be nothing more than rhetoric intended to justify the authority of organizations that did not have the material interests of the individual at heart.

Early Marxist-Leninists also believed that individuals had no need for religion on any level. But many Soviet citizens remained religious believers after the Russian Revolution, indicating that some individuals still wanted religion, even when it was not officially promoted by the state. Initially, Communist Party theorists posited that this was simply the result of ignorance. Just like healing incantations get replaced by modern medical treatments, religious beliefs would eventually be replaced by scientific knowledge, Communist Party leaders believed. From this perspective, "religious demand" was nothing more than a misplaced desire to explain and understand the material world. Hence, science could supply everything religion could, only better and more truthfully.

Contrary to this Marxist-Leninist perspective, classical and contemporary social theorists posit alternative conceptions of religious demand. Emile Durkheim famously equated religion with ritualistic activity.[20] Consequently, Durkheim indicated that religious demand was a universal need to participate in sacred rituals, where individuals derived a heightened sense of social solidarity and belonging. Based on this general understanding of religious demand, many practices, objects, and groups we don't normally think of as religious could potentially supply the universal need for ritual interaction. As such, social clubs with their initiation ceremonies, the sacred symbolism of a nation's flag, and habitual daily interactions can fulfill religious demand.[21]

Durkheim's ideas, although quite distinct, share an important commonality with the Marxist-Leninist approach to religion. Both perspectives indicate that humans have no natural affinity for supernatural concepts or intrinsic spiritual needs; in other words, religious needs are socially constructed. And for both, the otherworldly elements of religious organizations and rituals are actually peripheral to the main function and intention of religion. For Marxist-Leninists, religion was a pseudoscience used for the purpose of political exploitation, and for Durkheim, religion was an evolving expression of social solidarity. In the final analysis, Communist Party officials came to appreciate Durkheim's insight into the ritual elements of religion and decided that they could best subvert religion by stealing its rituals. This switch in perspective came as a result of observing religious persistence in the 1920s and early 1930s and explains the creation of an atheist alternative to religion.

However, Marxist-Leninists denied that the supernatural could be an important aspect of religious demand, mainly because they viewed the idea of the supernatural as so patently ludicrous. Contemporary theorists Rodney Stark and Roger Finke argue that explanations of God, gods, the afterlife, and spirituality are extremely important to understanding the allure and strength of religious traditions and groups.[22] The demand for religion, according to Stark and Finke, is a universal attraction to supernatural concepts, the very ideas Marxist-Leninists believed to be superficial and meaningless rhetoric. Consequently, Communist Party efforts to fulfill religious demand through scientific education and national rituals never really addressed this supernatural aspect of religious demand.

Soviet officials introduced their atheist alternative to religion through a push-and-pull strategy. First, particularly in the 1920s and 1930s, the Soviet regime pushed religious competitors out of the ideological market through sheer force and brutality. Second, throughout the entire pre-Gorbachev Soviet era, Marxist-Leninists attempted to pull in loyalists with the lure of utopian dreams and an atheist alternative to religion. This two-pronged strategy addressed and sought to undermine both the supply of religion and the corresponding demand for it.

BURYING THE COMPETITION

Mark Beissinger writes, "It is difficult to find any rationale for the bloody orgy unleashed by Stalin in the mid thirties."[23] Certainly, acts of terror by Stalin and other Soviet leaders were absurdly brutal by nature of their enormity alone. But the massive number of arrests and executions of political opponents follows a general logic of political survival in a turbulent era. It is vicious attacks on nonthreatening individuals that require a deeper understanding of the logic of the Communist Party. The most obvious example of brutal persecution of a politically submissive population is the mass terror waged against monks, nuns, religious clerics, and the religiously devout in the 1930s. If consolidating political power and stimulating economic development were the primary goals of Stalin and the Communist Party, they would have been more sensible to simply leave religion alone. Most probably, many mainstream churches would have fully legitimated Soviet rule if given some financial support. In fact, a few early Bolsheviks proposed turning the Orthodox Church into a "Red" church, but this idea was quickly dismissed; as a high-ranking Communist Party official explained in 1920, "The church is disintegrating, we must help with this, but by no means reconstitute her in a new form. . . . Our stake is on Communism and not on religion."[24] Consequently, the Communist Party remained steadfast in its plan to shut down religion and kill off religious leaders because early party leaders believed they were morally called to.

Consequently, religious groups were the victims of extreme violence immediately following the 1917 Russian Revolution. In the civil war that followed the revolution, Bolsheviks targeted Orthodox churches, monasteries, and clerics as potential sources of antirevolutionary activity. Church property was seized, and religious leaders, monks, and nuns were often killed in the process. The terror of the civil war sometimes spun out of control as murderous gangs took advantage of the melee: "In many cases the tortures, murders and vandalism were the autonomous initiative of local anarchistic bands of army and naval deserters calling themselves Bolsheviks."[25] In 1922, Patriarch Tikhon wrote a protest to Lenin that thousands of clergy were being killed and that over a hundred thousand religious believers had been shot.[26] His protest was ignored, and he was placed in exile. A decade later, Tikhon was executed.

In first decades of Soviet rule, religious leaders and advocates were sometimes brutally and publicly executed. Alexander Yakovlev, a former advisor to Gorbachev, explained the extent of the terror in the early days of the Soviet Union:

> The official term *execution* was often a euphemism for murder, fiendishly refined. For example, Metropolitan Vladimir of Kiev was mutilated, castrated, and shot, and his corpse was left naked for the public to desecrate. Metropolitan Veniamin of St. Petersburg, in line to succeed the patriarch, was turned into a pillar of ice: he was doused with cold water in the freezing cold. Bishop Germogen of Tobolsk, who had voluntarily accompanied the czar into exile, was strapped to a paddlewheel of a steamboat and mangled by the rotating blades. Archbishop Andronnik of Perm, who had been renowned earlier as a missionary and had worked as such in Japan, was buried alive. Archbishop Vasily was crucified and burned.[27]

Lesser-known clerics, monks, and nuns were imprisoned in the extensive Gulag system, where they ultimately met their demise through starvation, sickness, or mass execution.

Systematic religious persecution began in the 1930s and reemerged periodically according to the whims of Communist Party leadership. The intermittent yet ongoing violence was the direct result of religious persistence. Because Soviet elites argued that religion was "a cause and not merely the symptom of social problems . . . religious practices became the scapegoat of the Soviet ideological machine, they became the only readily admissible reason for the failure of the complete re-education of the masses."[28] To end this cycle of religious persistence, Emelian Yaroslavsky declared in the 1930s that "several hundred reactionary zealots of religion" needed to be exterminated.[29]

In pursuing these ends, the Communist Party was careful not to make its extermination project public. As Sheila Fitzpatrick notes, "Secret 'hard-line' instructions were issued to local party organizations but not published. When the antireligious drive inflamed the anger of the rural population, not to mention that of the Pope and other Western church spokesmen, the regime was able to back off from a policy that it had never publicly endorsed anyway."[30] In this manner, the Communist Party attempted to have its cake and eat it too by officially establishing religious freedom while covertly waging a massive war on all religion.

Although it is difficult to determine the exact number of individuals murdered during the Stalinist terror of the 1930s, the most recent figures indicate that more than 100,000 religious leaders were executed between 1937 and 1941. Former Soviet official Alexander Yakovlev had privileged access to private Communist Party documents before his death in

2005 and maintained that 85,300 clergy were executed in 1937, 21,000 in 1938, and 3,900 between 1939 and 1941.[31] Additionally, hundreds of thousands of individuals were sent to prison camps for "religious" crimes. Of course, many prisoners died during their sentence, making their prison term a type of drawn-out execution.

One surviving prisoner estimated the number of religious prisoners in the massive Shpalernaya Prison. "There were always in each cell ten to fifteen persons held in connection with cases involving questions of religion. And there were some of them in isolation cells, so that their number must have been about ten percent of all the prison inmates."[32] Other camps appeared to contain more religious prisoners; in a women's camp in Moldavia, one inmate indicated that "the majority of prisoners were believers."[33] Perhaps women tended to be arrested for religious reasons more than men; it is difficult to know. Regardless, two findings appear certain. First, hundreds of thousands of religious followers were imprisoned; and second, Communist Party officials indiscriminately attacked a wide variety of believers, from Russian Orthodox Christians to Jehovah's Witnesses to Muslims.

Mass executions on the scale of the 1930s terror never reappeared. Nevertheless, widespread imprisonment of individuals for religious reasons began again in the 1950s and 1960s. Baptists were arrested in large numbers during this time, and the Communist Party began to imprison Jews instead of allowing them to immigrate to Israel.[34] Officials also continued to humiliate and disgrace individuals in ways that were especially offensive to their religious beliefs. For instance, "The confinement of Russian priests at Solovky [a monastery] was an elaborate blasphemy. Detention in a monastery which from time immemorial had attracted numerous pilgrims and had now been converted into a concentration camp must have been felt by priests as a special insult. The administration, far from sparing their feelings, compelled them to witness the profanation of former churches. Along with other prisoners, priests were housed in the Troitskii and Preobrazhenskii Cathedrals. They were subjected to studied humiliation."[35] Prison guards targeted certain practices and fashions so that individuals would have difficulty expressing their religiosity in any form. Orthodox priests were forced to shave simply because their beards had religious significance, and guards made sure to work religious prisoners on religious holidays. The brutality and inhumanity of the Secularization Experiment in the 1930s cannot be overstated.

One harsh penalty for religious belief that continued throughout most the Soviet era was confinement within psychiatric hospitals. Because religion was officially viewed as illusory, religious believers could subsequently be deemed insane. Individuals arrested for religious reasons were sometimes examined by a psychiatric commission, which officially had the power

> to decide whether or not a person is mentally responsible. If they decide that he is not, a believer is not allowed to attend his own trial, and the courts do their best to keep out family and friends as well. Thus a trial becomes a formality. Relatives can appeal after the believer is sentenced to a psychiatric hospital. . . . Here a believer may be surrounded by patients with severe mental illnesses; many of them will have committed violent crimes such as rape, assault, and murder. . . . Nurses and medical staff are subject to the security demands of the institution, and find it difficult to act humanely towards patients even if they wished to do so.[36]

In the 1980s, Amnesty International examined a sample of 210 psychiatric patients in the Soviet Union; it found that 15 percent of the patients were sentenced to psychiatric confinement simply because they were religious believers.[37]

Although many religiously devout individuals lost their livelihoods or lives due to religious repression, most religious believers remained active members of society. Nevertheless, they were not immune from harassment if they decided to publicly express their religiosity. Admission of religious faith would negatively impact career options and social benefits. These more subtle tactics of social control existed throughout the Soviet era. In his two-year study of religion in Soviet society during the early 1980s, William Van den Bercken concluded,

> Social control is an important means of promoting atheism in society. . . . [Control] is aimed at religious life by means of the many group sessions Soviet citizens must attend in the workplace as part of the educational system. Groups discuss the "anti-social" behavior of religious believers who are subject to "comradely verdicts" . . . it is shameful for citizens to attend a church service or wear crosses; so to do is grounds for public criticism and depending on the gravity of the offence, sanctions involving the career. Controls within the Communist cadre groups also extend to members' family and friends: a party leader can be expelled because his son-in-law sings in church choir.[38]

The costs of religious expression in the Soviet Union were very high, ranging from actual physical harm and even death in the early years of Communism to insidious harassment by bosses, neighbors, and relatives for most of the Soviet era.

The Secularization Experiment included not only a wide range of coercive tactics intent on driving the individual from any public expression of religion but also a denial of meeting places for religious groups. In seizing all private property, Communist Party officials were able to determine the fate of all churches, mosques, and synagogues. In 1914, before Communist rule, there were approximately 54,000 functioning Russian Orthodox Churches; by 1941, only 4,200 churches remained open.[39] In 1941, less than 8 percent of the Russian Orthodox Churches functioning in 1914 were still in existence. The number of Russian Orthodox Churches then grew during World War II as restrictions on church activities were briefly lifted; this number subsequently shrank as postwar antireligious policies reemerged (see table 1). Monasteries and convents were also closed in great numbers; by 1964, only ten Orthodox monasteries and convents were still in existence from the hundreds that functioned before Communist rule.[40]

Churches were not only closed but, as an additional insult to the religiously devout, the structures were often converted into Communist offices or other buildings. Most dramatically, Communist officials remade the beautiful St. Petersburg cathedral of Our Lady of Kazan into the Museum of the History of Religion and of Atheism, which provided exhibits to demonstrate the "folly" of religion. In many cases, exquisite church buildings were simply demolished. The ornate and architecturally unique Cathedral of Christ the Savior was blown up to make way for a proposed shrine to Lenin. The monument was never actually constructed; instead, an enormous outdoor swimming pool was built on its site. Often material from a church was employed for other purposes; for instance, the Revolutionary Square metro station in central Moscow was constructed from the stones of the Danilov Monastery.[41] Church bells were confiscated and melted down for their precious metal, and holy relics were ransacked. "Icons were stripped of the precious settings; churches were looted of holy vessels of gold and silver, including jeweled boxes for the Eucharist and chandeliers from the fifteenth to seventeenth centuries. Solid gold crosses from the days of Ivan the Terrible and the first Romanovs were packed in boxes and sacks. Precious stones were gouged out, covers of Bibles were ripped off, all the gold and silver coins that could be found were confiscated. Ancient icons provided fuel for bonfires, books handwritten in Old Church Slavonic perished in the flames."[42] These acts of vandalism display not only a hatred for religious ideology but also an intense loathing of the existence of religious artifacts. Their symbolism alone was cause for fear, as if Marxist-Leninists themselves believed in an object's spiritual power to bring forth belief. In

TABLE I. SURVIVING CHURCHES

Year	Number of Russian Orthodox Churches
1914	54,000
1928	39,000
1941	4,200
1945	16,000
1948	15,000
1958	17,500
1966	7,500

SOURCE: Powell 1975: 41.

one especially fierce effort to eradicate religious possessions in the home, Communist Party officials falsely claimed that "an epidemic of syphilis in the countryside was being spread through the practice of kissing icons" and banned the ownership of Orthodox icons.[43]

Communist leaders also tried to discourage religious practices in the home, but these were far more difficult to monitor. Because religious activities needed to be officially approved by the government, private religious services were illegal and, if discovered, could result in sizeable penalties. In 1969, a covert religious practitioner wrote the following message to Russian Orthodox friends in the United States: "I was fined one hundred rubles in a single week for conducting services in my home; a short time later I was again fined one hundred rubles. This was when I was earning seventy rubles a month. My family, my children were sentenced to starvation."[44] This individual was never heard from again.

Non-Orthodox religious believers suffered similar fates. Mosques and temples were closed, and the cultural aspects of all religions were deemed corruptive. Soviets aggressively attacked many institutional arms of Islam. By the mid-1920s, Islamic courts ceased to have any official impact in criminal cases or civil suits, and Soviets had established Communist state courts throughout Central Asia. A record of functioning Islamic courts in Uzbekistan from 1922 to 1927 shows their rapid elimination (see figure 1).

In turn, Islamic studies were no longer an element in the education of Muslim youth, a deficiency that would have powerful implications for the practice of the Islam throughout Central Asia. For instance, Soviet schools reformed the instruction of indigenous languages, and, "through the so-called language and alphabet reforms, Central Asian youths were denied access to the very rich Islamic religious literary traditions written

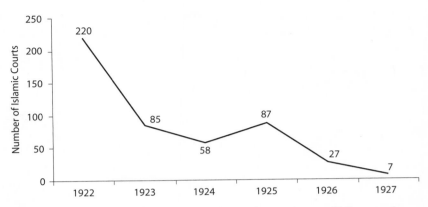

Figure 1. The Decline of Islamic Courts in Uzbekistan. Source: Keller 2001b: 148.

in the Arabic alphabet."[45] Approximately eight thousand Islamic primary and secondary schools were in operation in Central Asia before the Russian Revolution; by 1928, none remained.[46]

In Islamic communities, schools and mosques were mainly supported by revenue generated by *waqf* (clerical property). Without this independent resource, schools and mosques became dependent on Soviet officials, who closed both en masse. No Islamic schools survived the assault, and only a few official mosques endured. "In 1917, there were 20,000 mosques in Central Asia, but by 1929 fewer than 4,000 were functioning and by 1935 there were only 60 registered mosques in Uzbekistan [the largest of the Asian Soviet Republics, with over half of the Muslim population of Central Asia]"[47] Without *waqf*, imans and mullahs were unable to financially support themselves, and the number of official clergy dropped dramatically; many regions lost all registered imans or mullahs. In addition to losing their material resources, many Islamic clergy were arrested and imprisoned during Stalin's first purges. Unofficial clergy continued to minister to Muslims, but official clergy were effectively driven from their positions by financial necessity. By 1936, there were no registered Islamic clergy in the major urban centers of Central Asia.[48]

The repressive tactics of the Soviet government were quite successful in depleting the resources and places of worship of all the established religious traditions in the Soviet Union. In addition, Soviets threatened or punished religious leaders to discourage any attempts to criticize government policies and preach their faith. Coercion and overt repression played a central role in Soviet attempts to eliminate religion.

But as Communist Party authority in the 1930s encountered opposition from religious organizations and their members, particularly in rural areas, they began to supplement coercion with a crusade to teach the public that antireligious policies were not destructive but, in fact, for society's own good. In essence, Communist Party leaders realized that they needed to do more than shut off religious supply; they also needed to meet a lingering demand for religion. It is in this quest that the Secularization Experiment took a remarkable turn. As Isaiah Berlin aptly noted, Soviet Communism began to grow into a "new ecumenical organization, a kind of anti-Church."[49]

ATHEISM AS A NEW FAITH

The Church

How do you capture the hearts and minds of individuals and instill in them a deeply held faith formally unknown to them? Communist rulers encountered a culture in which religion was taken for granted. Russians, Ukrainians, Lithuanians, Central Asians, and the rest of the Soviet public may not have been the most religious people in the world, but they all lived in regions where religion was ubiquitous. Religious traditions had permeated the culture of the Soviet Union for centuries. Now, Communist leaders hoped to convince their citizenry that all things religious were evil and introduce them to a new "truth" — scientific atheism. As propagators of this antireligious message, Soviet officials resembled religious missionaries on a crusade to covert the masses. If missionaries promised locals an all-powerful God and a tempting afterlife, what would Marxist-Leninists offer?

In the 1920s, the Communist Party created an organization called the League of Militant Atheists to spread the message of atheism. This group referred to the Marxist-Leninist doctrine as *scientific atheism*. In general, scientific atheism combined a belief in socialist utopianism with an ethical mandate to proselytize the message of atheism. The role of the League of Militant Atheists was to teach the ethics of scientific atheism as a replacement for the moral teachings of popular theologies. They argued that religious doctrines created, to use Nietzsche's term, a "slave morality" that fooled religious believers into mistaking passivity for moral goodness. To dispel corrupt moral doctrines, the League of Militant Atheists set up atheist "cells," or houses, as a system of outlets where rural communities could learn about atheism and meet to discuss the fal-

sity of religion. For the most part, atheist cells presented antireligious lectures, distributed copies of *Bezbozhnik* (the atheist newsletter), elicited
testimonies from converted atheists, and showcased various antireligious
dramatizations. The league was determined to create atheist cells across
the entire Soviet Union to reach those citizens who were currently ignorant of atheistic science.

> What parishes are for the Church the cells were to be for the League of
> Militant Atheists, only cells were to outnumber the parishes at the ratio
> of sixty to one or so. The Five Year Plan of anti-religious propaganda which
> was adopted in 1932 and was to run until 1937 provided for the organiza-
> tion of 400,000 cells in town alone; not less than one cell was to be founded
> in each factory, government office and school. In addition, 600,000 cells
> were to be founded in the countryside, one cell in every inhabited locality,
> collective farm and machine tractor station.[50]

In total, the league proposed to establish one million atheist cells throughout the Soviet Union. This goal was never actually accomplished due to
the unrealistic ambition of the proposal, but the league received funding
and resources nonetheless.

In addition to setting up atheist cell houses to replace local parishes,
Soviets also used urban factories as alternatives to churches. Because the
revolution was based on proletarian solidarity, the factory edifice could
serve as a meeting and communal place for the worker class. Daniel
Peris, who researched the inner workings of League of Militant Atheists,
points out that the league's "antireligious propaganda suggested that factories were the proper substitute for churches as places of community,
faith, and purpose. Particularly in visual propaganda targeted at urban
audiences, factories effectively became the churches of a socialist era:
large, formidable enclosed spaces, often with a single piece of machinery
at one end serving as an altar to the god Industry. Bezbozhnik u stanka
[an atheist publication] regularly printed half and full-page multicolor
drawings of such factories."[51] Using a factory as a type of proletarian
church aligned with the ethic of a socialist revolution. Workers could
supplant the time they had formerly wasted with supernatural concerns
with factory work. Regarding resource allotment, commitment, and
importance, factories were a direct and real substitute for religious commitment. And factories also could potentially supply something that religious groups did — a common sense of purpose. With banners, lectures,
and group activities, Marxist-Leninists hoped to turn factories into
places that held real emotional belonging.

The Homily

Because of its official concordant with the Russian Orthodox Church during World War II, the Soviet regime briefly abandoned its overt proselytizing of atheism and Stalin abolished the League of Militant Atheists. Although the league never reemerged following World War II, the Knowledge Society, the Institute of Scientific Atheism, the Komsomol, the Pioneers, and a variety of "cultural enlightenment" institutions formed after the war to take over many of its functions.[52] An important purpose of these groups was to create and distribute antireligious propaganda. They, along with the Soviet school systems, distributed educational materials as the main means to convert the population to atheism. This tactic was based on a simple understanding of religious demand, that is, individuals were religious because they were ignorant.

Earlier, the League of Militant Atheists had viewed rural peasants as quintessential religious believers who only turned to God in times of need because they did not realize that science and technology could solve their health, economic, and agricultural troubles. Therefore, atheist conversion could be accomplished by exposing peasants to technological advancements. The president of the league proclaimed that "religion exists where knowledge is lacking, religion is opposed to science."[53] According to this view of religious demand, technology demonstrated that humans could work "miracles" that were not preformed by God and, consequently, serve the needs of the public better than God. For example, farming technology became a means to convince rural residences of their outdated reliance on religious concepts: "An anti-religious pamphlet printed in the first Five Year Plan period was entitled 'Prayers or Tractor' and a widespread poster crudely elaborated on the alleged contradiction between 'cross and tractor.' The alternative, 'religion or tractor,' with which the communists operated, never existed in the minds of the people for whom this propaganda was intended. The illusions about 'atheist tractor' were therefore soon shattered, especially when peasants affixed crosses to them and when priests celebrated thanksgiving services at their arrival in villages."[54]

As this instance demonstrates, for scientific atheists, the tractor proved that God was not in control of agricultural productivity. Militant atheists continued to pit technology against religion in many domains and provided testimonies from converts who claimed to have lost their religious faith when presented with technology. As one peasant stated in the official league journal, "I've become a complete [atheist]; electricity totally destroyed my belief in God."[55]

Militant atheists also believed that science disproved religion because God remained unseen, his miracles were never subject to empirical verification, and certain religious stories were scientifically inconceivable. Following World War II and after the dissolution of the League of Militant Atheists, Soviet officials started a campaign to produce natural-scientific arguments against belief in God. For instance, Soviet scientists placed holy water under a microscope to prove that it had no special properties, and the corpses of saints were exhumed to demonstrate that they too were subject to corruption.[56] These activities indicated that atheist propagandists held a very literal interpretation of religious language; for them, holy water and the bodies of saints were expected to hold some physical sign of their divinity. In addition, Soviet propagandists erected the Museum of the History of Religion and of Atheism to publicly exhibit the scientific impossibility of many religious ideas and stories. For example, one exhibit demonstrated that "the ark that Noah built could not have accommodated all the animals which then populated the earth."[57]

These instances reveal that Marxist-Leninists viewed religion simply as a pseudoscience. As such, the Soviet school system consistently promoted "atheistic science" to combat the effects of religion. The curriculum of scientific atheism resembled the curriculum for much of the Soviet educational system, as it was based more on memorization than critical analysis. For homework, schoolchildren were sometimes asked to convert a member of their family to atheism by reciting arguments that were intended to disprove religious beliefs. And schoolchildren often memorized antireligious rhymes, songs, and catechisms. Antireligious ideas infiltrated the most basic lessons in unrelated topics: "Physics, biology, chemistry, astronomy, mathematics, history, geography and literature all serve as jumping-off points to instruct pupils on the evils or falsity of religion."[58] Although many school subjects appear unrelated to religion, Soviets believed that any intellectual activity was intrinsically opposed to religion. The Soviet educational system officially stated that "the bringing up of children in the atheist spirit" was one of its primary missions.[59] University students were also required to actively propagate atheism and were told, "Those who refuse to make such practical application of their study [of scientific atheism] will lose their scholarships and must leave the university."[60] Special pressure was placed on academics and scientists to join the atheist educational organization Znanie, and, by the late

1970s, for example, over 80 percent of all professors and doctors of science in Lithuania became members.[61]

The course syllabi from the atheist universities of the Soviet Union indicate how the topic of atheism was presented as a historically logical outcome of scientific development; Soviet college students chose from the following course selections:

Physics: The place of physics in anti-religious propaganda. Connection between ancient myths and the endeavor of man to discover the causal relationship between various natural phenomena. The expression of primitive man's helplessness to establish the true, scientific reason for the phenomena. Scientific method in thinking as the foundation of godlessness.

Chemistry: Its importance for economic life in peace and war, in agriculture, and for working out a correct worldview. The part played by chemistry in the struggle against religious superstition.

Geology: Introduction to the Biblical religious point of view. Methods of geological reckoning of time compared with Church calculations. How old is the earth? Practical work for the study of the earth's surface. Belief in hell under the earth. Rejection of the religious explanation of the causes of earthquakes and volcanic eruptions.

Mathematics: Mathematics as a scientific method for studying the phenomena surrounding us. . . . Causes furthering the development of mathematics in antiquity and in our days. The "mathematical numbers" of pagan priests in ancient times. Legends about the supernatural origins of mathematical knowledge. The monopoly of mathematical knowledge demanded by pagan priests to enable them to oppress others.

Biology: A short history of biological science. The importance of biology for working out a dialectic-materialistic worldview. The importance of biology in medicine, technics, agriculture, and other branches of human life. Importance of biology for anti-religious propaganda.

Medicine: How religion looks on the cause of sickness. The modern scientific answer to this question. Contagious diseases. The origin and struggle against them. The founders of modern medicine. Serum, vaccination, and chemical therapeutics. Individual and social prophylactics. Religious ceremonies as a source of contagion.[62]

What stands out in these syllabi, in addition to the antireligious substance of each course, is the way in which the curriculum appears to ignore the objective, applied, and experimental essence of science. Instead, scientific findings are presented as correct or incorrect based on their supposed ideological positions. Religion is presented as the historic confounder of scientific advancement, with atheism providing the philosophical framework from which to conduct accurate science. In the end, it was atheist education that was supposed to lead to proper scientific, social, and philosophical thinking.

The Liturgy

Equating ignorance with religious demand became problematic when modern, urban, and educated citizens continued to observe religious habits, holidays, and life cycle rituals. In the early 1920s, Trotsky began to play with new symbols and ceremonial activities to help inspire troops in the newly formed Red Army; he introduced the red star as a unifying logo and a military oath.[63] Summarizing Trotsky's writings in *Pravda* at the time, Christopher Binns maintains that Trotsky

> argued that rationalistic anti-religious propaganda alone could not change the deep-rooted customs of family life. The Party must recognize "man's desire for the theatrical", his "strong and legitimate need for an outer mani-festation of emotion at regular intervals in order to relieve the monotony of life." Along with the theatre and cinema, secular festivals and life-cycle rites like those reported at the conference could help replace religion and alcohol in the satisfaction of these needs. Ceremonies could be detached from religion as the theatre had been from ritual. "In the course of years and decades" new customs would develop by a process of natural selection, "without bureaucratization, i.e. compulsion from above."[64]

Even though Trotsky would famously lose his initial influence over Soviet plans, his perspective on the importance of ceremonial alternatives to religion would become the centerpiece of the antireligious campaign.

Upon gaining power in 1918, the Bolshevik leaders immediately altered the Russian calendar from the Julian to the Gregorian system, a change that intentionally confused the Orthodox holiday season.[65] In addition, Soviets created work schedules that always conflicted with reli-gious holidays. From 1932 to 1940, they replaced the seven-day week with a six-day one: "five days of work, the sixth off. The antireligious propaganda believed this would be a most effective means of preventing believers from attending the Sunday liturgy. In addition, the 25th and 26th of December were proclaimed the Days of Industrialization with obligatory presence at work."[66] Many such strategies were employed to create confusion and push citizens out of traditional holiday activities. The following humorous example of how Communists in Poland covertly tried to discourage participation in a religious holiday demon-strates the clever efforts of Communist elites. "On Corpus Cristi [a Roman Catholic procession] at ten o'clock in the morning — when the processions begin — the Polish television service, which does not usually broadcast at this time, put on the popular American Wild-West serial *Zorro.*"[67] Even decadent American television was more preferable to Polish Communists than religious expression.

Nevertheless, these tactics were generally unsuccessful, as work absenteeism continued on religious days. In response, Yaroslavsky and other propaganda planners began to construct a growing calendar of Soviet ceremonies to replace religious holidays. New holidays directly overlapped with major religious festivals, and many new celebrations offered opportunities to joyously recognize Communist values. Table 2 lists the 1977 version of the Soviet calendar; as is shown, the number of Soviet holidays kept growing as the years passed. Most of these holidays were only celebrated by the section of the public to whom the holiday refers, such as Day of the Metallurgist, Day of Soviet Police, and Day of the Drivers.

In the first decade of Soviet rule, these substitute celebrations were quite rudimentary in their conception and execution. "As one peasant caustically remarked, they did not amount to much more than 'taking a red flag and running down the street.' "[68] But with time, participants developed more elaborate customs, often borrowing from local Christian or pagan rituals. For instance, "Instead of observing Easter, one model collective farm celebrated the Day of First Furrowing, during which the peasants lined up on both sides of the tractor and followed its progress, thus adapting the format of a traditional religious procession."[69] The level of mimicry was meticulous, ensuring that atheist rituals supplied the same elements and elicited the same responses as religious rites. But some people still "mistook Bolshevik processions for religious ones; the untutored peasants of one remote village, according to a contemporary report, 'took off their hats and devoutly crossed themselves' on seeing the approach of a column carrying colorful banners and portraits of august bearded figures (in fact of Lenin, Kalinin, and Lunarcharksy) unaware that it was a May Day 'manifestation.' "[70]

The pageantry and solemnity surrounding Communist holidays illustrate the importance of ritual solidarity in Communist society. Over the course of decades, most religious rituals were eventually replaced with atheist alternatives. Red youth ceremonies stood in for religious confirmations to instill a solemn devotion to Communism in future generations. Similarly, atheist funerals and even birth rituals (a response to baptism) replicated the sanctity of their religious counterparts while claiming a moral superiority. With no official reference to religious concepts, funerals were carefully worded to create a secular promise of immortal-

TABLE 2. SOVIET HOLIDAY CALENDAR
(WITH YEAR OF ENACTMENT, WHEN KNOWN)

January 1	New Year's Day (1919)
February 23	Day of the Soviet Army and Navy
March 8	International Woman's Day (1913)
March 18	Day of Paris Commune (1918)
March, third Sunday	Day of Workers in Housing and Communal Services (1977)
March 27	International Day of the Theater (1961)
April, first Sunday	Day of the Geologist (1966)
April 7	All-World Day of Health (1948)
April, second Sunday	Day of Forces of Anti-aircraft Defense (1975)
April 12	Day of Astronautics
April 22	Anniversary of Lenin's Birthday
April 24	International Day of Solidarity of Youth
May 1	Day of International Worker's Solidarity (1918)
May 5	Day of the Press (1922)
May 7	Day of the Radio (1967)
May 9	Victory Day (1945)
May 19	Birthday of the Pioneer Organization in the Name of Lenin
May 25	Day of Liberation of Africa (1963)
May 28	Day of the Frontier Guard
May, last Sunday	Day of the Worker in the Chemical Industry (1965)
June 1	International Day for the Protection of Children (1950)
June, first Sunday	Day of the Land Reclamation Worker (1976)
June, second Sunday	Day of the Worker in Light Industry (1966)
June, third Sunday	Day of the Worker in the Medical Services (1963)
June, last Sunday	Day of Soviet Youth (1958)
July, first Sunday	Day of International Co-operation (1923)
July, first Sunday	Day of Worker of the Sea and River Fleet (1976)
July, second Sunday	Day of the Fisherman (1965)
July, third Sunday	Day of the Metallurgist (1957)

ity. For example, one funeral rite offered, "Life continues, and everything that the deceased has managed to achieve will continue. His causes are alive in ours, his beginnings we shall complete, everything is left to man."[71] In this instance, the work of the individual attained an afterlife; his spirit lived on not in heaven but in the material world. In addition, funeral services often contained moments of silence as stand-ins for silent prayers.

July, fourth Sunday	Day of the Worker in Trade (1966)
July, last Sunday	Day of the Navy of the Soviet Union (1939)
August, first Sunday	All-Union Day of the Railway Worker (1936)
August, second Sunday	All-Union Day of the Athlete and Gymnast (1939)
August, second Sunday	Day of the Construction Worker (1955)
August, third Sunday	Day of the Air Force of the Soviet Union (1933)
August, last Sunday	Day of the Miner (1947)
September, first Sunday	All-Union Day of Workers in the Oil and Gas Industry (1965)
September 8	International Day of Solidarity of Journalists (1958)
September, second Sunday	Day of the Tank Soldier (1946)
September, third Sunday	Day of the Forestry Worker (1966)
September, last Sunday	Day of the Worker in Heavy Engineering (1966)
October, first Sunday	Day of the Teacher (1965)
October, second Sunday	All-Union Day of Workers in Agriculture (1966)
October, third Sunday	Day of Workers in the Food Processing Industry (1966)
October 24	International Day of the United Nations Organization (1945)
October 29	Birthday of the Komsomol (1919)
October, last Sunday	Day of Drivers (1976)
November 7	Anniversary of the Great October Socialist Revolution (1918)
November 10	Day of Soviet Police (1962)
November 10	All-World Day of Youth (1945)
November 17	International Students' Day (1941)
November 19	Day of the Rocket Forces (1964) and the Artillery (1944)
December 22	Day of the Worker in Power Engineering (1966)
December 25 and 26	Days of Industrialization

SOURCE: In *Nashi Prazkniki,* from Lane 1981.

The overt mimicry of religious practices was done quite plainly and deliberately. In fact, many atheist rituals largely involved the replacement of "Soviet Motherland" for "God" in the wording and the insertion of a picture or bust of Lenin in place of a religious symbol. The ubiquitous placement of pictures of either Lenin or Stalin grew out of an active attempt to replace religious icons. In Russian Orthodox homes, a single corner is usually dedicated to religious icons; a campaign to

remove these icons led to the introduction of "Godless or Lenin cor-
ners."[72] Instead of paintings of saints, individuals would display photos
of Lenin or various atheist propaganda trinkets. Christopher Binns notes,
"The first signs of the mounting hero-worship were observable in 1918–
19; Lenin several times voiced his distaste for this . . . [but] soon portraits
of Lenin were being carried by demonstrators or decorating public buildings."[73] But unlike the manufacturing of rituals, the cult of Lenin occurred almost spontaneously and against Lenin's own wishes.[74]

By the 1930s, Communist rallies included large placards of Soviet
leaders in the style of icon paintings. In fact, paintings of Stalin were
composed "in conformity with strictly specified canonical rule."[75] Soviet
stand-ins for God or saints illustrate that Communist propagandists realized that rituals require an object of devotion. The elevation of Lenin and
Stalin to saintlike status was embraced and promoted by Stalin. He
referred to himself as the father of his people, applying the full force of
the Soviet media to repeating the message that he alone could protect
Soviet citizens from the evils of the world. During his reign, citizens were
consistently admonished to "Be like Stalin!" and for a time after Stalin's
death, it was suggested that he be made an "eternal member" of numerous Soviet organizations.[76] In this way, Communist elites elevated Stalin
to transcendental status — truly rising above the confines of history.
Ultimately, Marxist-Leninists hoped that atheistic rituals and the elevation of leaders to cult status would ease individuals out of long-held traditional practices and provide a new source of symbolism, meaning, and
morality.

Stephen Kotkin writes that the cult of Stalin was effective due in part
to Stalin's charisma and talent for the theatrical:

> Stalin, who lived relatively modestly and dressed simply, like a "proletar-
> ian," employed a direct, accessible style and showed uncanny insight into
> the beliefs and hopes — the psychology — of his audience. Although initially
> portrayed as a political type, when the cult became functional in the 1930s,
> Stalin transformed into a warm and personal figure, teacher, and friend. . . .
> It is easy to make light of the many public effusions of love and gratitude
> for Stalin as enforced rituals agreed to by cynical people, but these express-
> ions were often deeply laden with affect and revealed a devout quality tran-
> scending reasoned argument.[77]

Nevertheless, the production of Stalin's cult and religiouslike rituals
appears to have strayed far from the initial Marxist-Leninist vision of
daily life under Communism. Certainly, "the regime's adoption of
numerous rituals in the personal and political realm ran counter to the

general antiritualistic orientation of most nineteenth-century European intellectual trends, including Marxism, and counter to the general processes of modernization characteristic of Western development in the twentieth century."[78] Within this context, the symbols, rituals, and moral codes produced by Communist Party elites appear ironic. But in trying to destroy religion, Marxist-Leninists discovered an unforeseen obstacle — religious demand. In trying to unravel the mystery of religious persistence, Communist Party officials recognized the powerful allure of ritual activity and charismatic authority, which they hoped to bend to their own ends. In pursuit of secularization, the Communist Party ended up creating a sacred church, homily, and liturgy of its very own.

IDEOLOGICAL EXCLUSIVITY

In arguing for the modern sensibility of atheism, Richard Dawkins asserts, "I cannot think of any war that has been fought in the name of atheism. Why should it?"[79] Dawkins poses a logical question that leads to a more empirical question: Why did atheists in the Soviet Union wage a war against religion and paradoxically produce a culture of symbols, ceremonies, and sacred texts that recreated most aspects of religious culture? Upon reflection, this intriguing and illogical development is not so surprising given a key characteristic shared by the doctrine of Marxist-Leninism and most religious theologies — *ideological exclusivity.* The exclusivity of a belief system and not its supernatural elements is what leads believers to go to great lengths to defend and fight for a cause. And in the end, Communist leaders created one of the most exclusive ideological systems of all time, one in which a handful of elites defined all appropriate perspectives on politics, art, culture, the supernatural, morality, and even time.[80]

Nearly seventy-five years before the Russian Revolution, Frederick Engels noted how Communist gatherings reminded him of church services. In 1843, at the age of twenty-two, he wrote, "These meetings partly resemble church gatherings; in the gallery a choir accompanied by an orchestra sings social hymns; these consist of semi-religious or wholly religious melodies with communist words, during which the audience stands."[81] Engels also observed that "frequently . . . Christianity is directly attacked and Christians are called 'our enemies.'"[82] By witnessing social activists, Engels realized that Communists were not bothered by churchlike settings, songs, or sermons but were openly hostile to religious concepts. What frustrated atheistic Communists about religion was not its communal or ritual aspects but its reliance on the concept of the supernatural — especially a supernatural entity that planned human behavior, rewarded individuals, and oversaw history. To Communists, religious belief systems were patently false because Communists believed that human behavior, earthly rewards, and history were actually controlled by economic relations, not by God. In this, they had absolute faith.

Faith in God can inspire extreme action. Throughout the centuries, committed believers have often suffered martyrdom for God. One constant in the study of religion is that the faithful often value their beliefs over their own lives. Believers get burned at the stake or thrown to the lions rather than deny their faith, the devout fight costly and bloody religious wars, and, in recent times, suicide bombers provide religious rationales for their dire acts. Of course, not all religious believers will risk life and limb for their theological convictions. Recent studies of religious groups find that "among religious organizations, there is a reciprocal relationship between the degree of lay commitment and the degree of exclusivity."[83] *Exclusivity* refers to how prohibitive a religious group is in allowing commitment to other gods or religious doctrines. Religious groups often explicitly denounce other religious perspectives along with philosophical and political systems of belief that they feel contradict their theologies. Generally, religious organizations understand that exclusive theologies are more powerful than nonexclusive ones. In contrast, openness to new ideas and tolerance of alternative views can lead to lower levels of commitment to a single ideology. All things being equal, the exclusivity of a doctrine is a primary determinant of its followers' devotion. As a humorist recently pointed out, suicide bombers don't tend to leave messages that state, "We are Unitarian Jihad. There is only God, unless there is more than one God. The vote of our God subcommittee is 10−8 in favor of one God, with two abstentions."[84]

With the historical development of monotheism, religious commitment to one religion became an all-or-nothing venture. Monotheism generated believers who could sustain religious covenants under extraordinary circumstances because, as Rodney Stark argues, monotheists face an absolute decision to either follow or abandon their one true god.[85] Subsequently, the exclusivity of monotheism gave religious groups the ability "to unite and mobilize humans on behalf of great undertakings, and to also plunge them into bitter and often bloody conflict."[86] Within all monotheistic traditions, exclusivity is a natural outcome of believing in one god. In turn, monotheistic religious groups often ban the exploration of ideas not directly approved by group teachings and condemn interaction with nonmembers, using the ultimate threat of their god's displeasure. Under circumstances of heightened exclusivity, religious believers will go to great lengths to defend their faith and are more willing to attack those who do not share their beliefs.

If a religious doctrine's exclusivity can explain its ability to ignite conflict with alternative religions and inspire sacrifice, the same might be said for secular doctrines. Of course, few secular doctrines are exclusive in a holistic sense. Faith in Keynesian economics does not exclude one from believing in evolution, drinking alcohol, or belonging to the Roman Catholic Church. In contrast, exclusive religious doctrines tend to dictate clear conceptions of social justice, moral evaluations of scientific efforts, and norms of social interaction. As such, the most exclusive religious doctrines will prohibit a host of political, social, and scientific viewpoints. Their exclusivity is therefore measured, in part, by the number of intellectual inquiries they attempt to control. In this, Marxist-Leninism was akin to many religious doctrines and qualitatively different from other political, economic, and social theories. It grew into simply one of the most exclusive political ideologies ever conceived.

Marxist-Leninism claimed to have exclusive access to the truth about the material and social world through the theories and writings of Marx and Engels. Their work was considered sacred—to be interpreted but never critiqued. Critical analysis within the Soviet context was impossible because the veracity of Marx and Engels was understood in the same way that religious believers view divine revelation. According to Marxist-Leninists, the truth was revealed in writing, and they were in the position to fulfill its prophesy.

Both Lenin and Stalin legitimated their power and influence through their ability to interpret Marx and Engels properly. While Stalin mainly claimed to understand Lenin's interpretation of Marx, he dominated intellectual and scientific discussions by publishing the only acceptable interpretation of the science of Communism. This work, *History of the Community Party of the Soviet Union: Short Course,* became the bible of the Soviet Union during Stalin's reign. One observer of political and intellectual life under Stalinism described its influence as follows: "The Short Course not only established a whole pattern of Bolshevik mythology linked to the cult of Lenin and Stalin, but prescribed a detailed ritual and liturgy. From the time of its publication party writers, historians, and propagandists who touched on any part of its subject-matter were obliged to adhere to every canonical formula and to repeat every relative phrase verbatim. The Short Course was not merely a work of falsified history but a powerful social institution."[87] Much like religion, Soviet Communism began with faith in a sacred text. And no other text could serve as a possible critique or alternative to the work of Marx and Engels.

Of course, many advocates of political and economic arguments confidently assert their veracity. For instance, political conservatives declare the constructive power of the free market, whereas political liberals dogmatically question the accuracy of this faith. But these positions are limited to the domain of economic theory and do not explicitly demand advocates to be loyal to an entire moral or philosophical worldview. In contrast, Isaiah Berlin explained that Marxism was "capable, at least in theory, of yielding clear and final answers to all possible questions, private and public, scientific and historical, moral and aesthetic, individual and institutional."[88] Marxist-Leninists could not consistently accept the veracity of certain aspects of their ideology while rebuffing others. Their ideology was an all-or-nothing venture that unequivocally discarded vast arrays of artistic, religious, literary, political, economic, moral, and philosophical traditions. In this, Marxist-Leninism may have surpassed the scope of even the most exclusive religious doctrines.

In addition to its massive intellectual scope, Marxist-Leninism quite brazenly claimed to be a science and dismissed alternative conceptions of social justice, metaphysics, ethics, and even aesthetics as "unscientific." Ernest Gellner explains that Marxist-Leninism was "a belief-system that claimed a monopoly of truth, but [a truth] that was built from what were, officially, *this-worldly* elements. . . . Though of course there were similarities between Marxism and other religions, at the doctrinal and intellectual level the proud boast of Marxism was that it had exiled the supernatural from social life. It claimed to be scientific."[89]

Alas, the "science" of Marxist-Leninism did not include what one normally thinks of as science — the rigorous testing of hypotheses using empirical data. Within the Soviet Union, the term *scientific* became synonymous with official state ideology, regardless of whether any systematic study had been actually conducted. Communist Party leaders probably thought that investigations into their philosophical claims may even have been a waste of time because they already were sure of their veracity. As Ota Šik argues in his detailed analysis of Marxist-Leninist theory, the most vulnerable part of this ideology was its "insistence on scientific justification."[90] Although the claim to scientism was certainly a source of vulnerability for Soviet apologists outside the Soviet Union, Soviet ideologues easily intimidated scientists and dismissed non-Marxist intellectuals within their borders. In the end, Soviet agencies, schools, and media all maintained that Marxist-Leninism systematically refuted all other "eternal truths" to create the "only scientific theory of how to recognize scientific truths."[91]

Marxist-Leninism's exclusivity is evident in the sacredness of its theory, the scope of its assertions, and its claim to ultimate truth. These doctrinal characteristics led Marxist-Leninists to behave in ways normally associated with religious extremists. First, committed Communists became determined to shut off all ideological alternatives to Marxist-Leninism. Their close attention to religious supply clearly indicates the rabid exclusivity of their atheism. They did not simply believe that religious belief was folly but were actually offended by the idea that religious belief could persist.

Although exclusivity explains the commitment of Marxist-Leninists to shut off the supply of religion, exclusivity does not imply popularity. The violence and relentlessness with which Communist Party officials attacked religion generated a great deal of animosity in religious communities across the Soviet Union. As it turns out, absolute certainty is often met with an opposing force of skepticism and resistance. Nevertheless, state authority can be a very effective means to shut down religion.

Second, Marxist-Leninism's exclusivity led atheist propagandists to completely discount the spiritual side of religious demand. At first, militant atheists assumed that religion was a pseudoscience that would be easily replaced with actual science. As such, individuals simply needed education and technology to fulfill their misplaced attraction to religious ideologies. Later, Soviet propagandists posited an additional feature of religious demand — the need for social solidarity through ritual activity.

Christel Lane, who closely researched how Communist Party elites distinguished between religious and secular rituals, finds that officials stressed "the effects of rituals and [and were] concerned with the achievement of value consensus and social solidarity . . . when Soviet ritual is under discussion. A Marxist approach, stressing the role of ritual in mystifying class relations and assisting domination of one class by another prevails when religious ritual or any form of ritual in capitalist society is at issue."[92]

In other words, Communist Party theorists advocated the awkward argument that atheist rituals promoted social *order* whereas religious rituals provoked social *disorder*. The defining difference in the effect of a ritual involved the object of the ritual — God or Communist society. Interestingly, this point of view attributes a primary significance to the object of ritual activity. Therefore, rituals were defined as good or evil, in the Soviet context, not based on their proceedings, structure, or ability to unite people but based solely on their reference to the supernatural. Outside observers could maintain that Soviet ceremonies were only religious ceremonies in disguise, but Marxist-Leninists viewed them as the antithesis of religion because they removed all references to the supernatural. Therefore, the campaign to replace religious rituals might properly be characterized as a fight over God — Soviets wanted to eliminate Christ, Yahweh, Allah, and any other type of god from ritual activity and Communist culture in general. Plainly speaking, Communist Party planners wanted to kill God and replace him with something perhaps even more omnipresent — Society.

Although Communist elites claimed that ideology naturally emerged from material conditions and social relationships, they were profoundly guided by their own ideological exclusivity. This was the real irony of Soviet Communism. In attempting to destroy religion, Soviet elites posited that belief in God was irrational and based in the stubbornness of tradition. In actuality, a stubborn belief in the evils of religion led Communist elites to kill hundreds of thousands of religious believers, destroy beautiful churches and mosques, dismiss the methods of science, present Soviet leaders as sacred figures, and regard Communist social theory as scripture. In sum, Communist leaders often ignored the material and social conditions of their world in favor of an ideal that only existed in their theories. Marxist-Leninists' distain for nonmaterialist worldviews ironically emerged not from a commitment to science but from the ideological exclusivity of their devotion to atheism. In this, they were akin to religious fanatics.

CHAPTER 3

Shutting Off Religious Supply

God is or He is not. . . . Since you must choose, let us see which interests you least.

— Pascal, *Penses*

Religious believers in the Soviet Union certainly suffered enormous penalties for retaining their faith, ranging from daily ridicule to imprisonment and sometimes even death. Religious persecution was intense, especially at the beginning of the Stalin's reign and during the Khrushchev era. With so much at risk, there appeared little reason to remain religious in Soviet society. Regardless, many individuals remained steadfast in their religious convictions. Unrepentant believers facing brutality and humiliation in the Gulag clung to their faith under the most extreme conditions. One witness recounted how his prison treated its nuns, who refused to work for the Communist "devils": "From time to time the commandant would visit their quarters with a whip, and the hut resounded with shrieks of pain: the women were usually stripped before being beaten, but no cruelty could dissuade them from the habits of praying and fasting."[1] Another prisoner in a Voronezh camp marveled at the ability of nuns to withstand standing barefoot on ice for hours as they held hands and continued to sing the Easter liturgy; this prisoner, who was a former member of the Communist Party, recounted: "Was this fanaticism, or fortitude in defense of the rights of conscience? Were we to admire them or regard them as mad? And, most troubling of all, should we have had the courage to act as they had?"[2]

Although the resolve of these defiant nuns' was certainly extraordinary, they had one another to reinforce their belief that God and justice were on their side. Because their small and loyal group was comprised of already devout believers, they were able to withstand incredible torture in a resolute commitment to their faith — a commitment that appeared inexplicable to the nonbelieving observer. The story of resistant nuns in the Gulag illustrates how small religious communities could survive the onslaught of the Secularization Experiment through inwardness and unity. In fact, small, tightly knit religious groups actually thrived under Communist oppression. Jehovah Witnesses, Evangelicals, Baptists, covert Muslim communities, and a host of other small religious groups and rural religious communities effectively recruited and retained members through their fearlessness and devotion to one another. The ability of these religious communities to evade authorities and remain true to their faiths actually inspired others' religious faith.

For historically dominant religious institutions, which had property holdings, professional clergy, and thousands of members, persistence necessarily extended beyond the boundaries of a small, closed, isolated community. Established Christian churches and landmark Islamic mosques were public spaces that could not easily hide their activities. Both the Orthodox and Roman Catholic Church also observed a strict religious hierarchy that required the official sanction of theological interpretations and religious rituals. These concerns made it impossible for religious practices to be legitimately conducted without notice; in fact, some underground clergy were defrocked for working outside the official chain of command. Without the option to conceal vital religious activities, mainstream religious institutions in the Soviet Union necessarily negotiated with Soviet officials to maintain their practices and very existence. To save their institutions, religious leaders decided between collaborating with Soviet demands and holding defiant stances, hoping to counter antireligious policies. The ability of these religious institutions to withstand and even combat religious repression depended on a number of organizational factors.

The Communist Party's attempt to shut off religious supply presents a unique opportunity to study how intense repression impacts the vitality of religious organizations. The Soviet government's intense effort to extinguish religion insured that many individuals disavowed their religious beliefs and memberships. But theological and organizational differences both played important roles in how successfully religious groups retained their members, and in some unique cases increased their members, during the Soviet era. Organizational structures were important in determining the extent to which a group withstood total absorption into the Soviet system. And theological requirements further dictated a religious group's ability to legitimately and effectively go underground. In the end, attacking religious supply created a multitude of religiously unaffiliated individuals, but it also had the contradictory effect of resurrecting the spirit of many believers.

THE RELIGIOUS LANDSCAPE

A growing body of research confirms that state regulation of religious supply will weaken levels of religious commitment and participation, all other things being equal.[3] States can manipulate religious supply in several ways. First, they can establish tax, property, and civic laws that favor certain religious organizations, enabling them to more easily mobilize resources. Second, states can provide churches with direct financial support. Finally, states can outwardly ban specific religious groups and imprison and sometimes even execute their members. In these instances, regulation becomes outright repression.

State support of a favored religious organization can produce a *religious monopoly*—a religious group that dominates a region so that the population has little or no exposure to alternative religious doctrines.[4] Before Soviet rule, most of the regions in the Soviet Union had some form of religious monopoly. In other words, religious traditions tended to "own" specific areas of the map. Russia was predominantly Russian Orthodox, for instance, and Lithuania was overwhelmingly Roman Catholic. The region that would become Uzbekistan was Islamic (see table 3). Estonia and Latvia were the most religiously diverse regions, with high percentages of Lutherans, Orthodox Christians, and Roman Catholics.

Often, religious monopolies only exist where public policies and tax systems support the dominant religious tradition. In these circumstances, religious organizations will begin to rely on state support instead of the donations and resources of their members. Therefore, state-supported churches have less incentive to maintain membership commitments and contributions. As political scientist Anthony Gill explains, "Although monopoly guarantees that religious consumers cannot defect to other faiths, a lack of pastoral attention to its parishioners will weaken the popularity and credibility of the church. Religious apathy and cynicism result."[5] This was certainly the case in imperial Russia, where the Russian Orthodox Church had been simply an arm of the czarist government since 1721. This state-supported religious monopoly had little motivation to generate active church participation. In fact, Russian Orthodox members rarely attended church at the beginning of the twentieth cen-

TABLE 3. MAJORITY RELIGION IN 1900
IN FUTURE REGIONS OF THE SOVIET UNION

Region	Majority Religion
Armenia	Orthodox
Azerbaijan	Islam
Belarus	Orthodox
Estonia	Lutheran*
Georgia	Orthodox
Kazakhstan	Islam
Kyrgyzstan	Islam
Latvia	Lutheran*
Lithuania	Roman Catholic
Moldavia	Orthodox
Russia	Orthodox
Tajikistan	Islam
Turkmenistan	Islam
Ukraine	Orthodox
Uzbekistan	Islam

SOURCE: Compiled from Barrett, Kurian, and Johnson 1980.
*Religious pluralism was high in Estonia and Latvia, but Lutherans comprised
the largest religious group (54 percent in Estonia and 45 percent in Latvia).

tury.[6] Similarly, the Roman Catholic Church received tax support in
Lithuania, and the Islamic regions of Central Asia actively suppressed
religious competitors.

The rise of the Communist Party and its radical religious policies drastically altered the religious favoritism that existed throughout the Soviet
Union. Although Communist Party officials claimed that they were putting an end to religious oppression, they were in fact replacing focused
religious regulation with universal religious repression. Many of the
dominant religions throughout the Soviet Union had benefited from state
support, which certainly helped the Communist Party to cripple their
religious institutions. No longer would religious monopolies receive outside money for upkeep, personnel, or programs.

Marxist-Leninists believed that religion had been artificially sustained
by state financial support. As we shall see, Communist ideologues were
not entirely mistaken in this belief; the extent to which religious groups
depended on state support largely predicted their ability to survive Soviet-
era religious policies. Nevertheless, many self-sufficient religious groups
existed, and Soviet leaders theorized that members of these groups would
abandon religion given other options. Accordingly, the joint impact of
industrialization, collectivization, and education would create a new

"Soviet Man" who was free from the psychological bondage of czarist Russia and the phantasm of antiquated religious beliefs.

In an intensive study of antireligious policy in Eastern Europe and the Soviet Union during the 1950s, Robert Tobias found that "what was happening in one region was not an isolated experiment. Public speeches, news releases, decrees, constitutional articles on religion, all had the ring of a common origin."[7] Although the tactics of religious repression certainly resembled one another, distinct differences in policy are apparent throughout the regions of the Soviet Union. In many instances, these differences were responses to the region's religious situation. The Orthodox Church was severely repressed throughout the Soviet Union, but by 1940, a disproportionate 63 percent of the remaining churches were located in the Ukraine.[8] In contrast, only 11 percent of the Orthodox churches in existence in 1940 were in the Russian republic. The Roman Catholic Church also suffered enormously under Soviet rule, especially in the Ukraine, Romania, and Eastern Germany. But in certain regions, such as Poland and Lithuania, the Catholic Church was able to deflect religious repression in ways unavailable to the church in other regions. And at first, Communist Party leaders were less inclined to attack Muslims in Central Asia due to the sheer size of the Muslim population. In sum, Communist Party officials generally sought to shut down religious supply but altered tactics based on the size of the population active in a particular religion and the local circumstances of political power.

To present the most general overview of religious change during the Soviet era, I offer a crude comparison of changes in the percentage of the population affiliated with the dominant religion of each region of the Soviet Union (see figure 2). The comparison shows the percentage of religious memberships in 1900, when Communists were still organizing in basement apartments, and in 1970, when the Communist Party was a well-established bureaucratic hierarchy controlling every level of society. Nevertheless, this analysis fails to account for important demographic shifts.[9] For instance, World War I significantly affected the religious composition of many regions of the Soviet Union, and Stalin's purges in the 1930s and the violence of World War II had profound effects on the makeup of the Soviet population. Regardless, a comparison of affiliations in 1900 and 1970 creates a general feel for the magnitude of the religious change that occurred in the first half of the twentieth century throughout the Soviet region.

In 1900, ten of the fifteen regions of the future Soviet Union had more than 85 percent of their populations affiliated with one religious group.

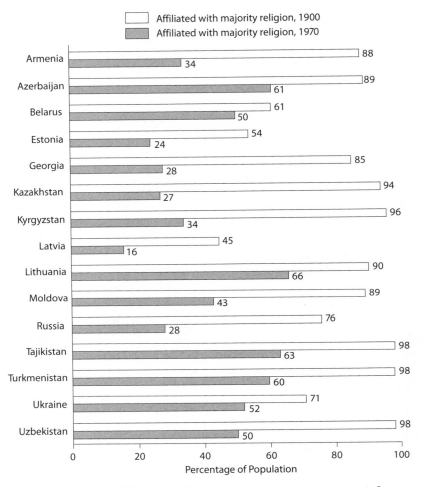

Figure 2. Change in Affiliations of Religious Majorities (1900 to 1970). Source: compiled from Barrett, Kurian, and Johnson 1980.

The Soviet regime universally attacked these majority religions, hoping to cripple their dominance. Their success varies by region markedly. Most Soviet republics underwent their severest religious repression before World War II. But it is important to note that Soviet republics were incorporated at different times after 1917. The Soviet Union absorbed the Central Asian republics by 1924, and the Baltic republics, Estonia, Latvia, and Lithuania, were the last to be annexed in 1940.

By 1970, the percentage of affiliations in the dominant religion had dropped in every region. A cursory glance reveals that the Orthodox regions of Armenia, Georgia, Moldova, and Russia lost a substantial percentage of their Orthodox populations. The Orthodox regions of Belarus and the Ukraine fared better. But Belarus and the Ukraine also had a smaller number of Orthodox Christians than any other Soviet republic in 1900; therefore, one might expect them to lose a smaller percentage of members.[10]

In contrast to all other regions, Lithuania retained a large percentage of its Roman Catholic population (66 percent). Like the Roman Catholic Church of Poland, the Lithuanian church impressively countered extreme levels of religious repression. Beyond the confines of the Soviet Union, the Polish Roman Catholic Church famously demonstrated how a religious institution could not only withstand religious repression but also strengthen itself in response to state oppression. Lithuanians were inspired and heartened by the Polish Catholic opposition movement and the support of Roman Catholics worldwide. These lifelines proved vital to the strength of Roman Catholicism in Lithuania.

The percentage of Muslims in Kazakhstan and Kyrgyzstan drops dramatically between 1900 and 1970. This decline is due, in part, to the forced migration of individuals during the 1930s, 1940s, and 1950s.[11] Hundreds of thousands of ethnic Russians and Ukrainians were transplanted into the Central Asian republics, so that the proportion of Muslims in these regions would have dropped even if Islamic groups sustained their memberships. In addition, Muslim affiliations are fundamentally different than both Roman Catholic and Orthodox affiliations; this is due to both institutional differences between the religions and important theological distinctions about the meaning of affiliation and religious identity.

Overall, it appears that the policies of Communist repression had a noticeable effect on religious affiliations. In this regard, the campaign to shut off religious supply was quite successful. Although a wide array of issues require further investigation, four initial questions spring from this general overview of changes in religious affiliations. First, what explains the weakness of the Orthodox Church? Did individuals who left the church convert to atheism? Second, why does the Lithuanian Roman Catholic Church appear so successful at retaining members in comparison to both the Orthodox and Muslim regions? Third, can the precipitous drop in the percentage of Muslims in Islamic regions be fully accounted for by migration patterns? In answering these questions, we can better understand how changes in religious supply affect religious vitality.

ORTHODOXY IN RUSSIA

In the years before the Russian Revolution, many Russians had become disillusioned with their political and cultural traditions. After the czarist regime fell, many appeared to believe in the promises of a new socialist utopia. In fact, Russian Communists were "able to persuade people far beyond the borders of the Soviet Union that a superior model of modernity had been discovered."[12] In addition, religion in Russia had been dominated by an extremely weak and entirely state-sponsored institution. The extent to which the czarist regime historically controlled the Russian Orthodox Church cannot be overstated. "Peter the Great had in effect made the Church little more than a department of state headed by a secular bureaucracy appointed by the Tsar himself. In exchange for loyalty bishops lived in luxury, but were captives of the State with their administrative authority severely restricted even in purely religious matters. The office of Patriarch had been suspended and in its place a synod of bishops, selected by the Tsar, was declared to be the supreme organ of government in the Russian Orthodox Church. In reality the synod was a state organ."[13]

When Communists took over the state, the Russian Orthodox Church became their unconditional property. Scholar of Russian religious history Sabrina Ramet elucidates: "The Russian Orthodox Church was subordinate and controlled by the Soviet State. Its chief newspaper was proofed by the KGB before publication. Its clergy were promoted, demoted, and assigned according to the preferences of state authorities. The curriculum and admissions at its seminaries were subject to the veto of authorities. . . . Some clergymen and bishops turned KGB informers. As for the patriarch, he was obliged to make 'positive propaganda' for the Soviet Union abroad."[14] The nine-hundred-year-old Russian Orthodox Church was transformed overnight from a powerful extension of the monarchy to a reeling giant, grasping for its very existence.

The Orthodox patriarch Tikhon resisted some of the changes imposed by the Communist state and was immediately replaced by Patriarch Sergeii; "the position assumed by Sergeii in 1927 implied unquestioning acceptance of society, evil or good. The Church could no longer stand in protest against social evil, but must tolerate and accept such evil as the price of remaining within society."[15] Collaboration or acquiescence became a necessary part of survival for anyone within the Orthodox Church. The Communist Party especially celebrated when a priest re-

nounced the cloth, but Sheila Fitzpatrick reports that a secret Soviet document from the 1930s indicates that Communist Party officials believed
that many more priests would leave the church if only they were offered
better jobs.[16] Some ambitious Orthodox clergy became proselytizers for
the League of Militant Atheists as they came to realize the new insecuri-
ties of their religious callings.[17] They essentially abandoned the old state
religion for the new one. Few clerical positions survived the initial Soviet
takeover of the church. There were more than fifty thousand Orthodox
priests before the Russian Revolution, and by mid-1939, there were no
more than three to four hundred clergy.[18]

If Soviets wielded such direct control of the Russian Orthodox Church,
why did they allow it to continue operating on any level? Although
Communist Party elites would have preferred to relegate the Orthodox
Church to the trash bin of history, they were faced with two nagging
problems. First, Orthodox culture was simply too ubiquitous. Churches,
monasteries, clergy, nuns, crosses, and other religious artifacts existed
throughout towns and villages across the vast regions of Russia, Armenia,
Belarus, Georgia, Moldova, and the Ukraine. Most community activities
were controlled by the church, and local religious leaders had enjoyed
influence over every area of social intercourse for centuries.[19] Although
Soviet officials easily cut off the head of the Orthodox Church, its massive
body remained a force to be reckoned with.

A comprehensive banning of such pervasive and long-held practices
would only uncover the government's inability to enforce its policies.
Therefore, Communist officials were forced to wash away the cultural
residue of the Orthodox Church piece by piece. Along the way, they discovered that many Orthodox clergy proved willing to help local Communist leaders, if only to retain their livelihoods. Thus, Soviet leaders
realized a second obstacle in their initial plans to bury the church — the
Orthodox Church could actually provide them with a service. In fact,
the Orthodox Church actively sought ways to be of use to the Soviet
state to prolong its life.[20] Consequently, the Soviet state began to use the
Orthodox Church to spread propaganda, spy on individuals, and generate support for the war effort during World War II. As one Orthodox
priest admitted during the Brezhnev era, "The 'catacomb' Church [resis-
tance], thanks to the diligent 'work' done by the KGB, is practically nonexistent."[21] While the Russian Orthodox Church survived in name, compromises with the state and evaporating resources robbed the church of
its vitality.

Church attendance is an excellent indicator of religious vitality. While individuals may affiliate themselves with a religious organization, many will not attend services or participate in other religious activities. Therefore, church attendance provides a general measure of how committed an individual is to her religious life. Sadly, longitudinal data on religious attendance is virtually nonexistent for the Soviet era. Nevertheless, longitudinal church attendance data can be constructed using retrospective data. While there are many methodological weaknesses of retrospective data, mainly because it relies solely on an individual's memory, the economist Lawrence Iannaccone demonstrated the validity of retrospective religious data from the *International Social Survey Program*.[22] Using questions concerning respondents' memories of childhood church attendance and their recollections of their parents' church habits, we can reconstruct attendance rates from 1925 to 1985. Figure 3 illustrates a massive decline in church attendance for Russian parents and their children.

Church attendance dropped dramatically in the late 1920s and continued to slowly decline until 1985. By 1970, only 4 percent of parents attended church, and in only half of those families did their children accompany them. This is a reversal of a universal trend that holds in all Western European countries — namely, that children will always attend church more than their parents if not at the same rate.[23] Children's higher attendance occurs because religious parents want to introduce their children to religious beliefs and practices and, in some cases, feel that church attendance is more important for their children than themselves. In contrast, many religious parents in Russia were not bringing their children with them to church. This fascinating trend is without any clear explanation. Most probably, religious parents hoped to spare their children the potential social and political costs of church attendance. That children did not attend church with their parents shows that Soviet religious and social policies were quite effective in dismantling an important mechanism of childhood religious socialization.

As the most public religious institutions, the few remaining Russian Orthodox churches were left essentially empty on Sundays. The overt collaboration of the church with Soviet officials frightened some believers and disillusioned others. But scaring people from church and turning them against religion are two very different things. Much evidence suggests that Communist officials were very good at the first, but how successful were they at the second? Reports from missionaries and religious

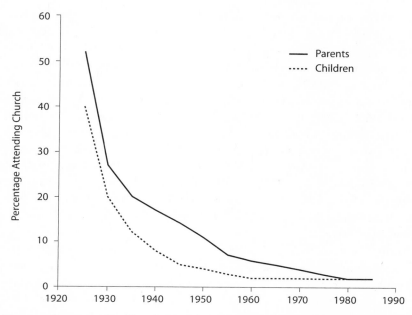

Figure 3. Retrospective Church Attendance Rates in Russia. Source: Iannaccone 2002, Complied from 1990 International Social Survey Program.

groups inside the Soviet Union indicate that many Orthodox members drifted toward smaller and more covert religious groups. Under the radar of Soviet repression, these new religious movements began to make inroads to a population that had remained staunchly Orthodox. In 1900, non-Orthodox Christian groups represented only around 10 percent of the Russian population.[24] These groups included Baptists, Evangelicals, Flagellants, Mennonites, Old Believers, Pentecostals, and Tolstoyans, to name a few that were most visible at the beginning of the twentieth century.[25] By midcentury and toward the end of the Soviet era, Hare Krishnas, Jehovah's Witnesses, Seventh-Day Adventists, and various charismatic sects entered the religious landscape. Quite interestingly, data reported by religious groups maintains that while membership in the Russian Orthodox Church rapidly declined under Communism, Protestants and various other Christian sects slowly brought in new members between the 1930s and 1970s.[26]

Small proselytizing groups partially thrived under Communism because the Orthodox Church was so severely impaired. Before the revolution, the czarist regime promoted the dominance of the Russian Orthodox Church while banning many of the small religious sects and cults.[27] Non-Orthodox religious groups actually celebrated the end of the czarist regime, knowing that the Soviets would not favor the Orthodox tradition. In 1929, Soviet Protestant groups proclaimed that the "history of the Reformation is well known. Through her, God broke the powers of darkness and fanaticism in the old church, and brought freedom to believe and think to ultimate victory. Now it's Russia's turn. After the world-shocking events of the last war and the Revolution, the evangelical movement is beginning to develop in the East in a very special way."[28] Protestants interpreted the language of Soviet religious law literally and responded to an official declaration of religious freedom with vigorous activities from thousands of Evangelicals and Baptists eager to proselytize their message. And for a while, they openly recruited members away from the Orthodox Church. "At the 1923 Baptist World Congress, the Russian Baptists report stated that 5,000 Baptist Sunday Schools were attended by approximately 300,000 boys and girls."[29] But indiscriminate persecution of all religious activity would quickly lead non-Orthodox groups to go underground.

Nonetheless, these groups were accustomed to religious regulation even before the rise of the Communist Party. Energetic religious sects had developed tactics to recruit and retain members under conditions of repression in pre-Soviet times. But Soviet religious regulation was different in one crucial way — it mainly repressed the monopoly religion! Consequently, non-Orthodox groups continued to work covertly but with the added advantage of recruiting Orthodox believers fleeing the rapidly collapsing Orthodox Church.

Stories of small Christian sects operating during the Soviet era illustrate their inventiveness in introducing nonmembers to their religious community and exchanging ideas with other religious groups. For instance, a Mennonite visitor to the Soviet Union in 1970 observed that a traveling Evangelical minister

> was forbidden to preach unless registered to do so in that locale. But when
> such a visitor was invited to give a greeting at a gathering, he managed
> to expand the greetings to a greeting from Jesus and the Epistles of Paul!
> Substitution Sunday schools were achieved by carefully planned birthday
> parties. The choir practice, with a protracted meditation in the middle,
> became a de facto youth meeting. A Christian wedding meant that unbeliev-
> ing friends and relatives would be present and would hear a Gospel invi-
> tation, and would see how the celebration was enjoyable without getting

drunk. And at funerals, churches still make sure that their best preachers and an adequate choir are on hand — here, too, the focus is often more on the living . . . than the dead.[30]

The size and flexibility of Protestant sects allowed them to operate in relative secrecy. One report from a Baptist missionary group claimed that two-thirds of all Protestant groups in the Soviet Union were unknown to authorities.[31] While this report cannot be confirmed, it is the case that many Protestants around the world took an interest in proselytizing efforts within the Soviet Union and repeatedly tried to penetrate the Iron Curtain.

Non-Orthodox groups may have exaggerated their successes to the outside world to build confidence and garner support, but Soviet officials also discuss the growth of new religious groups, which provides crucial support to their claims. Perhaps Communist Party theorists were willing to admit that Protestant groups were on the rise because there were ideological reasons to view this as a positive step toward secularization. The Soviet historian A. Barmenkov provided the Communist Party's official interpretation of increased sect activity by reasoning that this was simply a confused attempt by uneducated individuals to embrace Communist ideals. For him and other Marxist-Leninists, sects preached communal messages in the garb of religious language. While sect activity was certainly unwelcome, it was understood as an intermediary step toward total disillusionment with religion. Barmenkov explains: "The petty-bourgeois elements in the cities and in the countryside were attracted by the sectarian preaching of mutual assistance and voluntary sharing of property. And while people's religiosity in general did not increase at that time, the specific social processes in the classes led to the outflow of believers from Orthodox into sects."[32] For this reason, Soviet officials were mainly concerned with the Russian Orthodox Church and trusted that "temporary" sectarian growth was, in part, evidence of the success of atheist propaganda. Communist Party officials viewed the efforts of small Protestant groups as naive attempts at Communism or communal bonding in contrast to the overt imperialism of the Russian Orthodox Church. They trusted that sectarian groups represented the last gasp of religion as it receded from society. Therefore, many small religious organizations subsisted under the main thrust of Soviet antireligious efforts.

In addition, small non-Orthodox groups tended to advocate public obedience to the Soviet state. Evangelicals and Baptists promoted inward religiosity while encouraging the faithful to work hard in their public positions, even supporting military service. In this eyewitness account, an Evangelical minister and his congregation were faced with the order to work on a religious holiday. "Last summer, the Harvest Holiday arrived . . . the kolkhoz asked them to work a day or two more in order to finish the work. . . . The elder presbyter arrived, and setting an example by working himself, he encouraged the people to perform the task. There was great satisfaction while completing the work and a good witness was effected before the entire collective farm."[33] The willingness of many non-Orthodox groups to serve the Soviet project indicated that they realized that political opposition was futile and simply hoped to conceal their religious devotion while fulfilling the dictates of the Soviet government. In sum, most Protestants simply wanted to worship in private.

Ironically, the Communist Party initially invigorated sect activity by undermining the Russian Orthodox Church. Soviet policy had inadvertently done something in accord with the hopes of Russia's religious minorities—toppled the dominance of the Russian Orthodox Church. Based on a Marxist-Leninist understanding of the institutional basis of religion, Soviet leaders focused their antireligious efforts on religious organizations with political power and cultural import. While this strategy certainly worked to undermine the Orthodox Church, it failed to realize that religious demand could still exist even after a religious monopoly ceases to exist.

The acquiescence of the Russian Orthodox Church is unsurprising given its dependency on the czarist regime before Soviet rule; its institutional hierarchy and public presence made covert activities extremely difficult. As a result, Orthodox leaders and clergy routinely collaborated with Soviet officials to preserve their institution, even as they lost members and legitimacy.[34]

THE ROMAN CATHOLIC CHURCH IN LITHUANIA

One of most impressive stories of religious resistance to Soviet rule occurred outside the medieval city of Šiauliai, Lithuania. Townsfolk placed an array of crosses atop a nearby hill. Over time the number of crosses multiplied, thereby distressing Soviet officials, who promptly had the hill bulldozed. The crosses immediately reappeared and kept reappearing, despite ongoing efforts to remove them and guard the area. The phenomenon reached mythic proportions, and the amazing story of a hill that miraculously sprouted crosses spread throughout Lithuania. In the end, Soviets simply abandoned trying to tear them down. Today, visitors to Šiauliai can still visit the "hill of crosses" and marvel at the sight of thousands of crosses erected in direct defiance of forced secularization. The story of Roman Catholicism in Lithuanian is one of steadfast religious commitment in the face of unrelenting and brutal oppression, leading Pope Pius XII to call Lithuania "the most loyal daughter of Rome in the north of Europe."[35]

The tenaciousness of religious believers in Šiauliai represents the commitment necessary to persist under the cruel repression of Soviet antireligious policy. As one Lithuanian priest put it: "How much can preaching from some dozens of pulpits mean against the flow of lava [atheist propaganda] from the press, schools, television, radio, movie theaters, organization enterprises, lecture halls, various festivals, and speakers' platforms?"[36] Soviet law even forbade the use of microphones in Lithuanian Roman Catholic Churches because amplified sound would disrupt the surrounds and "lure" people away from other tasks.[37] But even under intense religious restrictions, Lithuania remained one of the most religious republics in the Soviet Union. This is in part because the Lithuanian Roman Catholic Church was the only institutional source of political dissent in a region where Soviet rule was plainly seen as imposed.

Using the same strategy that was successfully employed with the Russian Orthodox Church, the Lithuanian Communist Party intended to *absorb* the Roman Catholic Church into the state infrastructure and *materialize* religious activities.[38] *Absorption* refers to the seizure of church lands, buildings, and assets. Without these resources, it would be impossible for a religious organization to promote its message, hold services, and minister to its members. *Materialization* refers to the manipulation of religious doctrine to make it more compatible with a socialist worldview; in other words, Communists wanted to insure that lingering religious rhetoric was not overtly anti-Communist. This was done by requiring religious leaders to swear allegiance to the Communist establishment and openly support the basic premises of socialism. While Soviet officials were able to severely restrain the Lithuanian Catholic Church, they failed to absorb it as they had the Russian Orthodox Church and were never able to "materialize" Catholic doctrine or clergy.

Absorption of the Russian Orthodox Church occurred unconditionally because it had formerly been an arm of the state. In turn, Orthodox clergy more quickly succumbed to materialization of their religious doctrine, and many collaborated with Communist officials. The combined lost of autonomy with a loss of legitimacy due to collaboration destroyed the viability of the Russian Orthodox Church as a potential for religious indoctrination or political opposition. Absorption of the Lithuanian Catholic Church was a more difficult project. Soviet forces invaded Lithuania during World War II and established a military rule in which antireligious activities were imposed in relatively short time. Soviet troops flooded into Lithuania on July 15, 1940, and began the process of closing Roman Catholic seminaries and destroying religious books en masse. A Soviet publication announced to the population of the new Lithuanian republic that "the Militant Godless Movement has obtained the assurance of the Government that in the constitution of the new Soviet republics there will be a clause authorizing the Godless to organize all kinds of antireligious manifestations freely."[39]

Using the force of the military, Soviet Communists quickly robbed the Roman Catholic Church of Lithuania of many of its resources. The Soviet military confiscated the savings of clergy as well as the bank accounts of parishes and all religious institutions.[40] By stealing the savings of church leaders and individual parishes, Soviet forces left the Roman Catholic Church without resources, which were secured through private donation and not government subsidies.[41] Soviet forces also attempted to annex the Roman Catholic Church's recreational, educational, and charitable activities along with all its assets.[42] In response, Lithuanians waged an armed resistance to Soviet rule that lingered for several years but was eventually squelched by superior Soviet might.

The invasion of Lithuania left few Lithuanians in doubt that the Soviet government was not a liberator but rather an imposition. While the Roman Catholic Church certainly suffered great losses in human and material resources, the church avoided complete absorption into the Soviet government and developed a network of religious dissent known as the "church of the catacombs" that functioned out of Communist Party officials' view. The Lithuanian dissent movement was based around the organization of the Lithuanian Catholic Church, which retained many local parishes and a connection to the international Roman Catholic Church. A forty-year record of official dissent movements in Lithuania, including petition signings, dispersion of information, and marches, shows that 42 percent of these activities were organized by the church.[43]

During Soviet rule, the Lithuanian Catholic Church clergy continued to reject pressure from Communist Party officials to inform on their congregations or become "materialized" by Soviet ideology. Still, the Soviet regime kept the church on a tight leash. The work of the tenacious parish priests became increasingly difficult as the Lithuanian population urbanized; in 1951, 30 percent of Lithuanians were urban dwellers, and by 1975, Soviet industrialization plans increased urban centers to include nearly 60 percent of the population.[44] Urbanization frustrated Roman Catholics because they were not permitted to shift clergy in response to Soviet urbanization. By 1974, because of the restriction of church mobility, 13 percent of Roman Catholic clergy ministered to nearly 40 percent of the population.[45] As a result, even when Roman Catholic priests successfully resisted collaboration with Soviet officials, they often found their congregations moved to newly industrialized regions, and by law they could not follow.

Lithuania also became more religiously and ethnically heterogeneous due to migration patterns and mass imprisonments. This somewhat diminished the tie between the Roman Catholic Church and Lithuanian national identity. In the aftermath of World War II, approximately 250,000 people went west to repatriate in their ethnic homelands; 50,000 ethnic Germans (mostly Protestant) migrated west, and 200,000 Poles (mostly Roman Catholic) went to Poland.[46] In total, Lithuania lost around 10 percent of its population, many of whom were Roman Catholics fearing the return of antireligious violence as Soviet forces reoccupied Nazi-held territory. Once the Soviet military reestablished rule in Lithuania, they conducted mass deportations of "anti-Communists" to Gulags and certain execution; around 120,000 Lithuanians were sent to death camps from 1945 to 1947.[47] In turn, 225,000 people from other Soviet republics were shifted into the newly reacquired Lithuanian republic.[48] The end result of these forced migrations and deportations was a more ethnically and religiously diverse Lithuania.

By the 1960s, the Roman Catholic Church of Lithuania was a shell of its former self and faced a redoubled effort from state officials who sought to "enlighten" the public about the evils of religion. By 1960, 779 atheistic organizations, called "atheist houses," populated Lithuanian cities and rural areas.[49] Lithuania was actually a testing ground for atheistic recruitment, and Communist Party officials created an intense program of atheist education that provided a model for the rest of the Soviet republics. Lithuanian Catholicism served as a special target for atheist entrepreneurs. Defending its use of extensive resources, the central Lithuanian league of atheists, known as Znanie, claimed to steadily increased its membership through the 1950s, 1960s, and 1970s.[50]

Regardless of the massive attempts to dispel religious belief and expression from Lithuania, the Roman Catholic Church remained the only relatively autonomous institution in the Soviet Republic of Lithuania and was "by far the most prominent, best organized, and well-financed element of dissent."[51] Roman Catholics in Lithuania greatly benefited from the Roman Catholic Church's presence beyond the borders of the Soviet Union, outside the reach of Soviet Communism. The international church provided Lithuanians with moral and religious support in their struggle. In addition, the example of Roman Catholic resistance in Poland inspired Lithuanian clerics and parishioners to stand firm in opposition to Soviet rule.[52] The church ultimately became a symbol of Communist resistance and provided Soviet citizens with the only institutional means to voice their opposition to the government. As such, Lithuanians were attracted to the Roman Catholic Church for political as well as religious reasons.

The Roman Catholic Church of Poland most famously combined political and religious interests to help Polish intellectuals and labor leaders generate the hugely successful solidarity movement.[53] In fact, the Roman Catholic Church actually increased its number of churches, priests, and parishes in Poland from 1937 to 1969.[54] By identifying with Roman Catholics in Poland, Lithuanian opposition to Soviet Communism similarly developed a religious identity. As outside visitors to Lithuania recounted, "It has been observed that most Lithuanian dissidents are Roman Catholic; and even for nonbelievers, the Roman Catholic Church represents the aspirations of the nation."[55] In this way, Roman Catholicism gained respect from non-Catholic Lithuanians and provided a unifying force of opposition. However, the Lithuanian Roman Catholic Church suffered greater subjugation than its Polish counterpart due to Lithuania's isolation within the Soviet Union and the sheer intensity of its anti-Catholic policies. In turn, Lithuanian political opposition never reached the strength of the Polish solidarity movement, but the Polish example served as a prod and encouragement to embattled Lithuanians. In the end, their struggle to oppose secularization was unmatched by any other majority religious group inside the borders of the Soviet Union.

Throughout their domination, Catholic Lithuanians kept their eyes on the Roman Catholic Church for inspiration and hope. One Lithuanian observed that "the visit of the Pope to Poland in the spring of 1979 has as much impact on Lithuanian Catholics as it had in Poland itself."[56] The religious and institutional bond between Roman Catholic Churches throughout Eastern Europe and their tie with the Vatican continued to nourish the Lithuanian Catholic Church and diminish the legitimacy of Soviet rule in Lithuania.

Because the Roman Catholic Church remained relatively autonomous from Soviet control and in opposition to Soviet antireligious policies, it became a lasting symbol of everything that was not Soviet. Perhaps with time, Soviet repression would have reduced the Lithuanian Roman Catholic Church to a state of dissolution and submission similar to the Russian Orthodox Church's, but a combination of indigenous national resistance and greater institutional autonomy allowed Roman Catholics to wage an impressive resistance to antireligious tactics up until the collapse of the Soviet Union.

THE PARADOXES OF SOVIET ISLAM

Islamic groups throughout Central Asia had a much different relationship with and perception of Soviet Communism than Soviet Christians, be they Roman Catholic, Orthodox, or Protestant. Based on stereotyped notions of Islam, one might imagine that Muslims of Central Asia would react to Soviet antireligious policies by waging a deadly religious war, or *jihad*. Karen Armstrong points out that in Islam, politics is a "matter of supreme importance, and throughout the twentieth century there has been one attempt after another to create a truly Islamic state. This has always been difficult. It was an aspiration that required a *jihad*, a struggle that could find no simple outcome."[57] But the Communist Party's atheist crusade produced no *jihad* in the overwhelmingly Muslim regions of Central Asia. The absence of massive opposition to Communism suggests that Soviet Muslims were unwilling to fight for the political ideals of their religion. In actuality, Soviet Muslims did fight for their ideals — but as with all religions, the realities of Islam are more complex than the image of war-mongering Muslims suggests.

Muslims were certainly numerous enough to wage a massive *jihad* if they so desired. Changes in the proportion of Muslims in Central Asia mask the fact that the Muslim population grew throughout the twentieth century. Whereas the Republics of Central Asia went from 78 percent Muslim in 1926 to 55 percent in 1965, this decrease mainly reflects the number of Russians and other Eastern Europeans who were moved into the various Central Asian republics to farm, work in and manage factories, and administer public offices and schools.[58] In fact, the number of Muslims in Central Asia grew from around 10.5 million to 16 million over forty years (see table 4).

And Muslims had the highest birth rates of any group in the Soviet Union.[59] So while their proportion within Central Asia was decreasing

TABLE 4. CHANGE IN PROPORTION OF
MUSLIMS IN CENTRAL ASIA, 1926–1965

	1926	1939	1959	1965
Total population	13,671,000	16,624,000	22,978,000	29,080,000
Muslim population	10,670,000	11,200,000	13,650,000	16,000,000
Percentage Muslim	78	68	59	55

SOURCE: Bennigsen and Lemercier-Quelquejay 1967: 169.

due to the in-migration of non-Muslims, their proportion within the
Soviet Union was increasing due to higher Muslim birth rates. The
growth of the Muslim population all over the Soviet Union was such that
Communist Party demographers actually feared that the Soviet Union
would become a Muslim-majority nation by the twentieth-first century,
even though there were good reasons to question this assessment.[60]

Regardless of the increasing Muslim population, the Soviet government continued to pursue its antireligious agenda energetically. Soviets
shut down thousands of mosques, closed Islamic schools, and completely
abolished the Islamic court system, the institutional apparatus of sharia
law. How could the Soviets accomplish these measures without massive
resistance from the enormous Muslim population? The answer lies within
the political and social aspirations of Muslims within Central Asia.

Much has been made of the fact that Islam is not only a religion but
also a political doctrine. Islamic scholar Carl Brown explains this important difference between Christianity and Islam. "In Islam, unlike Christianity, there is no tradition of a separation of church and state. . . . One
simple reason for this difference between Islam and Christianity is that
Islam knows of no 'church' in the sense of a corporate body whose leadership is clearly defined, hierarchical, and distinct from the state."[61] The
political aspect of Islam stems from the tribal origins of the religion and
the distinguished talents of its founder, Muhammad, who excelled as
prophet, military general, and civic leader. As Mircea Eliade notes, "The
history of religions and universal history know of no enterprise comparable to that of Muhammad. The conquest of Mecca and the foundation
of a theocratic state proved that his political genius was not inferior to
his religious genius."[62] Combining his political and religious genius,
Muhammad was able to establish a vast Muslim empire governed by religious law — an ideal that would forever intertwine politics and religion
within the doctrine of Islam.

In contrast, no similar theocratic ideal exists in the history of Christianity. Early Christianity grew into an extensive network of religious communities that were later embraced by the Roman Empire. Since the initial rise of Christianity, Christian institutions were independent of state governments, producing a church-state relationship in which religious and political domains of influence were autonomous even while the religious and political institutions themselves were mutually dependent. "The medieval church-state arrangement and the modern idea of a secular state that is religiously neutral were both the results of working compromises. The more reasonable among the partisans of pope and emperor, just as later the more reasonable Catholics and Protestants, seeing that doctrinal purity and logical consistency spelled continued strife, settled for a nebulous but manageable middle ground between the extremes."[63]

Competition between Christian doctrine and European rulers' claims to legitimacy were sufficiently resolved through an understanding of separate yet symbiotic spheres of influence. Conflict between Christian institutions and political authorities occurred when either overstepped the boundaries of their domain, and these boundaries shifted as religious and political elites gained or lost power. Soviet Communism created a crisis in this dynamic relationship between the state and the Christian church by attempting to impose atheism on the population. Powerful Christian institutions found themselves in direct competition with the Communist state and had to fight for their very survival.

Unlike Christianity, Islam has no concept of the separation of church and state. The origins of Islam indicate how religious culture became intricately intertwined with political rule under Muhammad. The sharia, or Islamic law, provided the blueprint for religious governance and divided the world not into secular and religious spheres but into *dar al-Islam* (the land of Islam) and *dar al-harb* (the land of warfare). According to this theological perspective, regions in which Islamic law was not the rule of government remained embattled. After Muhammad, the complexity of governing expanding Islamic communities demanded a division of labor between ulema and sultan. And while the sharia provides a basic political theory for governance of an Islamic community, it does not outline the specifics of how to legislate and govern rapidly expanding states.[64] In the modern era, Islamic theorists are split on how to deal with the political import of the sharia. "Islamic intellectuals reacted to the West either, on the one hand, by syncretism, justified by seeing certain Western ideas as expressions of true Islam; or, on the other hand, by revivalism, going back to the sources of revelation."[65] Islamic revivalism takes the form of disparate fundamentalist groups that react to modernization rather than provide a means to reconcile Islamic ideals with modern realities. In turn, Islamic syncretism can take multiple forms, although it also draws on the early Islamic community for legitimacy. "Indeed, observers of Muslim political thought in modern times have often noted, sometimes with patronizing sympathy, sometimes with superciliousness, that those Muslims who seek democracy argue that Muhammad was the first democrat and the early Muslim community was the first democracy, those advancing socialism depict Muhammad as the first socialist and the early community as the first socialist state, and so on as political styles change. Even certain Muslim communists went so far as to urge that Muhammad and the early community prefigured the idealized communist society."[66]

Because Soviet Communism preached a decidedly anti-Western doctrine, it had an interesting appeal to Muslims, who were displeased with the imperialism of Western empires. Of course, Soviet Communism was also antireligious. Nevertheless, the civil war that followed the Russian Revolution placed Bolsheviks in no position to wage a war against Islam in Central Asia. Consequently, Bolsheviks attempted to appeal to Muslims by promising them political independence from czarist domination, religious freedom, and economic development.[67]

In fact, Lenin professed an admiration for Muslims who had revolted against imperialism and saw many Islamic folk heroes as emblematic of the human struggle against oppression.[68] In 1917, Bolsheviks made the following official announcement to Muslims of the former Russian Empire: "To all toiling Moslems of Russia and the East, whose mosques and prayer-houses have been destroyed, whose beliefs have been trampled on by the czars and the oppressors of Russia. Your beliefs and customs, your national and cultural institutions are declared henceforth free and inviolable. Organize your national life freely and without hindrance. This is your right. Know that your rights . . . are protected by the entire might of the revolution and its organs. . . . Support this revolution and its government!"[69] This announcement reflected the feelings and aspirations of Muslims across Central Asia. In Communism, many Muslims saw the opportunity for Islam to become once again a powerful force in a world that appeared to be leaving them behind.

Before Soviet Communism, a progressive Islamic movement known as Jadidism had already taken root. The scholar Adeeb Khalid explains, "The [Jadidism] movement derived its name from its advocacy of the *usul-i jadid,* the new method of teaching the Arabic alphabet to children. . . . Implicit in this concept was a new way of looking at the world. The most important item in the lexicon of Central Asian Jadidism was *taraqqiy*, a term that covered the notions of progress, development, rise, and growth. The Jadids' assimilation of the idea of progress, the notion of history as open-ended change, altered the way in which they saw the world and their place within it."[70] Quite naturally, the radical ideas of the Jadids were in opposition to the traditional and conservative forms of Islam in Central Asia and, with the development of Soviet Communism, strangely akin to much of the ideology of Marxist-Leninism. Rather than be washed away by Western forces and compromised by conservative Islam, Jadids hoped to influence and take advantage of the changing political tide in light of the Russian Revolution. These forward-looking Islamic thinkers attempted to "rationalize Islam, to purify it and bring it into line with the modern era."[71]

In the 1920s, the Jadids led many religious and cultural reforms with the support of Communist Party elites, who felt that these developments were an initial way to address the hopeless "backwardness" of Central Asia. Sultan Galiev was the highest-ranking Muslim in the Communist Party between 1920 and 1923. As a leading advisor to Stalin, Galiev argued that in Islamic regions, "We need to say openly, to whom it is appropriate, that we are in no way fighting against any religion, we are only conducting propaganda for our atheist convictions, exercising our right to do so."[72] But in addition to advocating religious tolerance, Galiev made a more dangerous political move in advocating an independent Communist state in Central Asia. In 1918, Galiev wrote, "We must unite the Muslim masses in a communist movement that shall be our own and autonomous."[73] This placed Soviets in a difficult position: A grassroots Communist movement was occurring within Central Asia but was taking on a nationalist and Islamic spirit.

By the late 1920s, Stalin decided that Central Asia needed to be purged of certain Islamic reformers. This decision demonstrated the insincerity of the initial promises made to Muslims by Bolshevik leaders. On numerous occasions, Lenin and Stalin expressed a desire to eliminate Islam while recognizing the importance of recruiting potentially supportive Muslims to their cause. Overall, Lenin and Stalin viewed Islam and the Muslims of Central Asia as primitive and extremely prejudiced against reason; therefore, as Stalin stated, Islam had to be destroyed "by indirect and more cautious ways" than those used against the Orthodox Church.[74] Once Stalin had secured power, he began a famous series of purges in a proactive measure to destroy any political competitors. Between 1927 and

1939, supporters of Galiev and his brand of Marxism were purged from the party. Galiev himself was arrested and sentenced to penal servitude; he was eventually executed in 1940.

By killing off many leading Muslims Communists, Stalin created a political dilemma. Replacing Muslim Communist leaders with Russian Communists insured that Islamic nationalism would not impact Communist ideology in Central Asia, but loyal Russian Communists were urgently needed in the newly formed Russian republic, and few had knowledge of the Islamic society they would be asked to rule. Nevertheless, many elite positions in Central Asia were given to Russians. But Muslim Communists were still needed to advise these leaders and often held leadership positions themselves. The Board of Muslims was created for the edification of Russian Communists concerning Islamic society, and many Communist Party members in Central Asia were self-identified Muslims; in 1918, half of the Communist Party of Turkistan was Muslim, and in 1924, the Bukhara Communist Party was 70 percent Muslim.[75] Under these circumstances, Soviet elites had to acknowledge that Muslim Communists were a reality that could not be wholly eliminated.

By the 1940s, Soviet Islam had lost many of its initial reformers but had solidified into a network of Muslim boards that were allowed to meet at the annual Central Muslim Religious Conference to discuss the state of Islam and its relation to Soviet Communism. Representatives of the Central Muslim Board showed support for the Soviet government and were often used to promote Soviet propaganda to Muslim citizens. During World War II, the Central Muslim Religious Board was employed extensively to unify Muslims against Germany. But an interesting balance existed within the board, trying to reconcile Soviet rule with Islamic law. In 1942, the Central Muslim Religious Board sent Stalin the following salutation: "Hearty greetings in the name of Muslims of the USSR to you . . . champion of the liberation of oppressed peoples and a man ever attentive to the need of the peoples. . . . May Allah help you bring your work to a victorious end."[76] As this message demonstrates, representatives of official Islam showed respect and allegiance to the Soviet government while also explicitly establishing the importance of their religious identity and the purpose of the Communist project in relation to a higher power. The message clearly suggests that Stalin would not accomplish his goals without the assistance of Allah. As one Muslim dignitary pointed out as late as 1970 at an international conference, "Soviet leaders who believe neither in God nor his Prophet nevertheless apply laws that were dictated by God and expounded by his Prophet."[77]

While Muslims of Central Asia were certainly denied national auton-omy under Communism, many of the initial goals of Jadidism came to fruition. Jadids wanted to modernize Central Asia, and Soviet Russia was providing them with the resources to do it. Therefore, Islamic national-ism did not automatically find itself opposed to Communist interests. In contrast, nationalists throughout Eastern Europe and many of the Soviet republics were at odds with the Communist agenda from the beginning and developed into the main expression of anti-Communist convictions. This is mainly because Eastern Europe was more industrialized than Central Asia; consequently, Communists sought different goals in these regions. Eastern European Communists wanted to unite the proletariat of all countries and shift the control of industry into the hands of its workers. But Central Asia had little industry, and Muslim Communists hoped to industrialize their regions to "catch up" to their Western coun-terparts. The act of modernizing Islamic society was closely linked to its empowerment in the world economy, and therefore Communism became an unintended means to realize this preexisting nationalist goal. And many high-ranking Central Asian Communist officials continued to express no contradiction between Islam and Communism.[78]

Certain Islamic leaders actively argued that Muslim home rule would be best achieved through participation in the Soviet project. For instance, the journal of the Tashkent Spiritual Directorate advises, " 'Believers who are good Muslims . . . must take part in building a new life and a new society in their own country.' This Directorate also encourages children to participate. For example, one Muslim leader in a sermon attacked a Baptist ban on Baptist children joining the Pioneers, he concluded: 'They are wrong. Our children must be Pioneers, members of the Komsomol and then of the Communist Party. Everywhere they must play a leading role.' "[79] Unlike Christian churches in Eastern Europe, which demanded an exclusive membership that could not be reconciled with Communist Party membership, many Muslim leaders viewed participation in Com-munist and even atheist organizations as a way to strengthen Muslim power. And Soviets continued to supply them with many incentives to remain loyal to the Communist project.

In line with Muslim nationalist goals, Soviets offered something that had not previously been available to Muslims — free public education on a massive scale. At the end of the czarist regime, less than three thousand Muslim children attended public school, but the Soviets prioritized edu-cation to the extent that by 1921, over eighty-four thousand Muslim children were enrolled in state public schools.[80] In time, all Muslim chil-

TABLE 5. INCREASE IN POPULATION WITH
SECONDARY EDUCATION, 1939–1970
(%)

	1939	1959	1970
Soviet Union	11	36	48
Latvia (most-educated republic)	18	43	52
Central Asian republics			
Kazakhstan	8	35	47
Kyrgyzstan	5	34	45
Tajikistan	4	33	42
Turkmenistan	7	39	48
Uzbekistan	6	35	46

SOURCE: Tuzmuhamedov 1973: 149.

dren attended free Soviet schools and by most accounts received instruction similar to that of more modernized regions of the Soviet Union.

Muslims certainly took advantage of the educational opportunities offered by the Soviet government. Central Asians were some of the least-educated people in the Soviet Union in the 1920s, but by the 1950s, they were receiving secondary educations at a rate comparable to the other Soviet republics (see table 5).

The Soviet government also industrialized Central Asia at an impressive rate. A comparison to other Central Asian countries reveals the industrial progress made by the Central Asian republics (see table 6). By 1965, the Central Asian republics had at least six times more per capita output of electricity than Iran, Pakistan, or Turkey. In addition, the Central Asian republics had substantially more tractors, doctors, and newspapers in circulation per capita than Iran, Pakistan, and Turkey combined. Finally, nearly 90 percent of Soviet Central Asians could read by 1965, while only 30 percent or less of Iranians, Pakistanis, or Turks were literate in 1964. These achievements were actively sought and encouraged by leading Muslims, who wanted to improve their lives and economic strength.

By 1970, Central Asian republics had established industries and an educational system; in turn, the need for skilled foreign workers and managers was no longer pressing. The Muslim population became more technologically advanced and urbanized, enabling them to fill elite roles within the Central Asian republics. This is evidenced by a study of technological and scientific workers in Uzbekistan between 1960 and 1975. The percentage of doctors in science, doctoral candidates in science, and

TABLE 6. MODERNIZATION OF CENTRAL ASIA,
IRAN, PAKISTAN, AND TURKEY

	Central Asian Republics		Iran	Pakistan	Turkey
	1928	1965	1964		
Per capita output of electricity, kwh	4	950	58	34	143
Number of tractors (per 1,000 hectares of sown land)	0.2	34.7	0.7	0.2	2.7
Percent literate over 9 years old	16	87	15	16	30
Newspaper circulation (per 10,000 population)	22	223	15	5	45
Number of doctors (per 10,000 population)	4.0	17.4	3.4	0.9	4.0

SOURCE: Tuzmuhamedov 1973: 141.

"scientific elites" who were Uzbek dramatically increased within the fifteen-year period of the study (see figure 4). While only 35 percent of all working scientists were Uzbek in 1960, 60 percent were Uzbek in 1975. In turn, the percentage of scientists in Uzbekistan who were Russian was shrinking.

The relationship between Islam and Communism was a growing process of give and take. Muslim leaders saw the long-term advantages of modernization, and Central Asia quickly became the most technologically advanced region in the Islamic world. Nevertheless, Central Asia lagged behind the industrial growth of other Soviet Republics, and an active debate still rages concerning the effect of industrialization on the long-term economy of Central Asia.[81] But while many Muslims sought entry into the economic and political structure created by the Soviet Union and succeeded in becoming part of the ruling and educated elite, they were simultaneously losing their Islamic traditions.

In 1929, the Soviet Union passed the Law on Religious Associations, which outlined how state officials were to monitor and control all religious groups. In Central Asia, Communists dissolved all Islamic courts; these courts oversaw criminal justice by upholding both customary law ('adat) and Koranic law (Shari'at). Bennigsen and Lemercier-Quelquejay argue that this assault was partially acceptable because it was supported by Muslim elites who viewed the Soviet reform as "merely one more engagement in the long war of the jadids to modernize the juridical structure of Islam."[82] In this case, the Communist anti-Islamic policy realized

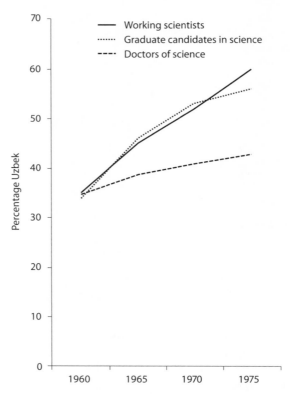

Figure 4. Change in Percentage of Scientists in
Uzbekistan Who Are Ethnically Uzbek (1960 to
1975). Source: Ro'I 1984: 55.

what some Islamic nationalists had hoped to accomplish as long ago as
the early nineteenth century. While the loss of Islamic courts was clearly
not supported by all Muslims, it is important to note that some Islamic
thinkers saw Communism as a means to settle centuries-long conflicts
within the Muslim community. As one Muslim scholar noted, Islam can
justify even "the rule of a usurper as a means of assuring the public order
and the unity of all Muslims."[83]

   Nevertheless, antireligious policies did sometimes produce active resistance and violence. Two recent books, *Veiled Empire: Gender and Power
in Stalinist Central Asia* and *The New Woman in Uzbekistan: Islam,
Modernity, and Unveiling under Communism,* detail the previously undocumented campaign, known as the hujum, to force Central Asian
women to unveil. While there is evidence that many women embraced

the hujum and gladly shed their veils, reactions across Central Asia in the 1920s were varied. In Uzbekistan, thousands of unveiled women were attacked, and many were raped as a commentary on their "disgraceful" appearance. While these violent reactions to the hujum were in opposition to official Soviet law, Marianne Kamp argues that these revolts were not really expressions of Communist resistance but rather "male efforts to reestablish the one aspect of social hierarchy that they had not yet lost."[84] Nevertheless, by the 1960s, the majority of Muslim women in Central Asia had unveiled and began participating in society in ways that were unimaginable in pre-Communist times.[85]

The Communist Party also attempted to alter the Islamic clan structure at the village level. The extended patriarchal structure of Islamic families throughout Central Asia was crucial to the transmission of local customs and daily rituals. Marriages were largely arranged, and married women were sent to live with their husbands' families. Resources were shared within this family unit, with the eldest male overseeing the distribution and application of finances. The introduction of Communism to local regions had mixed success in altering this family system. Bennigsen and Lemercier-Quelquejay explain: "The Soviet regime struck heavily at the large joint family, causing it to lose all economic significance. In spite of that, this type of family survived . . . in a modified form but still preserving its traditional characteristics in the formerly nomad districts. Here the large joint family persists more as an ethical than as a functional unit, in the sense that a number of customs survive despite prohibitions; but these are nevertheless gradually disappearing."[86]

The massive in-migration of non-Muslims also affected the Islamic family system simply by introducing Muslims to new levels of ethnic and religious diversity. The 1959 Soviet census shows that the percentage of interfaith marriages, which Soviets called "mixed" marriages, in Central Asian republics was quite high, between 14 to 18 percent of the population in urban centers, up from virtually zero a generation earlier.[87] The growing number of interfaith marriages indicates that local Islamic customs were often not observed by the 1950s and that the traditional Islamic family system was in crisis.

Although interfaith marriages were on the rise, certain clan and tribal relationships survived Communism amazingly well. In fact, leadership roles based on clan hierarchical systems tended to reproduce themselves within the Communist Party. "The tendency for kinship to permeate Soviet institutions was not confined to the local level but appeared at the highest tiers of authority such that the tribal structure has in some bizarre fashion fused with the party structure to form a single indissoluble whole."[88]

In terms of institutional change, the attempt to shut down religious supply appears to have had very mixed results in Central Asia. On the one hand, the Communist Party was quite successful at eliminating Islamic courts and schools, decreasing the number of active mosques, unveiling Muslim women, and weakening the Islamic family through a rise in interfaith marriages. On the other hand, the Communist Party merged with Islamic tribal structures, making "most party members, Komsomol, and *Znanie* sympathetic to the Islamic and nationalist causes and thus reluctant to vigorously [attack the beliefs of Islam]."[89] Institutionally and philosophically, official Islam fused itself to the doctrine of Communism.

Soviet Communism was a political reality to which Central Asian Muslims largely adapted. This adaptation was not unconditional, however. Muslims leaders found within the philosophy of Soviet Communism ideals that mirrored ideals of social justice within the Islamic tradition. For this reason, Muslim Communists argued that Soviet Communism was actually carrying out the will of Allah, albeit in ignorance. In addition, Muslims found that many of the social programs implemented by Soviets fit their preexisting nationalist and progressive goals. This further helped to solidify a working relationship between Muslims and atheistic Communists. No similar relationship developed between the Communist Party and any Christian group; in fact, Soviet Communism began its occupancy in many Christian regions by actively assaulting the local churches and religious leaders. But within Central Asia, Soviet Communists first appealed to the interests of Muslims before later attacking their traditional religious institutions under the banner of modernization.

A QUICK NOTE ON ANTI-SEMITISM

The amount of scholarly work on Soviet Jews is immense and overwhelms all other research on religion in the Soviet Union.[90] While the actual number of Soviet Jews pales in comparison to the number of Christian Orthodox, Roman Catholics, Protestants, and Muslims in the Soviet Union, interest in Judaism stems from the fact that anti-Semitism was a powerful ideological force in the twentieth century and that Jews were vastly overrepresented in an important and unique segment of the Soviet population — the urban educated classes. In fact, Jews comprised a large number of the elites within the early Communist Party.

A major source of scholarly inquiry involves the extent to which

Soviet policy was anti-Semitic. Clearly, Soviet rule violently targeted all religious groups within the Soviet Union, but many researchers and document compilers argue that Soviet officials targeted nonreligious aspects of Jewish culture and therefore practiced overt anti-Semitism. While Soviet leaders certainly denied anti-Semitic policies, especially after World War II, there is little reason to believe that the Soviet system was not anti-Semitic. But it is also clear that Soviet elites were anti-Christian, anti-Muslim, anti-Buddhist, and anti–all forms of religious expression. Regarding religious supply, Soviet officials attacked Jewish schools and places of worship with their usual aplomb.

But even though Soviet Jews constituted only around 1 percent of the Soviet population, they were a minority who were difficult to ignore based on their importance to Soviet intellectual, political, and cultural life. Soviet Jews mainly resided in large urban areas and represented 5 percent of the white-collar workforce.[91] Soviet passports also required Jews to be identified as having a Jewish nationality. Consequently, Jews tended to be more visible and central to the workings of the Soviet government than other religious minorities. In turn, Jews faced heightened scrutiny, and many decided to leave the Soviet Union when allowed to immigrate to Israel after World War II. Approximately 271,000 Jews emigrated from 1959 to 1985, with around 60 percent of those individuals leaving for Israel.[92] Overall, the Jewish population dramatically decreased during the Soviet era due to emigration, low birth rates, and intermarriage.

THE SIGNIFICANCE OF RELIGIOUS SUPPLY

A tourist in the Soviet Union in 1977 recounted this experience. "On a visit to Leningrad some years ago I consulted a map to find out where I was, but I could not make it out. From where I stood, I could see several enormous churches, yet there was no trace of them on the map. When finally an interpreter came to help me, he said, 'We don't show churches on our maps.' Contradicting him, I pointed to one that was very clearly marked. 'That is a museum,' he said, 'not what we call a "living church." It is only the "living churches" we don't show.'"[93] The Communist Party erased "living" churches from their maps as if that might erase religion from society. While complete secularization never came to pass, Soviet antireligious policies were quite successful in diminishing the power and dominance of traditional religious institutions. Soviets cut church attendance, greatly reduced the resources and activities of religious groups, and decreased the number of individuals affiliated with religious institutions. Nevertheless, "living" churches still operated within the Soviet Union, despite massive attempts to erase them.

The persistence of religion was based on the responses of religious groups to Soviet repression. Perhaps individuals would have retained some supernatural beliefs even if all religious groups had been disbanded; we may never know if religious belief can survive in the absence of any religious supply. For instance, would religious beliefs exist in a society that effectively banned religious supply for a thousand years? It seems that supernatural ideas and concepts might persist in some vague form. But during the relatively short reign of the Soviet Union, it was the continued existence and activity of religious communities that kept organized religion alive in the most hostile of environments. The survival of these communities took on different forms; in some cases, it was based in opposition to Soviet forces, and, in other cases, it relied on collaboration with its oppressors. The varied responses of religious groups to Soviet antireligious policy essentially depended on three factors: the group's structure, its visibility, and its theology.

The Roman Catholic Church of Lithuania represents the clearest overt resistance to Soviet rule. It asserted its institutional independence from the Soviet state and remained connected to the Vatican throughout the Soviet era. The ability of the Lithuanian Church to withstand total absorption into the Soviet state was premised on its autonomy before Soviet rule and its association with the international Roman Catholic Church. In contrast, the Russian Orthodox Church had no hope of asserting any opposition or independence to Soviet control because it was already subservient to the czarist state before the Soviet era.

For this reason, many Russian Orthodox leaders necessarily collaborated with Soviet officials to keep the church in existence. Consequently, the church lost its connection with the Russian people and its religious viability, even though it managed to survive in name under Soviet control. Membership dwindled, and attendance became virtually nonexistent. But the Russian Orthodox Church was not alone in making concessions to the Soviets, although it probably paid the highest price in its vitality. Both Protestant and Muslim groups cooperated with Soviet officials but without the same ramifications to their religious livelihoods.

Protestants were accustomed to regulation and repression throughout the Soviet Union. Unlike the Russian Orthodox Church, which relished its favored status in czarist Russia, Protestant groups sought not political sway but religious freedom. Many of these groups celebrated the demise of imperial Russia as an opportunity for religious liberty. When no new freedoms emerged, Protestant groups simply continued to minister in private while publicly striving to appear as model Soviet citizens. Their low visibility and political powerlessness justified the fact that they mounted no opposition movement to a repressive state. Baptists and Evangelicals never championed nationalist causes but simply sought to preach their religious message in any way possible. For this reason, their qualified acquiescence to Soviet rule never threw their credibility into question, and their proselytizing continued to meet with some successes.

Muslim leaders in Central Asia were fiercely independent and highly visible, but many embraced elements of the Soviet state because the Communist Party had something to offer them. Communist leaders promised to modernize Central Asia and provide the region with education, industry, and renewed vigor. In fact, Soviet rule successfully popularized literacy and education, improved health care, introduced modern science and technology, and expanded communication and irrigation infrastructures in Central Asia.[94] For these reasons, many Muslims accepted Soviet control to further their national and religious ends. Their compromise eliminated Islam from public discourse and reduced religious activity to the private realm. This led to no theological crisis for most Muslims, who held inner spirituality as the core element of Islam. In return, Central Asia was modernized, and many Muslims moved into positions of political power.

At the individual level, Soviet citizens responded to the activities of religious institutions and the actions of those around them. Religious leaders who collaborated with Soviet officials diminished the legitimacy of their religious institution. In contrast, the religiously devout who maintained their commitment with integrity often inspired respect and faith in others. Stories of religious conversions in prison beautifully demonstrate how nonbelievers were often stirred by the religious devotion of their fellow inmates. In one such story, an atheist prisoner continually taunts his religious inmate to the point that his religious faith is shaken. The atheist writes, "I felt no satisfaction in my victory. A horrible weight fell upon me. I felt sick, as though I had done something mean to someone. And he just kept on praying, but more calmly now. Suddenly, he looked at me and smiled. I was amazed at his face: there was something joyous about it, pure, as though it had just been washed clean. The weight immediately fell from my soul. I understood that he had forgiven me. And then a light of some sort penetrated me, and I understood that God existed."[95] In many ways, true faith emerges when under attack. Soviet repression was therefore the ultimate test of true religious faith.

Religious responses to the Soviet attack on religious supply reveal that religious groups and individuals make complex cost-benefit calculations. Some individuals accepted death as the price for their faith, but religious institutions tended to compromise and negotiate with Soviet forces in order to survive. This is not to say that public religious leaders were disingenuous to their beliefs; truly, anyone who practiced religion in the Soviet Union risked a lot for her faith. Instead, these compromises demonstrate that religious groups do not blindly march through the world but constantly seek to navigate a difficult balance between their theological concerns and institutional commitments.

CHAPTER 4

Hunting for Religious Demand

A philosophy whose principle is so incommensurate with our
most intimate feelings as to deny them all relevancy in universal
affairs, as to annihilate their motives at one blow, will be even
more unpopular than pessimism — that is why materialism will
always fail of universal adoption.

> — William James, *The Varieties of Religious Experience:*
> *A Study of Human Nature*

Neil Armstrong famously announced, "That's one small step for a man,
one giant leap for mankind" as his foot first touched the surface of the
moon. This line is well-known to generations of American schoolchildren, and it powerfully conveys the idea that technology helps humans to
realize their *worldly* dreams. Returning from the first flight into space,
the Russian cosmonaut Yuri Gagarin proclaimed that he did not see God
in the heavens. His statement was well-known to Soviet citizens and
sharply conveyed the idea that technology helps humans to discard their
otherworldly dreams.

Aeronautical technology was often presented as proof of atheism in
the Soviet Union. In Russian, there is only one word for both "heaven"
and "sky," and every flight into space was billed as an "assault on
heaven." The double meaning of this phrase was fully intended to indicate that Soviet technology had conquered God's supposed place of resi-
dence. Communist Party officials naively believed that religious ideas
could be proven false through scientific advancement. However, even
the most undiscerning religious believers easily accommodated their faith
to Soviet technology. As one little girl aptly responded to Gagarin's
inability to find God, "But only those with faith can see God."[1]

This child's retort characterized a major stumbling block for the science of atheism. How could Soviet scientists respond to religious ideas and beliefs that made no claims to science? In general, scientific attempts to address religion appeared to miss the point that most twentieth-century religious traditions were devoid of empirical assertions about the physical world. In addition, equating science with atheism was problematic when scientific setbacks occurred. For instance, some Soviet citizens indicated that the explosion of a rocket that resulted in the death of three cosmonauts was probably an act of divine retribution.[2] Because Communist Party officials depicted space travel as an assault on God's domain, God sometimes appeared to be fighting back.

In the face of scientific and technological advancements, atheist proselytizers could not understand what continued to attract individuals to religion. From a Marxist-Leninist perspective, religious ideology was pseudoscience, and believers were attracted to religious worldviews out of sheer ignorance. In other words, Communist Party ideologues viewed religious demand as a misdirected desire to understand the workings of the world. When scientific education did not appear to undermine ritual activity, church membership, and religious faith, Soviet officials began to alter this view of religious demand. Instead, they posited that religious individuals also sought group solidarity through joining church communities and participating in ritualistic activities. Therefore, Communist Party leaders decided to show religious believers that their longings to belong, worship, and celebrate could be fulfilled without the burden of religious concepts. Their scientific campaign to undermine religious belief turned into a godless religion with secular rituals, ceremonies, texts, saints, and revelations. By removing God from religious activity, Communist Party officials believed that they could meet the ongoing "irrational" demand for religion while erasing its harmful ideological components. To do so, they needed to pinpoint the deep psychological sources of religious demand.

Individual religiosity is usually measured by belief, behavior, and identity. But these aspects of religiosity are by no means in perfect correlation. Someone can believe in God and pray every day but never attend church or belong to a religious group. Conversely, another person may self-identify with a religious tradition but have no firm grasp of its theology or strong commitment to a religious community. The push-and-pull strategy of the atheism campaign attempted to address these many and sometimes competing facets of religiosity. By shutting off religious supply, Soviet rule sought to abolish religious practices, affiliations, and identities; this was done fairly successfully through coercion. But simple coercion was not

good enough—the Soviet project required faithful participants. Therefore, Communist Party officials hoped to convert the public to scientific
atheism; in theory, this would redirect religious demand and provide a
new source of meaning, belonging, and understanding.

In many ways, Communist officials hunted for religious demand by
simply mimicking different aspects of religion. Their experiments provide
a fascinating look into possible sources of religious commitment and
faith. In the end, Soviet rulers hastily dismissed the possibility that
humans might want or need God, and their intense desire to kill the idea
of God led them to miss a core aspect of religious demand.

THE DEMAND FOR IDENTITY

Religion provides individuals with a sense of identity. Religious individuals understand themselves as part of a larger community, and their
shared identity offers a sense of belonging, solidarity, and worth. To
undermine this aspect of religious demand, Soviet policy eliminated
many of the attractive characteristics of religious identity. Individuals
who continued to identify with religious groups were now subject to isolation and harassment—the very predicaments that religious affiliation
purportedly averts.

Religious affiliation in the vast regions of the Soviet Union was largely
taken for granted because it was ingrained in the cultural and social fabric of daily life. Most regions were dominated by powerful religious
monopolies, and religious affiliations were intricately tied to national
and ethnic identities. In Central Asia, the term *Muslim* distinguished
Central Asians from Russians and other Westerners. Similarly, to be
Russian meant being Orthodox, and Lithuanians were generally assumed
to be Catholic.[3] When the merger of national, ethnic, and religious identities occurs, it is uncertain what these labels mean in terms of religiosity.
Are Muslims, Orthodox Christians, and Catholics devoted followers of a
religious ideology or essentially nonreligious individuals who were historically tied for ethnic or national reasons to a religious identity? Communist Party leaders expected the latter.

In many ways, Soviet leaders were correct. To sever ties to religious
identities, they made religious membership and affiliation extremely
onerous. Threats of imprisonment, public ridicule, and employment discrimination made religious identities an unwanted burden and forced
many Soviet citizens in the 1920s and 1930s to reconsider the importance of religious affiliation in their lives. The universal decline of reli-

gious memberships, outlined in chapter 2, is evidence that a substantial number of Soviet citizens quickly discarded their religious affiliations in times of trouble. Had individuals with religious ties before Soviet rule vigorously protested antireligious policy, Communist Party leaders could not have regulated religion simply due to the ubiquity of religious identification. Instead, few Soviet citizens were willing to fight for their religious commitments, and these few, in turn, were overwhelmed by the power of the state. Many of the dominant religious traditions of the Soviet Union simply collapsed under state regulation, revealing their prior lack of vitality.

This result is not so surprising given that religious monopolies tend to be weak. It demonstrates that most religious affiliations before Soviet rule were culturally taken for granted rather than expressions of fierce dedication to a religious tradition. Nonetheless, not all individuals completely relinquished their religious affiliations, and some even remained committed to religious groups that were formerly monopolies. But in these cases, religious identity tended to attract individuals for more than just religious reasons.

For many Lithuanians, affiliation with the Roman Catholic Church came to represent political opposition to Communism. Due to its relative autonomy from state institutions and its connection to the international Roman Catholic Church, the Lithuanian Church was exceptionally difficult to absorb into the Communist state. Consequently, it maintained institutional independence along with some of its prior resources. Lithuanian nationalists viewed the Roman Catholic Church as the only national institution that opposed Soviet rule. As such, it became a resource and sanctuary for Lithuanians seeking national autonomy and a means to express political dissent. Soviet repression united religious and national interests in the minds of Lithuanians. In turn, the Lithuanian Catholic Church retained members for religious *and* political reasons, so that Communist Party actually broadened the potential appeal of Catholic identity instead of diminishing it.

This phenomenon was most evident outside the Soviet Union in the republic of Poland. The Polish Catholic Church has the distinction of being the only monopoly religion to actually gain members under Communist rule. In fact, the Polish Roman Catholic Church was so popular during the Communist era that it lost members when the antireligious policies of the Communism ended.[4] This instance demonstrates the potential political importance of religious identification. Under unique circumstances, religion attracts individuals simply for political solidarity, and in the cases of Poland and Lithuanian, Communist officials found themselves in an interesting paradox. Individuals were affiliating with religious groups *because* state policy discouraged it.

Communist Party officials did not encounter this problem when attacking other monopoly religions. Orthodox Church affiliations fell with no real oppositional movement to Soviet rule. As Orthodox clergy collaborated with Soviet officials and church resources were drained, Orthodox members abandoned the institution that could no longer provide religious services or social benefits and failed to offer any political alternative to Soviet rule. Orthodox identity was partially robbed of its meaning and purpose, and Orthodox Church affiliations dropped accordingly. And those who still yearned for religion tended to join underground Christian movements or worship in private to avoid harassment.

Like Catholic identity in Lithuania, Muslim identity weathered the storm of Soviet repression well. But unlike Roman Catholics, Muslims did not regard their religious identity as a marker of political opposition. Quite the contrary, many Central Asian Communist Party members identified themselves as Muslims, and Islamic leaders even controlled an official organization within the Soviet government — the Central Muslim Religious Board. In fact, Muslims voted overwhelming for the preservation of the Soviet Union in a 1991 countrywide referendum, revealing widespread reliance on and support of the Soviet system.[5] In Christian regions of the Soviet Union, religious individuals did not identify themselves as Communist supporters and did not join the Communist Party. For Christians, Communist and religious identities were mutually exclusive.

The term *Muslim* was employed by Communist Party officials to refer to the peoples of Central Asia. As such, it was utilized mainly as an ethnic identifier rather than an indicator of religious affiliation. While the terms *Orthodox* and *Catholic* had ethnic and national connotations, these identities were also linked to membership in either the Orthodox Church or the Roman Catholic Church. Therefore, the persistence of these identities was linked to these institutions. Centralization in the Roman Catholic and Orthodox Churches made "underground" religious affiliations difficult to sustain because religious activities required official religious approval. Within these religious structures, secrecy could be considered heresy. For instance, many underground Roman Catholic priests in Czechoslovakia were excommunication for violating church doctrine.[6] In Central Asia, Communist Party officials similarly attacked the institutional structures of Islam; they obliterated Islamic courts and schools and destroyed countless mosques. Still, Muslims retained their religious identities through a sense of ethnic solidarity and a more fluid understanding of religious affiliation.

The significance of Muslim identity during the Soviet era is a topic of debate. Some Islamic scholars feel that Soviets "did not inflict serious damage on the Islamic tradition" and argue that Islam remained actively "underground" throughout the Soviet era.[7] Others feel that Islamic groups "remained divided by clan loyalties and never developed a coherent ideology or leadership."[8] If one considers that religious identity and religious practice are independent measures of religiosity, both interpretations are correct. Muslim identity endured in the Soviet era, but many of the practices and traditions of Islam essentially lost their coherence and consistency as they went underground. Subsequently, individuals regarded themselves as Muslim, but it became increasingly unclear what this meant to their religious commitment and beliefs.

Some Islamic scholars argue that declines in religious practices had no effect on the persistence of Islam under Communism because there are specific religious rules that allow Muslims to abandon activities in religiously hostile environments. Normally, individuals are required to follow the five "pillars" *(rukns)* of Islam in order to be Muslims; however, these requirements can be waived under special circumstances. As Bennigsen and Lemercier-Quelquejay explain, "*Darl ul Harb,* faith without religious observance, is perfectly possible and even common, and . . . Islam, like Judaism, is a religion where the part played by spiritual leaders and religious institutions is only secondary, and therefore it is better able than Christianity to resist outside pressure."[9] Therefore, giving up religious practices or the dispersal of religious groups does not necessarily undermine individual Muslim identity. Personal religious identities survived as a real and popular option for Central Asians, who were predominantly Sunni Muslims of the Hanafi school. This school represents one of the most liberal religious orientations within Islam. Mehrdad Haghayeghi describes the significance of Central Asian theology: "Several Hanafi principles have been instrumental in providing a flexible framework for the practice of Islam, hence offering more freedom to the Central Asian believer. First, and perhaps the most critical aspect, is the qualitative distinction that has been made between faith (iman), and work or practice (amal). The Hanafis argue that if a Muslim wholeheartedly believes in God and the prophethood of Muhammad, but is negligent in performing his religious duties, he is not an infidel."[10] The theological distinction between faith and practice made it possible for

Muslims to retain their religious identities without active opposition to antireligious policies.

Because Hanafi Islam provided much greater freedom for religious believers to privately proclaim faith, Central Asians did not depend on professional clergy or a system of rituals to validate their religious identity. In contrast, the Roman Catholic and Orthodox Churches insisted on sanctifying rituals and rites preformed in their names. Unlike Catholics and Orthodox Christians, Muslims could decide for themselves what it meant to be religious. "In Islam, the means of crossing the boundary from non-Islam to Islam is relatively straight-forward: through the *shahada* or the profession of faith that 'There is no god but God, and Muhammad is the messenger of God.' This first pillar of the Islamic faith is the moral equivalent of a public declaration delimiting the borders of one's mind."[11]

Therefore, a private declaration of belief was enough to remain faithful. In many bizarre instances, self-identified Muslims publicly advocated atheism. As one committed Kazakh Communist explained, "I am an atheist but also a Muslim, because all Kazakhs are Muslims and I cannot deny my forefathers."[12] In fact, the phenomenon of the "nonbelieving Muslim" was widespread, according to Soviet publications.[13] This phenomenon demonstrates the nonreligious character of Muslim identity and the difficulty in assuming that Central Asians were any more religious than the populations of Christian regions of the Soviet Union. Muslims discovered a way to hold onto their identities while peacefully negotiating conditions of intense religious repression. As one Uzbek scholar, Tolib Saidbayev, explained, Muslims lived in "two dimensions — in the one, relating to the public sphere, Central Asians were thoroughly Sovietized in their attitudes, values and loyalties; in the other, relating to the private sphere, they retained a largely traditional outlook, their world shaped by customs and preconceptions that were rooted in Islamic practice."[14]

These two dimensions are most easily observed in the interaction between Muslims and the Communist Party. Communist Party members throughout the Soviet Union necessarily disavowed their religious affiliations or, at the very least, kept them hidden. But Communist Party members throughout Central Asia were self-proclaimed Muslims. In 1918, approximately half of the Communist Party members in Turkistan (a single, united Central Asian republic at that time) identified themselves as Muslims. Likewise, in 1924, the Bukhara Communist Party reported that 70 percent of its members were Muslims.[15] In 1965, an investigation into mosque attendance in Kazakhstan revealed that "every tenth participant was a member of the Komsomol."[16] And in 1985, a Soviet study reported that 14 percent of the Uzbek Communist Party and 56 percent of the Tajikistan Communist Party were "active Muslims," implying that they were "believing" Muslims.[17] Under these circumstances, it appears that atheistic Communism and Muslim identity were actually reconciled or at least loosened to produce the "Muslim Communist."

At the most basic level, religious identities indicate the direction of one's religiosity. Soviet repression was largely effective at reducing public declarations of religious affiliation and only failed when religious identities became synonymous with political dissent or customary ethnic identifiers. When forced to choose between religious commitment and social acceptance, most Soviets openly discarded their religious identities. Under these circumstances, state repression appears to be a successful means to scare individuals from their public religious attachments. Few were willing to fight for their religious identities, and the religious attachments that remained under Communism tended to exist covertly. As we shall see, the very fact that religious identities and activities went underground does not indicate continued religious fervor.

THE DEMAND FOR RITUAL

Communist Party officials viewed continued participation in religious festivals, holidays, and life event rituals, like baptisms and weddings, as real threats to their dreams of secularization. As with religious identities, these types of religious expressions may not indicate powerful religious commitments. For instance, what does getting married in a chapel say about a couple's religious dedication? Not much. In the same way, singing a Christmas carol does not indicate that someone is a devout Christian.

On the other hand, there are theoretical reasons to believe that religious activities are central to ongoing religious commitment. First, public expressions of religion demonstrate to participants that other individuals also believe in religious doctrines and that religious activity is socially acceptable and sometimes expected. As Rodney Stark explains, "Quite simply, an individual's confidence in religious explanations. . . . is strengthened to the extent that others express their confidence in them."[18] Rituals, ceremonies, and services are a primary means for individuals to communicate their religious confidence to one another. And in times of religious repression, ritual participation even more powerfully indicates that participants are dedicated to their faith. In the Soviet Union, seemingly innocuous religious ceremonies could acquire an air of rebellious piety.

Second, ritual activity generates religious capital. *Religious capital* consists of familiarity with church ritual and doctrine.[19] Economist Laurence Iannaccone finds that an individual's religious capital determines her ability to appreciate, value, and commit to religious concepts.[20] As such, confusion concerning religious concepts and ignorance of accepted ritual practices will reduce the religious confidence of individuals. Consequently, the Soviet attempt to discourage religious participation was at heart an effort to alter overall levels of religious capital through the promotion of religious ignorance.

In tandem, Soviet officials offered their own ceremonies and celebrations. The campaign to substitute atheist rituals for religious ones most clearly demonstrates the combined strategy to coerce and convert individuals. While banning religious practices, Soviets created ritual substitutes that appeared eerily similar to their forbidden counterparts. For instance, Soviet officials donned robes to sanctify the union between husband and wife in churchlike buildings complete with candles and altars emblazoned with Soviet symbols. Brides wore symbolic white as they affirmed their marital obedience before images of Lenin. As an added benefit, atheist publications promised that Red weddings produced longer-lasting marriages than religious ceremonies.[21] In theory, these types of Soviet rituals would redirect feelings of confidence, commitment, and belonging away from God and religion and toward the Communist Party and Soviet society in general.

Piecemeal data indicate that Soviets were successful at transitioning many citizens from religious to atheist rituals. The republic of Estonia collected data to trace the popularity of an atheist alternative to confirmation. During the 1950s, the Knowledge Society introduced a coming-of-age celebration called the Summer Days of Youth that was intended to mimic and replace church confirmations. Between 1957 and 1970, the number of religious confirmations subsequently dropped as participants in the Summer Days of Youth grew, most dramatically in the first three years since its introduction (see figure 5). The comparison of these data shows that atheist activists targeted specific religious practices to consciously produce substitute rituals. In addition, the transition could occur quite rapidly when funding and coercion of the state were in full play. The Estonian attack on confirmations appears to have been a remarkable success.

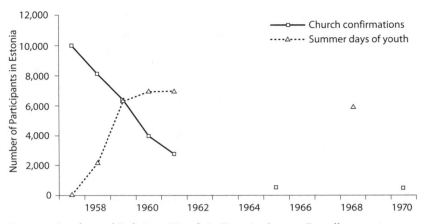

Figure 5. Secular and Religious Rituals in Estonia. Source: Powell 1975: 82.

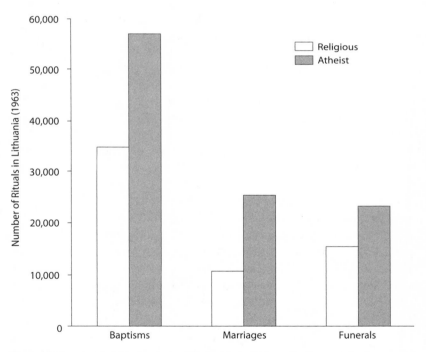

Figure 6. Baptisms, Marriages, and Funerals in Lithuania. Source: Anderson 1994: 46.

In Lithuania, Soviet administrators paid special attention to the practices of the Roman Catholic Church and waged a prolonged effort after World War II to promote atheist rituals. In 1963, data show that atheist baptisms, weddings, and funerals far outnumber religious alternatives (see figure 6). Once again, Soviet officials were specifically concerned with not only eliminating religious rituals but also transitioning individuals into atheist substitutes. While the number of Catholic rituals remains substantial and accounts for over a third of all life event ceremonies conducted, that the number of individuals participating in Catholic rituals still dropped when Catholic identity remained strong illustrates the power of the Soviet state to alter daily practices.

While quantitative and qualitative data show that most Soviet citizens switched from celebrating religious rituals to participating in atheistic rites, individual reports indicate that many did so apathetically.[22] For instance, Christopher Binns argues that dramatic increases in Soviet youth ceremonies tell us little about the ideological import of these activities; he adds, "It is entirely possible to ignore the ideological barrage as a necessary evil and to derive from such events simply pleasure at being the center of attention in a colorful gathering and at sensing the perfectly genuine human kindness and community concern displayed."[23] In his in-depth analysis of authoritative discourse in final decades of the Soviet Union, Alexei Yurchak similarly concludes, "In most contexts these unanimous acts, gestures, and utterances of support did not refer to the literal meaning of ideological statements, resolutions and figures."[24] In sum, many Soviet citizens willingly participated in atheist rituals but mainly for reasons other than to express their love of the Soviet state or their belief in scientific atheism.

But regardless of whether changes in ritual participation happened willingly or out of necessity, these changes would have a powerful impact on long-term levels of religious capital. Whole generations of Soviet citizens would not be baptized or confirmed, have church weddings, sing hymns, attend religious funerals, or celebrate religious holidays. Over time, the memory of religious activity was certainly lost for many Soviet citizens.

A change in ceremonial activity could have deep consequences for the collective memory of a population. Catherine Wanner argues, "We generally think of commemorations as a traditionalizing instrument used to reinforce the status quo by ritually enacting it."[25] But when a state attempts to radically alter the meaning and import of national or religious ceremonies, it can potentially confuse participants and even emphasize the fabricated pretense of the activity. For instance, regarding historical commemorations, Wanner points out, "When individual memories recall an account of events radically different from that advanced by the state in commemoration or recognize the occurrence of events that are denied by the state, the legitimacy of the state is undermined. Some commemorations actually served to inhibit the cultivation of a sense of Soviet nationhood and instead produced alienation, suspicion, and distain for the Soviet state."[26]

Similarly, the obvious mimicry of religious rituals with Soviet alternatives may have ironically kept alive the memory of religious ceremony it was ostensibly replacing. And atheist rites may have highlighted the loss of religious ideas and concepts and paradoxically increased the demand for them. The paradoxical nature of Soviet ideology and ritual behavior is nicely summed up by Yurchak, who argues, "The more meticulously and unanimously the system's authoritative forms were represented in language, rituals, and other acts, the more its constative meanings became disconnected from form and thus allowed to shift in diverse and increasingly unanticipated directions."[27] In the case of atheist rituals, the fact that they dogmatically eliminated God while reproducing religious ceremony produced an "emperor with no clothes" — something that everyone recognized but did not acknowledge.

Still, many Soviet citizens still practiced religious activities in private. Religious visitors to the Soviet Union often spoke of secret ceremonies and meetings in which religious believers covertly participated. In homes and hidden locales, important sources of religious capital were often maintained. And Protestant sects specialized in generating an underground system of religious services and activities. But Protestant sects and underground religious communities differed from the Orthodox and Catholic traditions because they had no commonly accepted style of worship or ritual. Consequently, small Protestant groups developed religious behaviors and ideas independently of one another, so their collective impact on society and culture was limited to insular and restricted social networks. While this certainly generated intense commitment within these confined social groups, religious expression necessarily remained fragmented and subject to drastic irregularities. Under these conditions, overall levels of religious capital would be difficult to consistently maintain and nearly impossible to increase.

The problem of underground religion is most evident in the impact of Communism on Muslims. Islam was better suited for covert activity than both Orthodox and Catholic traditions because it had no central author-

TABLE 7. HOUSES OF PRAYER

(1936 survey)

	Pre-1917	Closed	Open	Registered	Un-registered
Totaled Raion records (rural districts)	9,720	6,160	3,590	386	2,583
Totaled city records	10,489	6,544	3,724	686	2,588

SOURCE: Keller 2001b: 223.

ity. Therefore, Soviet repression could not simply cut off the head of the institution as it did with the Orthodox Church. Because local Islamic communities were free to function at will, Muslims faced no theological dilemma in worshiping in nonofficial mosques and with nonofficial clerics, who often improvised the content of their rituals. Unsanctioned mosques were commonly created and maintained in Central Asian villages. Often old or condemned mosques were utilized in place of newer mosques that had been occupied by Communists. Muslims also used *"mazars,"* tombs or gravesites imbued with spiritual power and often marked by piling stones into pyramid shapes. Interestingly, observers report that *mazars* were often "deliberately made to look neglected so that local officials (financial inspectors [were] especially feared) [would] take the *mazar* to be nonfunctioning."[28]

Central Asian historian Shoshana Keller compiled systematic data on covert Islamic operations from regional records. She assembled a list of unregistered mosques from local counts in both rural and urban areas in Central Asia during the mid-1930s (see table 7). Keller notes the limitations of her data, but one can assume that more unregistered mosques existed than were recorded. However, that the number of both registered and unregistered mosques in 1936 is a fraction of the number of mosques in existence before 1917 indicates that unofficial mosques could not fully replicate the extensiveness of Islamic mosques in pre-Communist times. And further closures of mosques occurred after 1936, with the most drastic assault occurring during the Khrushchev era. In Uzbekistan alone, 3,567 mosques (mostly unregistered) were closed between 1961 and 1963.[29]

Unregistered mosques were mostly managed by unofficial clergy. Keller also tracked the number of registered and unregistered imams and mullahs.[30] While she does not provide a comparison to pre-Communist times, her data indicate that unofficial clergy greatly outnumbered official clergy (see table 8). In general, unofficial Islamic clergy were young

TABLE 8. ISLAMIC RELIGIOUS LEADERS
(1936 survey)

	Registered Clergy	Unregistered Imans	Unregistered Ishans	Unregistered Mullahs
Totaled Raion records (rural districts)	108	1,151	118	806
Totaled city records	0	98	25	0

SOURCE: Keller 2001b: 230.

students or, conversely, retirees from traditional clerical families, but Sergei Poliakov argues that "the majority of such mullahs did not know dogma, the canonically approved rituals, or the prayers" of Islam.[31] While certain scholars maintain that unofficial clergy fulfilled their community's need for religious services,[32] the quality of these practices is unclear. In fact, observers of covert Islamic practices reported that pre-Islamic symbols and spiritual beliefs were often employed as untrained clergy improvised from a highly limited knowledge of their religious heritage.[33] In many ways, unofficial Islam resembled indigenous folk religions of Central Asia, and Sharin Akiner even asserts that during Soviet rule, "scarcely anybody, other than the ulama and religious trainees, knew even the basic Muslim attestation of faith: 'There is no god but God, and Muhammed is His Prophet.'"[34] Without this pillar of Islam, these individuals most likely would not be considered Muslim to other Muslims around the globe.

Even atheist activists took note of the beleaguered state of Islamic traditions. In an ironic twist, the League of Militant Atheists in Tashkent actually translated the Koran into Uzbek to introduce more Muslims to the Koran so that they could subsequently demonstrate fallacies in the text.[35] This bizarre reversal of religious instruction reveals how Central Asians held onto their religious identities while losing their religious traditions. And the Soviet League of Militant Atheists reported tens of thousands of members in the Central Asian republics in the 1930s and a miraculous growth rate, comparable to other Soviet republics.[36] Independent reports show that the proportion of atheists in Central Asia by 1970 was equal to that of the Soviet Union as a whole (see figure 7), but there is no way to determine if these atheists were ethnically Russian, Ukrainian, or native to Central Asia. Overall, atheist recruitment was as rigorous in Islamic regions as elsewhere in the Soviet Union.[37]

In addition, some Muslims actually admitted to being atheists, and

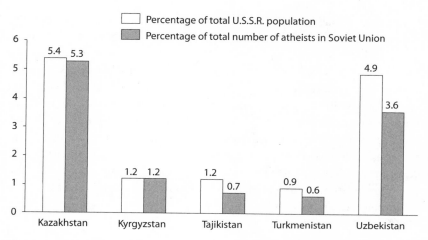

Figure 7. Proportion of the Total Population of Atheists Living in Central Asia (1970). Source: Barrett, Kurian, and Johnson 1980.

many Communist Party members openly retained their Muslim identity. This produced an ideological landscape with no clear victors. Soviet atheists were unable to disrupt Muslim identities even among leading Communists in Central Asia. And while Muslim identity resolutely persisted throughout the Communist era, Islam entered a long *jahiliyya* — the Muslim term for an era of religious ignorance. In the end, the Soviet era produced an unusual mix of Muslims estranged from their religious traditions and Communists claiming to be Muslims. This complex ideological knot is still in the process of unraveling years after the fall of the Soviet Union.

As the case of Islam under Communism demonstrates, the existence of underground religion is an uncertain indication of religious vitality during times of repression. In forcing religion underground, Soviet leaders succeeded in greatly reducing levels of religious capital in all regions of the Soviet Union. Along with the suppression of religious activity, Soviet officials also compelled most Soviets to participate in atheist rituals and ceremonies. In some circumstances, the Soviet ceremonies struck a chord with the population and probably inspired true devotion to the state. For instance, the commemoration of World War II reflected a very meaningful event for Soviet citizens, who suffered inconceivable hardships during the war; consequently, "Victory Day commemorations kept alive a mythology of Soviet grandeur, of solidarity among the *sovetskii narod,* and of a sense of self as citizen of a superpower state."[38]

But as a whole, Soviet ceremonies appeared unsuccessful at generating collective effervescence or the intense devotion common in many religious gatherings. Based on a review of Soviet survey data on Red ceremonial activities and his own observations, Christopher Binns argued, "What people like about these events are meeting friends, being the object of attention or concern, festivity, color and variety. Ideological content — Marxist-Leninist ideals, patriotism, etc. — is completely absent from the replies, even the dislikes: it appears to be virtually ignored."[39] In the end, the Soviet ritual project was successful only to the extent that it forced individuals to alter their public behaviors but ultimately failed to effectively foster a source of meaning and purpose to correspond to atheist ceremonies and rituals.

THE DEMAND FOR GOD

In the Soviet Union, the doctrine of atheism was taught in schools and advocated in the public media. Atheist missionaries preached their philosophy in the remote regions of the Soviet Union and established thousands of atheist cells to function like local parishes. Life event rituals and national celebrations were imbued with atheistic symbols and meaning. In sum, atheism was a ubiquitous concept in the daily lives of Soviet citizens.

With the support and funding of the Soviet regime, the League of Militant Atheists launched the first sustained atheistic crusade in the history of the world. The league intended to totally secularize Soviet society by the mid-1930s. According to the league's own count, this voluntary organization steadily grew since its formation in 1926 (see figure 8). Realizing in 1931 that approximately half of its members resided in Moscow and Leningrad,[40] the league set out to convert citizens in rural regions of the Soviet Union. By 1932, the league boasted over 5.6 million members. A growth from 100,000 to 5.5 million members within the course of six years is quite impressive but most likely an egregious lie. Daniel Peris argues in his detailed account of the league's activities that its membership records were predominantly falsified.[41] Peris's claim garners support if one compares the membership of the League of Militant Atheists to membership in the Communist Party. In 1932, the Communist Party only had around 1.8 million members. It seems dubious that an atheist group created by the Communist Party to propagate active atheists would have recruited three times as many members as the Communist Party itself.

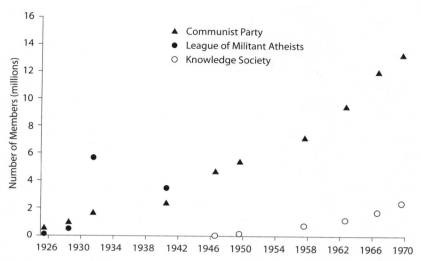

Figure 8. Active Atheists and Party Members (1926 to 1970). Sources: for the League of Militant Atheists, Pospielovsky 1987: 60–61; for the Knowledge Society, Powell 1975: 50; for the Communist Party, Scherer 1984: 30–31.

Nevertheless, the Soviet government appeared confident that a decade of educational enlightenment and modernization had washed away centuries of belief in the supernatural and decided to collected data on religious belief in 1937. Although no detailed results from the 1937 census can be reported because data analysis was quickly aborted, Soviet documents indicate that over half of the entire Soviet population admitted to believing in God.[42] Considering the overtly antireligious stance of the government, religious belief was probably underreported.

The president of the League of Militant Atheists, Yaroslavsky, explained that most (around two-thirds) of these religious believers resided in rural areas.[43] Yaroslavsky's qualification of the results was intended to show that cultural "backwardness" existed mainly in the countryside where peasants had not yet learned the fallacy of faith. Even though Yaroslavsky was quick to explain away the persistence of religious belief, his results indicate a dramatic drop in religiosity when one considers that in 1900 nearly 100 percent of the people who lived in regions that would eventually constitute the Soviet Union were religious adherents.[44]

Because previous generations had expressed almost universal affiliation with some religious tradition, one could interpret the 1937 Soviet census as indicative of a colossal success. But Soviet leadership felt differently. Stalin and others within his regime viewed these results as a dismal failure.[45] While Stalin's expectations concerning the speed of atheist conversion may have been overly self-assured, there are reasons to question the auspicious drop in religious belief. First, Soviet social scientists were displeased with the results and vaguely reported the findings; this is in marked contrast to detailed reports of other statistics on industrialization and population movement and indicates that some data was hidden. Second, reports of religious participation from religious groups inside the Soviet Union indicate that religious belief was probably a good deal higher than the Soviet census indicated. Finally, by 1937, Soviet citizens were aware of the high price of appearing to hold "counterrevolutionary" opinions. Under these circumstances, responses to religious belief questions are highly dubious.[46] Nevertheless, by 1937, the Soviet government at least appeared to have succeeded in reducing the number of individuals willing to admit belief in God.

Before 1937, the Soviet regime had closed thousands of churches and removed tens of thousands of religious leaders from positions of influence. By the midthirties, Soviet elites set out to conduct a mass liquidation of all religious organizations and leaders. This decision stemmed from a violent dissatisfaction with the census results. Because religious faith was thought to be the result of social inequality and an opiate of the oppressed masses, officers in the League of Militant Atheists found themselves in a bind to explain the widespread persistence of religious belief in 1937. Therefore, "they made a tactical move of proclaiming religion as a cause and not merely the symptom of social problems . . . religious persistence became the scapegoat of the Soviet ideological machine, [religious believers] became the only readily admissible reason for the failure of the complete re-education of the masses."[47] According to this argument, Communist society failed to secularize because religious faith prevented Communism from attaining its economic and industrial ideals, which, in turn, would effortlessly secularize society. To end this cycle of religion, Yaroslavsky declared that "several hundred reactionary zealots of religion" needed to be exterminated.[48]

The brutality of the Great Terror of the 1930s cannot be overstated; as greater numbers of Soviet archives are opened to the public, thousands of documents reveal the unmitigated horror.[49] The latest estimates indicate that thousands of individuals were executed for religious crimes and hundreds of thousands of religious believers were imprisoned in labor camps or psychiatric hospitals.[50] Nevertheless, Communist elites came to realize that their harsh dealings with religion were not proving an effective means to convert individuals to the truth of atheism. Reports within the

Soviet government indicated that purging religious believers was actually backfiring. One 1939 report read: "During the previous years a number of priests and religionists were declared counter-revolutionaries and many more churches were closed but it now appears that in many cases this was carried out by the enemies of the people in order to increase hostility to the Soviet government."[51] As this report reveals, the "enemies of the people" were those who persecuted religious individuals; therefore, the blame for religious persistence and growing hostility toward the Communist Party was attributed to Yaroslavsky's own organization, the League of Militant Atheists. During the final months of the Great Terror, even the Communist elites within the League of Militant Atheists were under heavy fire.[52] As was often the case in the Stalinist era, those most committed to a cause became the scapegoat for unachieved goals; in this instance, committed atheists became the "cause" of growing opposition to secularization. On the eve of World War II, widespread killings of religious believers ended. As Soviets faced death from a foreign invader, atheist conversion was put on hold and the League of Militant Atheists was disbanded.

After the war, the Knowledge Society was formed to take over the functions of the defunct League of Militant Atheists. The society offered not only atheist education for youth but also various extracurricular activities, like the Summer Days of Youth. By the 1950s, each of the union republics had its own Knowledge Society, and there were branches in every region, territory, city, and district.[53] Their reported membership grew consistently from 1947 to 1970 (see figure 8). But as the Communist Party swelled in numbers, the Knowledge Society never grew to the size of the League of Militant Atheist at its reported peak in 1932. Clearly, there are many reasons to question the membership figures of atheist groups inside the Soviet Union. These groups were under pressure from Soviet leaders to covert the masses and could easily claim unverifiable members in faraway reaches of the country. Regardless, the Knowledge Society only reported around 1 percent of the Soviet population as active members in 1970. Perhaps Knowledge Society leaders had learned from the mistakes of the League of Militant Atheists and had decided to lower their sights.

In the late 1960s, the Soviet government collected data indicating that the message of scientific atheism had been disseminated more successfully than the number of Knowledge Society members would suggest. A survey of sixty thousand people living in the Voronezh region of the Russian Federative Soviet Republic included one religion question. Soviet researchers divided their sample into the following five groups: (1) convinced religious believers, (2) wavering religious believers, (3) nonreligious people, (4) convinced atheists, (5) active atheists; for comparative purposes, I combine the first two categories as "religious" and the last three categories as "nonreligious." Soviet findings appear to show a low percentage (22 percent) of religious believers (see table 9). This is a considerable drop from the 56 percent as religious believers reported in the 1937 census, although one cannot assume that the exceptionally rural region of Voronezh is representative of the Soviet Union as a whole.

Nonetheless, Soviet leaders were more pleased with these results than with the 1937 census data. Of special interest was the finding that religious believers were overwhelmingly rural, illiterate, and unskilled. This supported the idea that religion was the product of ignorance, isolation, and helplessness. The Soviet historian A. Barmenkov later explained that "the toiler, tied to his plot of land, benighted, frightened and ignorant, was a victim of superstitions."[54] Therefore, Soviet theorists posited that technology, education, and urbanization would eventually erode that remaining fifth of the population clinging to "superstition."

But there are reasons to question the results of the Voronezh survey. First, independently collected data from religious groups around the Soviet Union at this time indicate that religious believers constituted around 52 percent of the Soviet population (see Barrett comparison data in table 9). Second, the Voronezh study reports that 12 percent of the sample were "active atheists," meaning that these individuals diligently spread the message of scientific atheism to convert others. But this would mean that approximately 29 million Soviets were atheistic proselytizers, a number far greater than the 1.8 million reported members of the Knowledge Society at that time. It seems unlikely that so many Soviets would be actively promoting atheism while not affiliated with the official organization of scientific atheism. The other unlikely possibility is that all of the atheists in the Soviet Union lived in the Voronezh region. Consequently, one should treat the findings of the Voronezh survey with deep suspicion.

Looking at levels of atheism indicators reported by groups unaffiliated with the Soviet government, the data indicate that slightly less than a fifth of Soviet citizens claimed to be atheists by 1970.[55] This percentage matches the findings from the Harvard Interview Project conducted a decade earlier, which estimated that around one-fifth of Soviet workers genuinely supported the ideology and policies of the Soviet regime.[56] The

TABLE 9. VORONEZH REGION SURVEY, 1965–1967, BY PERCENTAGE

(n = 60,000)

	Religious	Nonreligious	Active Atheists*
Whole sample	22	78	12
Barrett comparison (1970)	48	52	not applicable
Region			
Rural	33	67	not applicable
Urban	15	85	not applicable
Gender			
Women	31	69	9
Men	11	89	15
Education			
Illiterate	69	31	not applicable
Primary	26	74	not applicable
Secondary	1	99	not applicable
Postsecondary	0	100	not applicable
Occupation			
Unskilled farmer	31	69	4
Skilled worker	6	94	9
White-collar worker	3	97	20
Technical specialist	0	100	42

SOURCES: Region, Marshall 1971: 60; gender, Fletcher 1981: 88; education, Fletcher 1981: 92; occupation, Fletcher 1981: 104.

*Also included in nonreligious column.

contentious fact that around a fifth of Soviet citizens were atheists could be read in one of two ways. On the one hand, no other country in the world purported to contain as high a proportion of atheists as the Soviet Union; therefore, the results indicate success on the part of the Soviet government to convert at least a portion of its citizenry. On the other hand, over fifty years of vigorous religious repression combined with active atheistic proselytizing, not to mention numerous social and economic incentives to convert to atheism, only induced one out of five people to claim to be atheist. Considering the effort employed, these results appear unimpressive.

Evaluating the success of the atheist conversion project is difficult. Because Soviet social scientists had a clear incentive to find religious belief in decline, Soviet data is highly dubious. In addition, Soviet citizens were under strong pressure to falsify their true opinions. Religious believers could be discriminated against in schools and workplaces, imprisoned, and even killed, indicating that many probably lied about their religious opinions. Consequently, Soviet data should be weighed against the trickle of information that foreign visitors collected; of course visitors, especially those with religious agendas, had incentives to overestimate the importance and vitality of religion. Truly, no one source of data from the Soviet era is fully reliable. In his analysis of large-scale preference falsification, Timur Kuran admits that it is very difficult to demonstrate when the public is lying to protect itself.[57] Nevertheless, Kuran argues that swift changes in opinions that correspond to changes in social controls reveal that public opinion has been exaggerated. In the Soviet Union's case, the end of religious repression was followed immediately by a sizable drop in atheism. As Kuran would posit, this provides some crucial evidence that most self-proclaimed atheists were either hiding their real beliefs or, at the very least, were very weak supporters of scientific atheism.

A comparison of levels of atheism in 1970, 1990, and 2000 shows the rapid decline of atheism throughout the Soviet Union (see figure 9). On average, around 18 percent of citizens in the Soviet Union were atheists in 1970. In keeping with Lithuanian exceptionalism, only 10 percent of Lithuanians, who were mainly Roman Catholics, were convinced atheists; most Orthodox and Islamic regions have nearly double the percentage of purported atheists. These percentages fall precipitously in 1990. At this point in time, the Soviet Union was collapsing, and large numbers of individuals had already relinquished their ties to atheism. Such a dramatic shift confirms that many atheists privately held reservations concerning their stated belief. The number of atheists falls further between 1990 and 2000.

In surveys conducted in 1991, Russians were asked to account for dramatic increases in the number of individuals who claimed to be religious. Twenty-three percent of the population felt that religious change was due to actual conversions, and 29 percent felt that most recent religious converts were really individuals who were simply hiding their religion under Communism.[58] While it is difficult to know how many former atheists were falsifying their true beliefs, it is very telling that after Communism, both Communists and non-Communists were equally likely to have switched from nonaffiliation to affiliation.[59]

These data highlight the failure of scientific atheism to establish committed followers. In other words, atheist education and propaganda had *no* lasting effect on the belief systems of most Communist citizens. Why

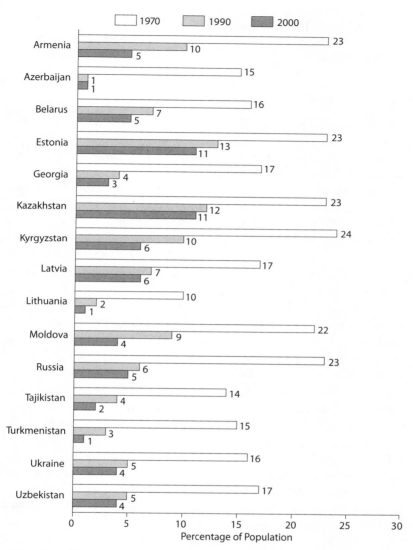

Figure 9. Percentage of Atheists in Each Soviet Republic (1970, 1990, and 2000).

were Communists so unsuccessful in convincing people of the truth of atheism? Answering this question is complex. As Yurchak maintains, "Elements of 'belief' and 'disbelief' [in Soviet ideology] appear to have coexisted within everyone, along with a certain residual resentment."[60] And because the Soviet Union conducted the first concerted effort to proselytize atheism, there are no comparison cases. However, because the atheism campaign so consciously mimicked religious activity, we can compare it to the successes and failures of religious movements to uncover the sources of its ultimate failure.

A FAILED CRUSADE

What's wrong with atheism? Atheism is the conviction that God and the supernatural do not exist. In the abstract, atheism appears as plausible, if not more so, as belief in God; neither can be scientifically proven or falsified. All the same, less than 1 percent of the world is atheist.[61] This is not to say that 99 percent of the world is devoutly religious, but rather that very few individuals are willing to explicitly deny the existence of God or some form of supernatural essence. Perhaps religious concepts have some instinctual appeal to the human mind; in other words, individuals naturally demand religious ideas. As Edward O. Wilson maintains regarding the United States, "The inability of secular humanist thinkers to satisfy this [religious] instinct, even when evidence and reason are on their side, is surely part of the reason that there are only 5,300 members of the American Humanist Association and 16,000,000 members of the Southern Baptist Convention."[62]

While it is difficult to measure the religious instinct, religious ideas clearly have the upper hand in institutional support. Powerful churches, synagogues, mosques, and temples around the globe vigorously promote the message that God or gods exist and require one's attention. In addition, these institutions have lengthy histories of political and social influence. Conversely, there are a few fleeting atheist organizations and nearly no outlets of atheistic proselytizing. Atheists do not come to one's door. They do not ask for donations. They do not request one's faith. Soviet leaders understood this and sought to change it. Their experiment in secularization turned the tables on religion's institutional dominance by giving all the resources and authority to atheists.

With that authority, atheist proselytizers faced the same issues and dilemmas as religious missionaries. The first and probably most important challenge that missionaries face is gaining the confidence and trust of their would-be converts. Rodney Stark asserts that the central proposition in gaining converts is this: "Conversion . . . occurs when, other things being equal, people have developed stronger attachments to members of the group than they have to nonmembers"[63] Successful religious missionaries take time to get to know individuals and form close attachments with them. Mormon missionaries currently in Eastern Europe find that teaching English as a second language provides access to individuals interested in American culture and enables them to develop close friendships. This method is very common, and foreign missionaries often take years to establish themselves among a population — learning the native language and working side by side with would-be converts to generate social contacts and friendship networks. These activities are important because they build trust and ultimately confidence in the religious messages espoused by proselytizers. Anthony Gill and Erik Lundsgaard observed the growth of religious competition in Latin American and found that "clergy have long had an incentive to engage in behaviors that build trust on a smaller scale. It is not uncommon for many clergy to take vows of poverty or engage in other costly activities (i.e., itinerant preaching) to signal that they are sincere in their beliefs and are not just selling 'snake oil.'"[64] Essentially, successful missionaries go to great lengths to demonstrate that they are friendly and sensitive to the concerns of their would-be converts. In turn, this enhances their credibility and the probably that others will listen to their message.

Regarding some of the most successful missionaries in the world, Stark and Finke report that "even today, when there are more than ten million Mormons worldwide, networks are the basis of conversion, as revealed in records kept by a Mormon mission president in 1981–82. When Mormon missionaries make cold calls, when they knock on doors of strangers, this leads to a conversion once out of a thousand calls — and never immediately, only after a long series of contacts as a friendship is established. However, when missionaries make their first contact with a person in the home of a Mormon friend or relative of that person, that results in conversion 50 percent of the time."[65] The pattern of Mormon growth confirms that the success of Mormon conversion is greatly increased when the messenger is familiar, even when the message isn't familiar. Total strangers dispensing exotic ideas will have great difficulty instilling confidence in their would-be converts.

The Communist Party's violent campaign against religion damaged its image as a friend of the ordinary Soviet believer. Of course, some Soviet citizens certainly despised religion as much as Communist Party elites, but much of the population still admired clergy and went to them for advice and assistance in times of need. The imprisonment and execution of religious community leaders sent a clear message that the religious public should fear the Soviet regime. In addition, Soviets destroyed centuries-old churches and mosques, demonstrating that they had no sympathy for those who held these places dear. The strong-arm tactics of

Soviet forces undermined their projected image as liberators and indicated that they only sought to coerce people away from religion instead of attracting them to atheism. With time, Stalin realized that coercion could create a religious backlash and redoubled efforts to campaign *for* atheism instead of against religion. While repression of religion continued after the 1930s, more resources and efforts were placed toward atheistic proselytizing.

The tactics employed by the League of Militant Atheists never attempted to establish close ties to local communities. Instead, the league waged "shock brigades" in which massive amounts of atheist propaganda were distributed in short bursts. Daniel Peris explains, "The League itself was a reflection and victim of the greater campaignism within Bolshevik political culture, which produced short attention span and limited material support. . . . This style of operation was particularly inappropriate for tasks that could not be completed in a week or a month or could not be measured as easily as the production of cement."[66]

While atheist campaigners could report that they disseminated high volumes of atheist propaganda like *Bezbozhnik,* the atheist newspaper, and held thousands of atheist rallies, these activities merely scratch the surface of successful missionary work. Without ongoing contact and trust, individuals felt unfamiliar with and distant from atheist messages, regardless of the force of the atheist campaign. In the minds of Soviet organizers, propaganda "shocks" represented the most effective means for spreading the atheist message. While this may have introduced new ideas into many communities, it did little to establish an active following for atheistic ideas or to recruit local activists.

In addition, rural Communist Party offices were pressed to find atheist crusaders to produce the requisite atheist propaganda in each region and were obliged to import antireligious experts from urban areas.[67] One satirical Soviet cartoon depicts rural Communist Party officials praying to God for an atheist lecturer to visit their region. These traveling atheist lecturers rarely built up social ties to enhance their credibility and often preached messages that were highly problematic. Atheist lectures dismissed complex religious ideas while maintaining that technological and scientific advancements obviously disproved the validity of religion. They repeated the official Soviet position that "religion exists where knowledge is lacking, religion is opposed to science."[68] Consequently, lecturers and proselytizers espoused a completely materialistic or literal understanding of religious concepts.

In most cases, atheist proselytizers had little knowledge of actual religious doctrine. In fact, a visitor to the Soviet Union in the 1960s reported that "no atheist ringleader has ever dared to allow those under him to study the Bible, even for the purpose of spying out the enemy's territory in order to more easily conquer it."[69] Under these conditions, atheist recruiters were largely ignorant of the nonempirical tenets of religious belief, which led them to attack the supernatural only using empirical arguments.

Concurrently, professional scientists realized that they had nothing really to say about religion. While they were making rapid advancements in physics and chemistry, Soviet scientists rarely accepted the enticements of available funding and career promotion to work on the "science" of atheism. By the 1970s, "very few persons register[ed] for graduate work in scientific atheism in the Institutes of the USSR Academy of Sciences or in the faculties of higher educational institutions. In the period of 1957–63, only three doctoral dissertations and some sixty candidates' theses dealing with scientific atheism were defended. . . . The lack of scholarly research and interest, combined with faculty and student indifference to atheist themes in their regular classwork, suggest that the effectiveness of university based anti-religious programmes is likely to be quite limited."[70]

The lack of any intellectual interest in scientific atheism left the work of antireligious propaganda to individuals who knew little about religion or science. Atheist preachers who held "intellectual revivals," fashioned after religious revivals, displayed their ignorance through an inability to properly impart what scientific atheism meant and how it explained the world. One observer noted, "Often the intellectual revival embarrasses the lecturers with difficult questions. They are, for instance, asked, 'Why are our youth so rough? Why have we so many neglected children?' These are wounding questions in a Communist society where there should be no laziness or neglect. Sometimes members of the audience point out that recent discoveries in physics are incompatible with the official materialism, or that men are able to perceive only phenomena but not the essence of things. Faced with such questions the propagandists are completely at sea."[71] While atheist lecturers proclaimed that religion was based on ignorance, they repeatedly demonstrated their own incapacity to address the most basic questions from their would-be converts. In his detailed history of the League of Militant Atheists, Daniel Peris concludes that "the background, training, and work experiences of the League's cadres made the successful delivery of the regime's message of atheism highly problematic."[72]

Because atheism was supposed to be scientific, atheist promoters were wed to the use of science to prove atheism—essentially, an impossible task. This led to difficulties as actual scientists shrewdly avoided the topic altogether. In the end, atheistic "science" became an ideology that avoided scientific method entirely. Scientific atheists may have initially discussed evidence for atheism, but they soon fell into an ideological stance that did not allow for any actual discourse. A lack of any serious engagement with tough theological and scientific questions produced an atheist message with no real content. Soviet historian William Van den Bercken finds that "Soviet atheism admits no serious differences of opinion, no skepticism vis-à-vis the monocausal explanatory theory of historical materialism. Each and every book repeats the old truths and is a variation on the same theme, a re-establishment of principles ... the avoidance of confrontation with those who think differently, the fear of direct challenge, must surely indicate an unvoiced realization that the doctrine is not up to it."[73] In the end, atheist propagandists had no clear or resounding message to relate to their captive audiences. On the one hand, they hoped to demonstrate that science was opposed to religion. But they applied no actual scientific methods to demonstrate their antireligious assertions. On the other hand, they demanded an unquestioning faith in atheism without any real evidence for it. By not being able to respond to simple questions or allow for open discussion of concerns, scientific atheists appeared insecure about their own doctrine. This could not have generated confidence in their would-be converts.

The multiple problems that plagued the atheist campaign stemmed from the imposition of scientific atheism on a population from official channels. Communists did not attempt to engage the hearts and minds of would-be converts but expected individuals to simply bend to their brutish recruitment tactics. In marked contrast to most modern religious campaigns, Communists forbade any attempts to innovate ideas and never implemented tactics of recruitment based on personal interactions with the population. In this, scientific atheism shared the weaknesses and problems of sluggish monopoly religions, which rely solely on political favoritism for subsistence and are apathetic to the needs of their congregations. Like the lazy clergy in a monopoly religion, atheist propagandists were disinterested in explaining or improving their message and cared nothing for the lives of their would-be converts. Instead, they relied on state funding and merely carried out the orders of Communist Party elites without much passion or real understanding of how conversion works.

SOURCES OF FAITH

In addition to employing poor recruitment and educational strategies, atheist proselytizers had nothing to offer individuals that would actually require their *faith*. In searching for religious demand, Soviet officials discovered many of the social and cultural allures of religious identity and belonging. But they failed to recognize the importance of otherworldly incentives in generating faith.

Social rewards and pressures certainly entice individuals to participate in religious groups. Religious members benefit from friendships, career contacts, and social support by joining a group; conversely, leaving a religious group can lead to social isolation and stigma. These social benefits and costs might explain why many individuals join and stay in religious groups, but they cannot fully explain why individuals believe in religious concepts. In other words, belief is not a necessary component of receiving the social rewards of religious group membership — an individual can easily be an active member of a church while not believing in its religious dogma.

In terms of social rewards and costs, scientific atheism matched and even surpassed religion. Membership in atheist organizations and the Communist Party offered many social rewards, while religious commitment carried high social costs. Soviet citizens could improve their career opportunities and social networks by relinquishing their religious identities and practices. But most religiously nonaffiliated Soviet citizens did not believe in the doctrine of scientific atheism. And even individuals who claimed to be convinced atheists abandoned scientific atheism once official sanctions against religious membership disappeared. This indicates that most reported atheists had no actual faith in their doctrine because they abandoned it in response to free expression. In contrast, millions of religious believers in the Soviet Union maintained their religious commitment at a time when the outward expression of religiosity could result in imprisonment and sometimes even death.

Faith requires more than the enticement of social rewards or the strain of social pressures. Individuals can fake faith to garner benefits and avoid costs. Religious doctrines can inspire true faith because they offer something that can *only* be obtained through faith. As Stark and Finke explain, "Religions offer many rewards here and now, but the truly potent religious resource is *otherworldly rewards*."[74] "Otherworldly rewards" are the heavenly delights religious believers expect to receive in the afterlife along with the sense of purpose and meaning believers derive from envisioning a religious cosmic order. Unlike social and economic rewards, otherworldly rewards require faith to be obtained. The enticements of heaven or a loving God are meaningless if one does not believe in them.

One can join a church to gain entrance into desired social networks without believing in church doctrine. One can pretend to pray to demonstrate one's piety and integrity to others. But in traditional monotheistic religions, God will not reward a person with blessings or eternal life if she has been faithless. Because God is all-knowing and all-powerful, individuals cannot hide their doubts or falsify their preferences. That God judges, punishes, and blesses provides religion with an extremely powerful source of monitoring. For this reason, Stark and Finke argue that otherworldly rewards are the most potent of all religious resources because they ensure that faking religious belief will never be sufficient in obtaining the most valuable benefits of religion.

Although faithful individuals contemplate an otherworldly realm, their faith has real-world consequences. Belief in the afterlife, God's grace, or a divine plan can transform individuals by generating a host of new incentives for action and instilling a powerful sense of individual purpose. Individuals who believe that God wants them to go to church will be more devout church participants than those who attend simply for social and material benefits. It is their lack of faith that defines religious free riders — those who want the benefits of religion without the costs. Religions can cultivate dedicated followers who behave selflessly because devotees view worldly costs as necessary for their ultimate salvation. The biblical story of Job illustrates this core idea that unswerving faith is the central and most important aspect of religious belief. Job refused to renounce his belief in God in the face of terrible life tragedies and demonstrated that religious faith does not depend on earthly rewards.

Marxist-Leninists wanted to inspire a Joblike faith of their own. They sought to convince their citizenry that Communist ideals were bigger and more important than the daily plight of individual citizens. As Sheila Fitzpatrick notes, "According to the 'Radiant Future' story, Soviet people could be confident that there would be rewards because of their knowledge of historical laws, derived from Marx."[75] In fact, Soviet citizens were expected to suffer gladly in pursuit of these higher ideals. But unlike religious ideals, which posit perfect justice in the afterlife, Marxist-Leninists had to persuade Soviet citizens that Communist utopia was a real and attainable goal. And this goal surpassed the utopian promises of religion because it existed in this world.

While Communist Party leaders offered promises of earthly utopia, Mircea Eliade keenly points out that their language conjured up familiar religious images and myths; he writes,

> Marx's classless society and the consequent disappearance of historical tensions find their closest precedent in the myth of the Golden Age that many traditions put at the beginning and the end of history. Marx enriched this venerable myth by a whole Judaeo-Christian messianic ideology: on the one hand, the prophetic role and soteriological function that he attributes to the proletariat; on the other, the final battle between Good and Evil, which is easily comparable to the apocalyptic battle between Christ and Antichrist, followed by a total victory of the former. It is even significant that Marx takes over for his own purposes the Judaeo-Christian eschatological hope for *an absolute end of history*.[76]

Those who believed in the Marxist-Leninist concept of the "end of history" were expected to lay down their lives in pursuit of this higher goal. Individual stories from the Soviet era demonstrate that some citizens were willing to make great sacrifices for their Communist ideals. Millions of Soviet soldiers and civilians fought and died for their country during World War II. However, it appears likely that most Soviet citizens fought in defense of their homeland rather than out of love for Communist society; in fact, Stalin realized the value of nationalist and religious rhetoric to motivate his armies and briefly lessened restrictions on the Orthodox Church to help the war effort.[77]

Nevertheless, Communist ideals were real for many Soviet citizens, and some were willing to give their lives for the dreams of the revolution. For instance, Zinoviev recounts how his cousin reacted to state persecution with unexpected enthusiasm. "A relative of mine, who knew that he was due to start a long prison sentence in a year's time, was (as people often were under Stalin) suddenly appointed to run a large factory. He grabbed the opportunity because, for him, the challenge of that single glorious year was worth more than a thousand years spent in uneventful living. 'I know they will kill me — but this year is going to be my year,' he said. He was filled with the consciousness of making history."[78] As this recollection indicates, certain individuals were inspired by the idea that they were contributing to a social cause of great historic significance.

In fact, the strictly controlled ideological landscape of the Soviet Union offered many individuals little choice but to grasp onto worldly utopian dreams. Isaiah Berlin maintained that Stalin and the early Soviet regime realized that "the discussion of ideas — disputes about issues apparently remote from politics, such as metaphysics or logic or aesthetics — was, by promoting the critical spirit, in principle more dangerous to despotic regimes engaged in a struggle for power than belief in any form of authoritarianism."[79] Consequently, Soviet citizens were punished and persecuted for what they believed rather than simply how they behaved. This left little room to ponder the meaning of life in an ideological world that presented everything in black and white. Nikolai Bukharin, a high-ranking Soviet official who was sentenced to death by Stalin, explained the extent to which Communist ideology ruled his life:

> For three months I refused to say anything. Then I began to testify. Why? Because while I was in prison I made a reevaluation of my entire past. For when you ask yourself: "If you must die, what are you dying for?" — an absolutely black vacuity suddenly rises before you with startling vividness. There was nothing to die for, if one wanted to die unrepented. . . . And when you ask yourself, "Very well, suppose you do not die; suppose by some miracle you remain alive, again what for?" Isolated from everybody, an enemy of the people, an inhuman position, completely isolated from everything that constitutes the essence of life.[80]

Without an attachment to the Soviet project, Bukharin could find no meaning in his life or death. Through this form of intense ideological repression, Soviet rule attempted to demand and enforce faith. Historian Ian Buruma laments that the most tragic aspect of the Soviet project was that "you had to convince your torturers not only that you had renounced your evil thoughts and become a believer, but that you had done so in all sincerity. This was mental torture of the worst kind, for people were forced quite literally to lose their minds."[81]

Extremist religious cults try to control their members by disturbing sleep patterns or drugging individuals into trancelike states, but these manifestations of religious coercion are rare and tend to be short-lived. Instead, religious groups tend to foster faith through a belief system that posits a loving and caring God. For a variety of social, psychological, and personal reasons, most individuals are attracted to a religious worldview and develop a relationship with God that is necessarily based on faith. This relationship provides meaning, purpose, and comfort to religious believers. In attempting to re-create a religiouslike faith in their citizens, Communist Party leaders applied tactics more similar to extremist cults than traditional religion. By bullying and tricking their captives into worshipping them, Soviet elites sometimes succeeded in their goal of dominating the minds of their citizens. For instance, the Soviet population's outpouring of grief after the death of Stalin was genuine in most cases.

But without the dictates of the Soviet government, few held onto a faith in atheism. In dramatic contrast, Soviet citizens did not need the church, synagogue, or temple to retain their faith in God.

RELIGIOUS DEMAND

"Religious demand" is a vague and ambiguous concept and lies at the center of a contemporary debate concerning the sources of religious change. According to theorists who posit a universal religious sentiment, religious demand is defined as a basic existential need for meaning and understanding that is common to all cultures and historical eras. According to this theoretical assumption, religious demand is never supplanted by scientific innovations because science cannot address the core ethical and teleological issues explained in religious doctrines. Conversely, modernization theories assume that the importance of religion becomes diminished as scientific worldviews replace religious ones and technology saturates people's daily practices. While the actual mechanism of secularization is obscure, there is a sense that new technologies, cultural diversity, and scientific education create, as Peter Berger says, a "crisis of credibility" for religious believers.[82] Much of the debate comes down to this — are low levels of religiosity explained by religious regulation and repression (the suppression of religious supply) or by a growing sense that religious ideas, practices, and goods are worthless (the decline of religious demand)?

The Secularization Experiment was an attempt to secularize a society by eliminating both the supply of and demand for religion. The Soviet assault on religious supply was predominantly successful. But Soviet elites also wanted to capture the hearts and minds of the population and explored the various sources of religious demand to undermine them. At first, Marxist-Leninists were convinced that individuals essentially clung to beliefs that were cultural and socially dominant. Marx explained that religion

> is the self-consciousness and self-feeling of man, who either has not yet found himself or has already lost himself again. But man is no abstract being, squatting outside the world. Man is the world of man, the state, the society. This state, this society produce religion, a perverted world consciousness, because they are a perverted world. Religion is the general theory of that world, its encyclopedic compendium . . . its enthusiasm, its moral sanction, its solemn completion, its universal ground for consolation and justification. It is the fantastic realization of the human essence because the human essence has no true reality.[83]

For Marx, religious faith was the product of individuals reacting to a perverted or irrational social world. Therefore, changes in social and economic structures would bring about changes in individual beliefs.

Central to this theory of secularization is the idea that religion becomes more implausible as humans learn more about the economic and social world. Peter Berger similarly explains how religion is eventually replaced by science in modern environments: "The sinking of [God's word] into implausibility left an empirical reality in which, indeed, 'God is dead.' This reality then became amenable to the systematic, rational penetration, both in thought and activity, which we associate with modern science and technology. A sky empty of angels becomes open to the intervention of the astronomer and, eventually, of the astronaut."[84] Interestingly, Berger's argument that angels get replaced by astronauts appears strikingly similar to the Soviets' belief that their space program was actually an "assault upon heaven," or, in other words, a disproof of the religious notion of heaven above. But as became evident throughout the Soviet Union, space travel, technological advances, and widespread communication did not eliminate religious demand.

What Soviet elites failed to understand was that most traditional religious doctrines tend to be nonempirical: They do not claim to be scientific. In turn, new scientific interpretations of empirical phenomena need not diminish the plausibility of nonempirical doctrines. Although nonempirical doctrines, such as most religious explanations, are inherently implausible because they cannot be proven true, they similarly cannot be proven untrue. As such, most religious ideas are immune to scientific findings and technological advances. Instead, the plausibility of religion occurs through interaction with others. As sociologist Darren Sherkat argues, "Religious goods are not simply 'experience' goods which must be consumed in order to be evaluated; rather, these goods must be experienced in communities which direct us on how to evaluate them."[85] And community rituals, celebrations, and rites have historically provided a means to communicate religious ideas to individuals and to experience religious feelings and emotions.

With a growing awareness of the power of religious ritual activity, Marxist-Leninists came to view religious practices as a basic source of religious demand. Individuals enjoyed and valued ritual behavior but were inadvertently indoctrinated into a false belief system. To undermine these negative effects of religious rituals, Communist Party elites created rituals of their own. But Soviet rituals differed from religious rituals in one key way. Religious rites have a distinct object — God or some supernatural essence. Individuals pray to God, celebrate his grace, ask for his forgiveness, and make covenants with him through religious rituals. Soviet rituals mimicked religious ones down to specific ceremonial details but removed the primary rationale for ritual activity. Without God, it was unclear what Soviet rituals meant. Soviet rituals may have been intended to mean nothing. In other words, Soviet officials thought that rituals themselves were somehow important to individuals, and they were merely supplying an outlet for ritual needs. While the rhetoric of Marxist-Leninists indicates that they thought that Soviet rituals were social gatherings intended to build social solidarity, the content of actual Soviet rituals reveals a different agenda. To copy religious rituals, Soviet officials were forced to substitute something for religious symbols and references to God. These elements of religious ritual ultimately communicate the purpose of the ritual and the object of devotion. Soviet officials replaced God in rituals with references to either the Communist Party or Lenin and Stalin.

That some visitors to Lenin's mausoleum crossed themselves in reverence to the author of Soviet Communism demonstrates that, in the minds of many worshippers of Lenin, their commitment to Communism was a new form of religious faith. The incessant atheist mimicry of religious rituals and symbols confused religious believers, many of whom viewed the heroes and ideals of the Soviet Union as something magical or mystical. But the otherworldly elements of Soviet prophesy and rituals lacked something central to monotheistic worldviews — an otherworld. In contrast to the message of most religious doctrines, Soviet rhetoric and rituals indicated that justice, freedom, self-realization, and happiness were to be experienced in this world.

Scientific atheism was intricately linked to the Soviet dream of utopia. Long-standing religious traditions avoid prophecies that can be directly tested; in other words, successful religions do not predict the foreseeable future. Because the problems of a failed prophecy are extremely difficult to overcome, Rodney Stark argues that religious movements succeed to the extent that "their doctrines are nonempirical."[86] Nonempirical doctrines easily avoid inconsistencies with sensory experience, at least in having to accurately explain certain empirical occurrences. And the world's most popular theologies assert almost exclusively nonempirical claims. The central tenets of Christianity, Islam, Judaism, Buddhism, and Hinduism focus on issues such as immortality, salvation, spiritual enlightenment, and moral goodness — none of which is empirically testable.

Similarly, successful political ideologies tend to be nonempirical.

Michael Mann's sweeping study of the sources of social power from Mesopotamia to the nation states of sixteenth-century Europe highlights that political ideologies draw on systems of morality and not science to justify power relations. This is a key to their success, as Mann observes, "Knowledge purveyed by an ideological power movement necessarily 'surpasses experience' (as Parsons puts it). It cannot be totally tested by experience, and therein lays its distinctive power to persuade and dominate. But it need not be false; if it is, it is less likely to spread. People are not manipulated fools. And though ideologies always do contain legitimations of private interests and material domination, they are unlikely to attain a hold over people if they are merely this. Powerful ideologies are at least highly plausible in the conditions of the time."[87]

Research into the persistence of utopian movements also confirms the problems of making testable promises. In a review of a number of studies of utopian communes, Rodney Stark and William Bainbridge find that religious communes have much greater life expectancies than secular ones.[88] They explain that "in the case of religious utopias . . . the new community is not the ultimate aim. Rather, it is simply a preliminary station where members can attempt to live in accord with divine will, while waiting to fulfill their truly utopian life in the world to come."[89]

In contrast, secular communes strive to create a utopian ideal on earth. This ideal becomes less plausible as commune members realize that their daily experiences are not in accord with their definitions of utopia. Religious communes can provide the more plausible explanation that a real utopia only exists in the next life (a nonempirical realm). Ironically, this enables religious utopian groups to become more committed to what is expected to be an understandably flawed utopia. Due to this focus on the afterlife, religious communes tend to posit more plausible earthly goals than secular utopias.

Soviet Communism suffered the same fate as most nonreligious communes. Soviet elites eventually were unable to back up their many claims about society, the economy, and religion. And while scientific atheism mimicked religious doctrines in its dogmatism, claim to sacredness, and attachment to ritual activity, it offered no otherworldly rewards. In their hunt for religious demand, Marxist-Leninists never considered the role of otherworldly rewards. Unlike religious faith, which offers a host of spiritual and afterlife benefits, faith in scientific atheism provided believers with nothing beyond the self-assurance that they knew the "truth" and that history would prove them right. For this reason, scientific atheism was a tough sell. It required a blind commitment to something that was

not very personally appealing — a temporary existence without any purpose beyond the contributions one made to a future earthly utopia.
While Communist Party elites wanted to inspire selfless dedication to the
Communist project, they offered an ideology that essentially told the
individual that she was a minor and disposable player in a larger historical drama.

Whereas many religious ideologies also maintain that the individual is
insignificant in comparison to God, God paradoxically cares for and
rewards the individual for her faith. Not surprisingly, a caring God garners more commitment than an uncaring historical process. The significance of God and the afterlife in the popularity of religious belief was
wholly ignored by Soviet propagandists. By focusing solely on the material and social elements of religion, Soviet elites failed to realize the existential and personal aspects of religious demand. And perhaps faith in
God was so difficult to dislodge because it reflects the simple human
desire for a happy ending — a desire for which Communist Party elites
could never find an adequate substitute.

CHAPTER 5

After Atheism

When militant atheism planted itself in our society, a vacuum
was formed in the souls of the people.

— Patriarch Aleksi II, in a sermon, quoted in Davis 1995

As one Hungarian proverb claims, "In the course of eating comes the
appetite." A desire, in short, can be a product of its object. In religious
terms, we might say that humanity's innate need for explanation and
purpose is activated and stimulated by religious descriptions of cosmic
order and ultimate meaning. In other words, religious suppliers (groups
or individuals who posit religious explanations of the world) fulfill an
underlying and constant religious demand (the human need for meaning). The Secularization Experiment essentially shut off religious supply
but failed to undermine the persisting religious demand. As religious
knowledge and participation declined in the absence of religious supply,
deep-seated beliefs in God and the supernatural continued to provide
Soviet citizens with a vague sense of something beyond the confines of
their proscribed lives. When religious restrictions were lifted after the
Soviet era, a flood of religious suppliers found themselves in the midst of
one of the most religiously fertile areas of the world. And in the course of
active missionizing came a renewed religious appetite.

The religious revivals occurring in the former Soviet Union and the
former Eastern Bloc countries demonstrate the effectiveness of simple
religious supply on religious vitality.[1] Religious leaders and missionaries
report that their activities easily generate interest and enthusiasm about
new opportunities to participate in church communities. For example, a
representative of the Christian Peace Conference visited Hungary in 1986
and reported the following incident of religious growth:

One pastor told me he announced the day and time of the first confirmation class of the year, but not a single student showed up. He then checked the church records and identified 25 children who had been baptized 13 years earlier. He called on each family and urged the parents regardless of their own belief or lack of belief to encourage their children to attend and to develop a basis for their own decision making about religion. As a result of these calls 22 of the 25 young people are now members of the confirmation class.[2]

This instance of religious growth did not occur because individuals or family members sought out religious instruction. Nevertheless, when given the invitation to join in religious activities, individuals gladly responded. With very little effort, the pastor of this story transformed his confirmation class from zero to twenty-two students. If you magnify this occurrence to the thousands of religious leaders and educators acting under reemerging autonomy, a religious revival happens. This is what occurred throughout the former Communist world.

The post-Communist religious revivals demonstrate the ineffectiveness of decades of antireligious policy and active promotion of atheism. In fact, Andrew Greeley found in 1991 that younger birth cohorts in Russia are more likely to believe in God and be converts to this belief than middle-aged cohorts, indicating that the massive atheist educational system was fruitless.[3] Nevertheless, the Soviet era still affects the substance and direction of religious revivals. Communist Party officials unwittingly introduced new levels of religious pluralism into the religiously homogeneous regions of the Soviet Union while also intentionally increasing ignorance concerning religious traditions and theology. There are theoretical reasons to expect that these changes greatly contributed to renewed religious fervor. In other words, Soviet antireligious tactics oddly enough provided both local and foreign religious activists with millions of eager converts.

RIPE FOR REVIVAL

Areas inhabited by religious monopolies are often ripe for religious growth. Religious monopolies occur when religious groups dominate a society through a combination of state support and state regulation of minority religious groups. Before 1917, most of the regions of the future Soviet Union contained distinct religious monopolies that successfully regulated their would-be religious competitors and relied heavily on government funding. These powerful religions were lulled from their peace-

ful slumber by the Russian Revolution. They were replaced by a new ideological monopoly of even greater intensity. Isaiah Berlin noted that
"under the worst moments of tsarist oppression there did after all, exist
some areas of wholly free expression; moreover, one could always be
silent. This was altered by Stalin. No areas were excluded from the
Party's directives; and to refuse to say what had been ordered was insubordination and led to punishment."[4] The problem with both the religious
monopolies of the czarist era and the Soviet ideological monopoly is that
they relied completely on the suppression of free thinking for their dominance, eventually leading to their dissolution under conditions of intellectual freedom.

By simply altering religious policy, Soviet leaders undermined the
sources of religious homogeneity in the various regions of the Soviet
Union. Dominant religious groups, in most Soviet states, lost over 30
percent of their members by 1970. Soviets focused their atheist attack on
the monopoly religions of each region and successfully diminished the
political and cultural importance of dominant Christian churches and
ubiquitous Islamic institutions. Surprisingly, smaller religious groups
were able to maintain their memberships and sometimes even increase
their size under Communist rule. One could think of sect joiners as those
avoiding the very public attacks on dominant religious institutions by
hiding in the cracks with covert and underground religious minorities. In
the end, as Soviet rule sought to destroy and replace religious monopolies, it inadvertently set up new religious alternatives as Soviet citizens
navigated the rapidly changing ideological landscape.

Before Soviet rule, Baptists and Evangelical groups subsisted across
the European regions of the Soviet Union but began to expand slightly
under Communist repression.[5] In addition, Hare Krishnas, Jehovah's
Witnesses, Seventh-Day Adventists, and various other charismatic sects
found ways to begin penetrating the Iron Curtain. New seeds of religious
pluralism were planted when a multitude of foreign missionaries descended upon the former Soviet empire in the wake of the fallen Soviet
ideological monopoly. But could these seeds blossom in a land fertilized
with decades of antireligious propaganda?

With new access to the former Soviet population, new missionaries
worked hard to establish ties to local communities and even attempted to
gain influence with newly created local governments. For instance, the
Unification Church (Moonies) actively campaigned for politicians in
Yekaterinburg with the hope of establishing favorable political relationships.[6] Although attempts to gain political influence have been largely

unsuccessful, they indicate the enthusiasm and ingenuity of missionary groups. Foreign missionary efforts also tend to receive generous funding from international organizations, which appreciate the potential for growth in former Soviet lands. Overall, foreign religious movements grew substantially in the early 1990s; in 1995, over three thousand missionaries alone from twenty-five Western agencies spread throughout the Soviet Union to assemble new congregations (see table 10).

In addition to foreign-led movements like Scientology and the Aum sect Shri Chinmoy, many new religious groups have originated within Soviet borders. The Rerikh movement, the Great White Brotherhood, the sect of Vissarion, and the Center of the Mother of God are just a few of the many indigenous groups that have sprung from a combination of Orthodox, pagan, and New Age beliefs. Although domestic religious movements tend to have fewer resources than foreign missionaries, they have the advantages of preexisting social ties to local populations and a better understanding of Soviet ideology and culture. For instance, the Bogorodichny Tsentr, the Center of the Mother of God, grew from an Orthodox tradition. The group's prophet, Veniamin Bereslavsky, spoke to the "mother of God" and recorded her revelation concerning the spiritual transformation of the Orthodox faith. The revealed milestones to transformation are all Russian-specific and include "1) the appearance in March 1917 of the icon 'Dershavnaya'; 2) the mighty victory of Mary over the 'red communist dragon' in August 1991; 3) the birth of the Church of the Uncorrupted Virgin (the Center of the Mother of God)."[7] In addition, the group prophetically asserted that the fall of Communism was part of God's ultimate plan. This aspect of the group's theology is especially attractive in post-Communist times and enhances the legitimacy of the group's religious vision.

In addition to the creation of indigenous religious groups and the influx of religious missionaries before and after the fall of the Soviet Union, religious and ethnic pluralism grew throughout the Soviet era due to the systematic movement of peoples. Most significant to this discussion, Soviet officials placed hundreds of thousands of ethnic Russians and Ukrainians in Central Asia; by 1989, the Soviet census indicated that ethnic Russians constituted 19.3 percent of the entire population of five republics of Central Asia.[8] This massive displacement of people, especially in 1930s, 1940s, and 1950s, drastically changed the ethnic makeup of Central Asia and fostered greater religious diversity, or at least the integration of people with very different religious histories. "In this context occasional tensions arose between religious groups within Christian-

TABLE 10. WESTERN MISSIONARIES, 1995

Agency	Missionaries
Assemblies of God	28
Biblical Education by Extension	12
Calvary Chapel of Costa Mesa	8
Campus Crusade for Christ	23
Child Evangelism Fellowship	25
Christian and Missionary Alliance	39
Church of Christ	104
Church of Nazarene	16
Church Resource Ministries	17
Evangelical Free Church Mission	12
Frontiers	118
Greater Europe Mission	18
International Teams	20
Institute in Basic Life Principles	320
InterVarsity Christian Fellowship	32
Lutheran Church, Missouri Synod	32
Navigators	193
OMS International	87
Operation Mobilization	40
Salvation Army	50
Seventh-Day Adventists	49
Southern Baptist Convention	80
United World Mission	18
Wesleyan World Mission	38
Youth with a Mission	1,600
Total	3,190

SOURCE: Meadows 1995: 10.

ity and also within Islam in terms of jostling for their 'share of the market.'"[9] Nevertheless, the Soviet era was one of general religious decline, even as religious pluralism and religious integration increased.

Religious pluralism is expected to cultivate religious growth only in circumstances of religious liberty.[10] As more religious groups come into contact, theorists hypothesize that religious groups will more actively and effectively compete for members; this economic model of religious growth suggests that religious demand — the religious appetite — responds to religious activity. Based on the expectations of this theory, the Communist Party unintentionally planted the kernels of future religious growth by destroying dominant religious traditions, displacing religious majorities, and indirectly fostering sect and cult activity. But the realization of religious growth also entailed the lifting of regulations on all religious activity. This occurred when the Soviet Union collapsed.

Therefore, the end of Soviet Communism provided two basic circumstances theoretically ideal for religious growth: millions of religiously
unaffiliated individuals and a free religious environment where no one
religious group enjoys political favoritism.

THE ADDED EFFECTS OF RELIGIOUS IGNORANCE

Although Soviet repression of monopoly religious groups generated new
levels of religious pluralism, the incessant promotion of antireligious
propaganda in schools, workplaces, and the media produced high levels
of religious ignorance. In other words, because Soviet citizens had little
exposure to religious texts, experts, and practices, they knew very little
about the specifics of religious worldviews. Positive depictions of religion
were only publicly available through certain cultural or artistic goods
that passed the criteria of censors and only vaguely referenced religion.
For example, Metropolitan Kirill maintains that the Soviet public derived
much of its meager knowledge of spirituality from the religiously inspired
work of Dostoevsky, which remained available under Soviet rule; he
writes, "Soviet power could not prevent people from reading Dostoevsky, even though he was not studied at school. This great writer was a
profoundly religious man, and his works are imbued with Christian
ideas. The instructions of Starets Zosima in *The Brothers Karamazov*
were largely borrowed from the writings of early church fathers, in particular from St. Isaac the Syrian, a Christian mystic of the seventh century. So while works by the holy fathers were not published and the
writings of St. Isaac the Syrian were impossible to obtain, Dostoevsky
was widely read and appreciated."[11] Although certain religious aspects of
Soviet culture persisted from a previous era through works of art, architecture, and social customs, the particulars of intricate religious faiths
were essentially lost. Even if Soviet citizens remained open to certain
religious ideas or traditions, they tended to be unacquainted with them.

In Central Asia, many individuals who identified as Muslims were
largely ignorant of the basic tenets of Islam. Similarly, most Soviet Christians lost touch with many of their religious practices and community
activities. Soviet children rarely attended church or participated in religious celebrations and rituals and were subject to a vast number of
classes in atheism. After seventy years of religious repression, many in the
Soviet Union had little or no firsthand contact with an active religious
community and consequently had no detailed knowledge of religious
subjects. As Sergei Filatov pointed out, in the post-Communist era, "reli-

gion in general had been rehabilitated, but ignorance regarding religious matters was so great among the Soviet people, from the president of the USSR down to ordinary citizens, that few could tell the difference between Syoko Asahara and Reverend Moon, on the one hand, and the pope, Patriarch Aleksii II, and Billy Graham, on the other."[12] In the language of economic and sociological theorists, Soviet citizens by 1989 had very little religious capital.

Religious capital, the individual's familiarity with and connection to a religious tradition, predicts patterns of membership and conversion. In general, individuals will be less likely to convert to a religion that is wholly different from their childhood religion. Theorists argue that this holds true mainly because individuals rarely invest the time and effort to learn a completely new worldview. Instead, religious converts normally do not move far from the religious tradition they are exiting. Conversely, new and different religions or religious cults do best with people who have little religious capital; in this case, converts need not relearn an entire religious system because they begin with none. Therefore, a lack of religious capital does not predict an aversion to religion but rather a potential openness to atypical religious ideas. If this is the case, then the Soviet population in 1989 represented a sea of possible converts for a wide host of religious missionaries.

In Central Asia, Muslims lost many of their religious customs and institutions along with their ties to developments in Islam in other countries. Some non-Soviet estimates of Islamic religious activity indicate that as few as 20 percent of Muslims in the Soviet Union recited their required five daily prayers *(salat).*[13] But beyond that, Adeeb Khalid argues, "Muslims did not so much lose the ability to understand the literal meaning of the Qur'an or prayers as the implicit cultural knowledge, acquired in the family of the maktab [religious school] during childhood and thus assimilated at the level of instinct."[14]

Nevertheless, an omnipresent sense of Muslim identity persisted in Central Asia. But as Michael Rywkin argues, the term *Muslim* in Central Asia is a "symbiosis between the national and the religious that is accepted as fact by both Muslims and settlers."[15] Islam initially became an ethnic marker throughout Central Asia through a prolonged interaction with Russians. When imperial Russia army occupied Central Asia, Muslims of that region came into close contact with Russian institutions and culture for the first time. From this new frame of reference, Islam "came to be used as a generic term to refer to everything that was perceived to be local, not foreign."[16] Subsequently, Muslims, Russians, and eventually

Soviets viewed Islam as an ethnic identity regardless of very distinct differences in religious practices, commitment, and religious organizations within Islam. "During the first six years of the new regime (from 1918 to 1923) the term 'Muslim' was used in official Soviet texts to designate all the Muslim nationalities of the USSR. A 'Muslim' Red Army and a 'Muslim' Communist Party were in existence for a short while. Muslim administration was carried out by 'Muslim Commissariats' and in 1918 the Central Muslim Commissariat in Moscow represented the embryo of a 'Muslim government.' "[17] As such, Muslim identity would have persisted even as religious practice became nonexistence.

Nevertheless, new religious freedoms have led Central Asian Muslims to reexamine their religiosity. Their return to religious practices is a process of regaining their Islamic religious capital. M. Nazif Shahrani aptly points out, "The phenomenon of 'resurgent' Islam in Central Asia, which has attracted much attention in the West, has little to do, however, with Islamist political movements in other parts of the world. It is fundamentally a popular and, to a large measure, provincial or rural educational effort to reclaim Islamic knowledge and learning and to gain the right to practice Islam in public without fear of intimidation."[18] When restrictions on religious practice subsided, Muslim leaders immediately began to organize efforts to educate the population about Islam. The process of reeducation is complex, as Muslims confront new information not only about the complex theology of Islam but also concerning political developments in Islam around the world. For instance, "One Tajik intellectual interpreted rhetoric about the importance of supranational Islam to mean primarily that newly independent Tajikistan, which faced enormous economic problems, would be able to obtain loans through 'Islamic banks' at interest rates far below prevailing world levels."[19]

Although confusions and debates pertaining to many social, political, and religious concerns persist, Central Asian Muslims have reattached themselves to the basic rituals and activities of Islamic life. Immediately after the fall of the Soviet Union, "the observance of various Islamic practices and rituals in Central Asia such as daily five-times prayers (salat), fasting during the month of Ramadan, payment of Sadaqa (voluntary contributions for the maintenance of mosques), [and] attendance at the mosques during the important Muslim festivals like Qurban Bayram, Mawlud, and Idul-fitr have acquired legitimacy with great fervor. Similarly, observance of the main family rituals such as circumcision, religious marriages and burials, which were done secretly during the Soviet period, have been legalized."[20] The return of fundamental elements of Islamic culture indicate that Muslims are eager to learn about and develop their religious lives and that decades of religious ignorance have not generated religious apathy. Instead, Muslims must now contend with new and diverse forms of Islam. This has led to conflicts as Muslim fundamentalists clash with ex-Communist Muslims to define and control Islam's future in Central Asia.

Mainstream Christian groups also lost touch with religious changes in the rest of the world. Instead of looking outward, religious leaders frequently compromised their theological teachings by actively collaborating with Soviet forces. Religious integrity and resoluteness often suffered under the demands of immediate survival. Theologian Karl Barth wrote the following warning to a Christian collaborator: "You are at the point of making an article of faith of your agreement with Communism, of making it part of the Christian message. You are at the point of wandering into an ideological Christian wonderland. How is it that you put socialism on your banner as if it were a perfect thing? How can you dare to put it on the banner of Jesus Christ? How can you claim in your propaganda that socialism is heaven on earth and is thus identical with what you find in reality . . . I am very much concerned about this and ask you to rethink your theology radically."[21]

Barth pondered how rich and expanding theologies could endure Soviet coercion. Religious traditions that survived Soviet domination encountered a very different world in 1990, as they had to contend with both newly emerging post–cold war issues and modern lifestyle changes. The Russian Orthodox Church appeared especially ill-equipped to address these changes. In the years following the end of Communism, "the overwhelming majority of the current 119 bishops of the Moscow Partiarchate were ordained to the episcopacy prior to August 1991. This suggests that each of these bishops was carefully screened and vetted by both the ideological apparatus of the Communist Party and the KGB. It need hardly be noted that a flourishing of religion in the USSR was *not* an aim of those two bodies."[22] After the Soviet system collapsed, Archbishop Kirill of the Orthodox Church summarized an anxiety shared by religious leaders of many faiths; he realized his "Church now has much to do in order not to fall behind."[23]

Like new economic entrepreneurs in the former Soviet Union, religious groups had to learn to cope with foreign competition and a free market. The dearth of religious capital among the Soviet population made the work of traditional religious groups more difficult as new and inspiring religious ideologies entered the landscape. Because they represented the exciting world on the horizon, foreign religious groups appeared to hold an advantage over traditional Islamic and Christian groups in their worldliness and knowledge of religious missionizing. Fervent Islamic movements from southern Asia and the Middle East have introduced Central Asians to distinctly twenty-first-century Muslim attitudes concerning the immorality of the West and the Israel-Palestine conflict. Similarly, Christian missionaries appear savvy about life in the high-paced world of global capitalism in ways that scare and confuse the traditional religious groups of the former Soviet Union.

PLURALISM AND RELIGIOUS GROWTH

Religious revivals that occurred throughout the former Soviet Union have been systematically documented.[24] Increases in religious memberships, beliefs, and participation correspond directly to the lifting of Communist religious regulations. Religious growth took place all over the former Soviet Union. On average, around 20 percent of the population of each former Soviet state has taken up some form of religious affiliation since 1970.[25] Although the Soviet Union remained essentially in tact until the early 1990s, the lessening of religious restrictions within the Soviet Union began in the early 1980s.[26] Therefore, one can most dramatically see the extent of these religious revivals by comparing levels of affiliation from 1970 to 1995. Although each region differs in its proportion of religious members in 1970, a substantial increase in memberships occurred in every region over the following twenty-five years. The most dramatic instance of religious growth occurred in Armenia due to a unique setback suffered by the Armenian Apostolic Church in the early twentieth century and its current restoration (see figure 10).[27]

But who is winning in this competition for souls? Are the religious missionaries, new Christian sects, and foreign Islamic movements dominating the religious market? In a comparative analysis of Lithuania, Latvia, and Estonia, Steve Bruce found that "of these three countries with in many senses similar recent histories, Lithuania is markedly more religious than the other two and it is the one with the most homogeneous religious culture."[28] Bruce maintains that religious pluralism does not explain growing religiosity in Lithuania. Although Lithuania is unique because it is the only former Soviet republic that is predominantly Roman Catholic, and Roman Catholicism has proved an exceptional case for many reasons, Bruce uncovers a finding that loosely holds true for the rest of the former Soviet Union: Religious pluralism does not predict levels of religiosity or religious change.

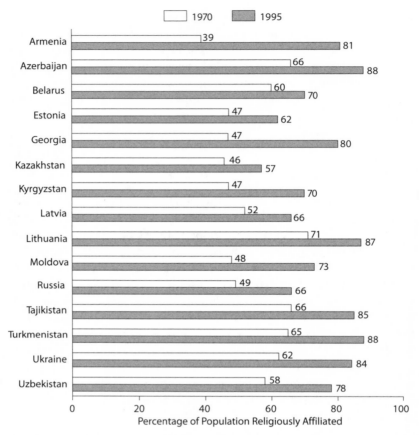

Figure 10. Change in All Religious Memberships (1970 to 1995).

The case of the former Soviet Union is ideal to test the expectation that religious pluralism generates religious growth. Certainly, religious growth across the Soviet Union occurred after religious regulations were lifted, but different regions of the former Soviet Union have varying degrees of religious pluralism (see table 11) and religious growth.[29] Therefore, one can calculate the relationship between these two variables to determine the extent to which pluralism fosters growth. The results do not support theoretical expectations. There is no statistical relationship between the number of distinct religious groups and the increase in religious memberships in each region.[30] Figure 11 depicts this relationship visually to illustrate the point more clearly. No obvious visual pattern emerges from the data, revealing that regions with more

TABLE II. PLURALISM AND REPRESSION STATISTICS

Country	Religious Pluralism (Measured by Herfindahl Index)[a]	Religious Repression[b]
Armenia	0.39	4
Azerbaijan	0.15	5
Belarus	0.66	5
Estonia	0.78	1
Georgia	0.60	4
Kazakhstan	0.65	4
Kyrgyz Republic	0.42	4
Latvia	0.81	3
Lithuania	0.28	2
Moldova	0.73	4
Russian Federation	0.62	4
Tajikistan	0.10	7
Turkmenistan	0.12	7
Ukraine	0.69	3
Uzbekistan	0.19	6

[a]The Herfindahl Index = $1 - \Sigma p_i^2$, where p_i is the proportion of religious adherents that belong to a religious group, i, a value of 1, means each individual belongs to a different religious group, and a value of 0 means the entire population belongs to one religious group.
[b]Repression scores taken from Marshall 2000; 1 = most religious freedom; 7 = least religious freedom.

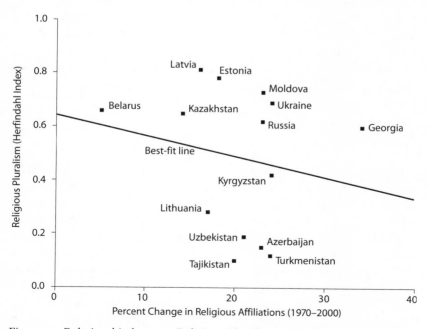

Figure 11. Relationship between Religious Pluralism and Religious Growth.
Note: Armenia is not included in this figure because it is an outlier in religious growth.

religious diversity are somewhat less likely to experience religious growth. In other words, pluralism appears to have no effect on religious growth.

The Islamic regions of the former Soviet Union stand out as the least pluralistic yet the most religiously active. But there are a few important qualifications to this finding. First, the measure of religious pluralism used in figure 11 does not account for pluralism *within* Islam. Therefore, predominantly Muslim regions appear nonpluralistic, even though they may contain very intense rivalries between competing Muslim groups. Second, dramatic demographic changes occurred in Central Asia during the 1990s. The latest estimates indicate that over a million ethnic Russians and Ukrainians left the region in the past decade.[31] Consequently, the proportion of Muslims increased simply due to demographic shifts. In sum, measures of religious growth and religious pluralism in Central Asia are highly problematic.

Nevertheless, if one looks only at the Christian regions of the former Soviet Union, religious pluralism is still unrelated to religious growth. The underlying cause of this finding is that traditional religious monopolies are growing as fast as new religious movements. Contrary to common predictions, traditionally dominant religious groups, like the Orthodox Church, have reestablished a monopolylike status in regions of the former Soviet Union and currently attract a larger portion of new religious converts. Subsequently, religious growth is occurring even when religious pluralism is low. Why former religious monopolies have reemerged when conditions appeared to favor new religious movements requires some explanation.

THE RETURN OF MONOPOLY RELIGIONS

The reestablishment of religious monopolies has several possible explanations. First, this phenomenon could be viewed as the failure of nonmonopoly groups. In many cases, Western missionaries do not understand the circumstances of their would-be converts. Observers of foreign missionaries find that "the greatest flaw may be inadequate to nonexistent country-specific and culture-specific preparation; that is, woefully insufficient study of pertinent languages, literature and history."[32] How can foreign missionaries appeal to individuals who have had years of indoctrination into the tenets of scientific atheism? The effects of Soviet Communism on the population are complex and may have rendered many individuals with unique psychological and emotional needs with which missionaries are unaccustomed. Although there is certainly some truth to this argument, religious missionaries have successfully adapted their tactics to a wide variety of cultural and historical circumstances. Therefore, one should expect that motivated religious groups will eventually overcome their misunderstandings and false starts as they learn more about their would-be converts.

A more satisfying explanation recognizes the historic tie between certain religious traditions and the ethnic and national identities of the regions.[33] For instance, if Central Asians conceive of themselves as Muslims, then they will be more attracted to Islamic religious activities even when they have little knowledge of the tenets of Islam. This is true throughout the former Soviet Union as newly emerging nations attempt to define their national identities through references to their pre-Communist past. As one Russian historian states, "The historical faith of Russia is Orthodoxy, and Orthodoxy is deeply embedded in the Russian soul. It defines a Russian's sense of nation, history, and identity, even when the individual is not devout."[34] Similarly, Lithuanians are Catholic and Uzbeks are Muslim in their ethnic and national understandings of self. These bundled identities certainly influence individuals' religious decision making. Under circumstances of newly acquired religious liberty, perhaps Russians are more likely to walk into a Russian Orthodox Church.

Certainly, the fusion of religious, national, and ethnic identities influences individual action, but, perhaps more important, it has affected the political policies of post-Soviet nations. These identities became crucial guides to how church and state relations would emerge. "The collapse of the Soviet Union . . . completed the fragmentation of religious policy, and left religious groups in fifteen different states each with their own ideas on how to handle religion."[35] At first, most states simply maintained an acceptance of complete religious liberty, but religious policy soon became more complex as traditional religious communities reasserted their historic ties to political power. In response, politicians utilized favorable relations with religious groups to legitimate their power and distance themselves from the militant atheism of a prior era.

In the case of Russia, the Russian Orthodox Church immediately established a close connection to government officials in the final days of perestroika as opportunities presented themselves. In 1990, the Orthodox patriarch Aleksi II met with the prime minister of Russia; they "spent several hours discussing crime, freedom of conscience, business, charity, labor productivity, property and taxes. Future meetings are being planned. The two men, who are approximately the same age, have taken entirely different paths in life, but, despite this, find they have a lot in common."[36] This meeting marked the beginning of newfound respect for the Russian Orthodox Church. Russian leaders publicly began consulting with Orthodox religious leaders, and by 1992, newly elected Russian president Boris Yeltsin was attending religious services and asking for Orthodox blessings. The public appearances and rhetoric of Yeltsin allied him closely with Orthodox leaders and demonstrated his moral convictions. When three young defenders of the Russian White House were killed in 1991 during the August coup, Yeltsin's apology to their parents was steeped in religious symbolism. Yeltsin said, "'Forgive me, your president, that I was unable to defend and save your sons.'"[37] As Billington goes on to explain, "'Forgive me' is what one Russian says to whomever is next to him before taking communion and what that other Boris, Tsar Boris Godunov, said to all the Russian people in the last words of the greatest of all Russian operas. Power was being relegitimized morally. Someone not to blame was assuming responsibility in a society where no one in power had ever accepted responsibility for anything."[38] Yeltsin's political and personal conversion demonstrated the importance of moral and religious sources of legitimacy for the post-Soviet government. And the Russian Orthodox Church was happy to oblige.

In fact, some members of the Russian Parliament expressed concerns about the growing relationship between the Russian Orthodox Church and the Russian Federation. "Parliamentarian Marina Salye alleged that Boris Yeltsin kept trying, by various means, to turn Russian Orthodoxy into a 'religion of the state.' She said, 'In a multinational and multiconfessional state such things are dangerous and actually violate human rights.' She expressed her bewilderment on learning that Patriarch Aleksi II was included in a protocol list of state officials. She was indignant when at the school where her grandson was a pupil all children were blessed by a Russian Orthodox priest on the first day of school."[39] For politicians such as Yeltsin, ties to the Russian Orthodox Church helped them to distance themselves from their Soviet past and its atheist legacy. Consequently, the Russian government was eager to grant the church special status and privileges.

In turn, the Russian Orthodox Church was quick to take advantage of its political utility. Of great concern to Orthodox leaders were the influx of foreign missionaries and the vigorous activities of Protestant groups. "Indeed, [the Orthodox] complain that the Protestant fundamentalists behave in Russia as if it had never known Christianity and was a country of pagan savages."[40] The Orthodox community assumed that religiously unaffiliated Russians should be theirs for the taking in post-Communist times. And the success of non-Orthodox Christian groups proved too traumatic to bear. Soon after the advent of religious liberty, "an influential body of opinion began to proclaim that the freedoms had gone too far, that they threatened the true traditions of Russia, and that something must be done to curb them. Such attitudes are to a certain extent understandable and justifiable, though the methods attempted to bring some control to into the anarchy were unbelievably crude."[41]

In fact, Russian Orthodox metropolitan Kirill argued that Russia was the "canonical territory" of the church and should not be open to other religious missionaries.[42] And the Moscow patriarch evoked the Epistle of St. Paul to the Romans to defend the church's position on outlawing foreign religious groups; the passage states: "It is my ambition to bring the gospel to places where the very name of Christ has not been heard, for I do not want to build on another man's foundation."[43] The fervor of Orthodox claims that non-Orthodox religions are invasive and socially destructive indicates a high level of fear among Orthodox leaders of religious pluralism. Essentially, the Russian Orthodox Church wanted to return to the religious homogeny of czarist Russia; as one Orthodox expert noted, "The Church in 1988 remained in many respects exactly as it had been in 1917; and in 1917 it had been in many respects exactly as it had been in 1721 when Peter the Great had made it into a department of State."[44] Orthodox leaders wanted nothing less than to once again become a state church.

In response, the Russian Duma revised the Bill on Religious Freedom in 1997 to create a new policy of religious restriction that in many ways resembled the laws of czarist Russia. "The 1997 law effectively establishes three classes of religions in Russia: (1) the Russian Orthodox Church and its members, which receive full legal protection and various state benefits; (2) various 'traditional' Christians, Muslims, Jews, and Buddhist groups and persons, which receive full legal protection, but fewer state benefits; and (3) all other religious groups and persons, which receive only a pro forma guarantee of freedom of worship and liberty of conscience."[45]

Russian officials now deny religious minorities access to public spaces and make the registration of new groups extremely difficult. In contrast, Orthodox Churches receive public moneys and are included in government decision making. "Sociologist Sergei Filatov regards [the new religious law] as so repressive as to be inoperable. He predicts that authorities will exploit it to keep minority churches intimidated, and at the mercy for the extortion of bribes in exchange for the privilege of building a church or renting a hall. It will also place many churches at the mercy of the good will of the local Orthodox bishop or priest."[46] Under these circumstances, non-Orthodox missionaries in Russia fight terrible odds. And missionary watch groups relate news of ongoing repression of their activities daily. One Russian Pentecostal recently lamented, "Can you imagine — I, an evangelical Christian, or even an atheist, is working and paying taxes to build a new Orthodox church which is going to fight us?"[47]

In such an environment, it is no surprise that religious growth is occurring mainly in Russian Orthodox quarters.[48] Zoe Knox warns, "The Moscow Patriarchate's privilege is such that Orthodoxy can be described as a 'pseudo-state church.' The danger of such a status is demonstrated by xenophobes' discourses which wed Orthodoxy with platforms and ideologies incompatible with civil society."[49] In the final analysis, the new religious monopoly of the Russian Orthodox Church threatens not only religious freedom but democratic freedoms in general.

A similar relationship exists between favored forms of Islam and governments in Central Asia. A decade after the fall of the Soviet Union, Communist elites continue to rule Kazakhstan, Kyrgyzstan, Tajikistan, Turkmenistan, and Uzbekistan by applying "repressive campaigns to eliminate all forms of opposition, subverting democracy and elections almost as meticulously as the Soviets did and eliminating their political opponents through assassination, imprisonment or exile."[50] Although greater religious freedoms were assumed following the emergence of state independence, each of these Central Asian countries returned to strict religious laws that favor Islamic groups with current links to power. In fact, many Communist mainliners have claimed a faith in Islam to legitimate their grip on power.[51] These leaders hope to establish a tie to mainstream Islam while actively crushing more politically radical Muslim groups. Ironically, conflicts between Islamic groups have "served the interests of post-Soviet power elites by enabling them to consolidate their hold on the state apparatus as guarantors of peace and security in their own nations. Readily accepting Western assertions concerning Iran's possible involvement as a principle supporter of Muslim extremism in the regional conflicts, the post-Soviet Central Asian leaders have adopted a particularly harsh attitude toward any organized form of Muslim activism."[52]

In both Kazakhstan and Kyrgyzstan, the government "unofficially distinguishes between 'traditional' and 'nontraditional' religions, suggesting a de facto inequality."[53] Religious freedoms are more harshly

denied in Turkmenistan and Uzbekistan. This is done through constitutional articles that require respect for "national traditions"; this results in
the severe persecution of most religious groups.[54] Non-Muslim religious
sects and cults are often harassed; for instance, as recently as June 2004,
Uzbek officials imprisoned Jehovah's Witnesses for nothing more than
proselytizing. In general, "the major religious groups, Islam and Eastern
Orthodoxy, suffer fewer problems as long as they do not criticize the
government."[55] Therefore, Muslim groups can flourish, provided they
remain deferential to the ruling elite.

Despite the apparent fervor surrounding the end of Soviet religious
regulations, Central Asian Muslims did little to bring about the political
change that permitted their new religious freedoms. "Rather, it was the
breakdown of Soviet central authority that provided an almost effortless
opportunity for independence. Unfortunately, the rapidity with which
political freedom was brought to bear left these republics ill-prepared to
fill the ideological void created in the collapse of Marxism."[56]

Without any clear opposition movement to Communist rule, Central
Asian republics have been slow to change their governing structures.[57]
This is due in part to the political coalition of official Islam and Communism during the Soviet era. Religious leaders and advocates are not
quick to upset a political system that they have long legitimated. And
"the fusion of the [Islamic] clanic structure with the Communist hierarchy . . . [has] meant that clanic relations have been preserved throughout
the period of 'modernization' of Central Asia."[58]

In educating Muslims about their newly acquired religious traditions,
Muslim leaders grapple with balancing the status quo with growing
interest in Islam around the world. In fact, the current tension between
Islam and the Western world is emerging in the newly independent
Central Asian states as Muslims struggle to understand what it means to
be a committed Muslim in the modern era. New divisions between "radical" and "establishment" Muslims create religious conflict that Muslims
never experienced under Soviet rule.

"The growing popularity of militant Islam . . . springs directly from the
refusal of the Central Asian regimes to broaden the political base of their
governments, allow democratization, and lift bans on political activity."[59]
In Tajikistan, the Islamic Renaissance Party (IRP) fought for political
recognition in the bloody Tajikistan civil war. Although the IRP represents
the radical religious element in Tajikistan, it never advocated the formation of an Islamic state. In fact, IRP leaders argued that "Tajiks were so
poorly informed about Islam that the establishment of an Islamic form of

government was impossible in the near term."[60] Nevertheless, Communist mainliners aligned with "official" Islamic leaders fought to end the IRP quest for political recognition.[61] By the end of the war, the IRP was granted membership in the coalition government of Tajikistan. In this case, religious pluralism was only recognized through violent opposition.

To avoid more civil unrest, other Central Asian states will need to recognize Islamic groups that question state rule and the relationship between old Communist rulers and traditional Muslim authorities. In many ways, established Islamic leaders in Central Asia hope to model their political and social status after the Russian Orthodox Church. By utilizing the power of state authority, they may diminish the activities of not only non-Muslim groups but also "radical" or "oppositional" Islamic groups. As in Tajikistan, the effects of this tactic may prove dangerous.

As Muslim and Christian groups jockey to influence state policy, one finds that traditionally dominant groups are successfully returning to their past favored statuses. Political actors seeking to distinguish themselves from the antireligious policies of the Soviets have generally favored religious groups that claim a connection to the regional ethnic and national identity. The result is a reemergence of repressive religious policies that tend to favor one religious group.

As might be expected, the least religiously restrictive regions of the former Soviet Union are also the ones that are the most pluralistic. Estonia and Latvia do little to regulate their religious markets, and both countries have no clear majority religion. A statistical analysis of the different regions of the former Soviet Union confirms this trend — regions with the most repressive religious policies tend to contain the most religiously homogeneous populations.[62] The regulation of minority religions provides significant advantages to majority religions. The relationship between religious regulation and the growth of a majority religion is highly correlated.[63] Countries with more religious restrictions will tend to have more rapidly growing majority religions, and figure 12 confirms the benefits of religious regulation for the favored religion.

By seeking restrictions on their competitors, dominant religious groups act in accordance with theoretical predictions. Regulation clearly works to their advantage. Through the regulation of smaller religious groups, dominant religions can better exploit the opportunities left by the collapse of their powerful atheist competitor. In the end, the seemingly strange reemergence of monopoly churches has occurred not through religious innovation but through political favoritism.

If traditional patterns of religious dominance fully reestablish them-

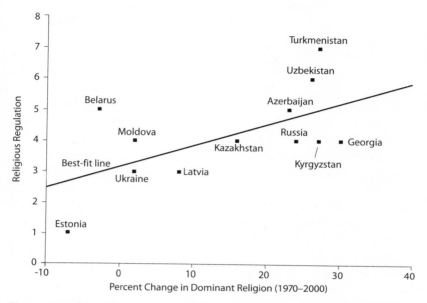

Figure 12. Relationship between Religious Regulation and Majority Religions. Note: Armenia is not included in this figure because it is an outlier in religious growth; Lithuania is also removed.

selves, we can expect a religious landscape that appears eerily similar to that of pre-Communist times. Current increases in religious diversity will fall, and the religious vitality of the immediate post-Communist era will similarly decay as the peoples of the former Soviet Union return to their past religious-ethnic identities. The return of religious monopolies and traditional religious identities is one of the most fascinating reversals of the goals and efforts of the Secularization Experiment. Nevertheless, as religious monopolies flourish, religious fervor will wane—a prospect that would not dishearten Marxist-Leninists.

REVIVAL TESTIMONIAL

Monopoly religions do not occur without state assistance. Although certain religious traditions may have historical connections to ethnic or national identities, state intervention is necessary to ensure that these religious traditions hold their decided advantage over all others. Because monopoly religions tend to be propped up by states, they often become inactive and generate little religious turnover. The religious monopolies of the former Soviet Union are surprisingly vigorous, however, gaining thousands of new members and growing by leaps and bounds. This flies in the face of the label "lazy monopoly." Monopolies around the former Soviet regions have been able to grow so impressively because of the religious vacuum generated by seventy years of intense religious repression. Nevertheless, these groups still require the assistance of new governments to take advantage of this vacuum and to avoid losing their many new members to upstart religious sects.

But how did historically dominant groups, who were decimated by Soviet repression, regain their former favored status after the fall of Communism? Part of the explanation involves the persistence of national, ethnic, and religious identities throughout the Soviet era. The existence of these identities demonstrates the ultimate failure of a central Soviet goal: to undermine ethnic loyalties, regional cultures, and feelings of nationalism. In achieving this goal, they failed. Religious, ethnic, and national feelings continued to be bundled together, and their persistence has led to numerous conflicts throughout the former Soviet Union and Eastern Europe. During the fall of Soviet Communism, Uzbeks and Kirgiz feuded in the Osh conflict of 1990; Armenia and Azerbaijan went to war; a battle between the Ossetians and the Ingush broke out in the North Caucasus in 1992; and the Chechen War grew throughout the 1990s. These incidents illustrate the immediate reassertion of ethnic and national divisions after seventy years of hibernation.

The return of religious monopolies is further evidence of deep-seated cultural differences within the Soviet population. Even as Soviet citizens lost their religious capital, they retained a sense that their national and ethnic character was tied to a particular religious tradition. Consequently, religious and political actors utilized these general perceptions to build coalitions between state and religious institutions. Today, many of the regions of the former Soviet Union contain governments that support a favored religion. In turn, these traditional religions gladly legitimate their supportive governments.

One of the surprises of the post-Communist world is how deeply religious, national, and ethnic identities were embedded in the psyches of Soviet citizens. Why did decades of reeducation, propaganda, forced migration, industrialization, and urbanization do so little to dispel the nineteenth-century identities of the Soviet public? Perhaps the Communist Party simply tried too hard. In the case of religion, Soviet leaders did not *just* want to diminish the role of religion in people's lives; they also hoped to eradicate all references to religion from the social world.

This proved impossible. Religion was too ingrained in the fabric of society to be washed away by an oppressive government. Maybe the Soviet government's failure to erase religion revealed the importance of religion in ways that previously had been hidden. Although individuals throughout the Soviet Union were not exceptionally religious by world standards, forced secularization exposed the many religious rituals, beliefs, and customs that surrounded their lives.

The forced promotion of scientific atheism kept religious ideas and symbols at the forefront of Soviet society. To dispel religious beliefs, Communist Party officials created a public discourse concerning the falsity of religion that may have unwittingly kept religious ideas alive. Metropolitan Kirill describes an instance of this when Soviet propagandists attempted to utilize a monastery as an atheist museum; he writes that the museum guide "tried to persuade the group that the magnificence of the church was created not because of but in spite of Christianity, which she maintained did not allow architects and icon painters to express themselves fully. But speaking about the architecture and icons, she willy-nilly spoke about the Gospel, and what she said and the icons and the architecture themselves came out as a witness to Christ — and that witness was so much more powerful than . . . scientific atheism!"[64]

While keeping religion at arm's length, Soviet officials also kept religion in view through an incessant negativity about the religious past. Traditional pre-Communist patterns of religiosity indicate that most individuals took their religious identities and beliefs for granted. Soviet rule forced citizens to evaluate the substance of their beliefs in new ways and ironically led some individuals to grasp onto identities that had little significance in their daily lives. In some sense, religious apathy was something better left alone, and by beating a dead horse, atheist propagandists called attention to religious concepts and identities that were in many ways forgotten.

Although a desire may often be the product of its object, a desire may also respond to a forced separation from its object; in other words, separation from religion may make individuals long for it more passionately. Religious vigor responds to religious promotion, but the Soviet case demonstrates that religious curiosity and concern also responds to antireligious pressure. Even though they certainly would not have attained their goal of total secularization, Soviets may have done a greater disservice to religion by actually supporting it. In fact, some Bolsheviks proposed the co-option of the Russian Orthodox Church immediately after the Russian Revolution. According to this plan, Soviets would simply continue to fund the church and demonstrate how Christian theology was a naive or primitive version of Marxist-Leninism. In fact, maybe Marxist-Leninism could comprise a third book of the Bible — the true ending? This strategy would be similarly employed in Islamic regions, where Soviets would discount religious particulars in favor of the religiously uniting rhetoric of Marxist-Leninism; Central Asian Muslims were already enamored with Communism anyway. Simultaneously, Soviet officials could brutally repress all religious alternatives. In the end, the Soviet government could oversee the training and placement of clergy and infuse all religious services, rituals, and ceremonies with Communist images and ideas.

The example of state religious monopolies around the world suggests that this might have been a successful strategy, or at least more successful than scientific atheism. State-supported religions tend to produce populations that rarely go to church or express strong religious beliefs.[65] Therefore, Soviet support of religion could have further diminished religious activity and interest throughout the Soviet Union and removed any ability it had to oppose the government. Religious elites would necessarily have legitimated the Soviet system because they would have been dependent on it.

But Communists were guided by their belief in scientific atheism, which precluded the acceptance of religious ideas and practices. In many ways, Soviet elites already had their own religion — scientific atheism — and they were unwilling to compromise it. A firm and unrelenting faith in the evil of religion led Soviet leaders to commit vast resources and exert violent efforts to destroy religion, even as these efforts proved counterproductive. Paradoxically, the fervor with which Soviets attacked religion may have indirectly conveyed the importance of religion. Subsequently, religion continued to play an active role in Soviet society through antireligious propaganda, covert religious activity, and religious opposition to Soviet rule.

In the twentieth century, the story of religion throughout Soviet Union is one of religious monopolies — their virtual destruction under Communist rule and their remarkable reemergence after Communism. These results demonstrate how religious demand persists even under the most repressive conditions and how church-state relationships determine the form and expression of religion in society. The new monopolies of the post–Soviet Union will not inspire religious vitality in their populations, but this is not their main goal. Instead, these religious organizations seek political favoritism and will achieve it through their willingness to trade on their historical connection to national identities in the pre-Soviet era.

CHAPTER 6

The Social and Political Resilience of God

There are many good laws, the importance of which is known to the sagacious lawgiver, but the reasons for which are not sufficiently evident to enable him to persuade others to submit to them; and therefore do wise men, for the purpose of removing this difficulty, resort to divine authority.

— Machiavelli, *The Discourses*

Living in a social experiment can be demanding. As Alexei Yurchak explains, "The Soviet citizen was called upon to submit completely to party leadership, to cultivate a collectivist ethic, and repress individualism, while at the same time becoming an enlightened and independent-minded individual who pursues knowledge and is inquisitive and creative."[1] And regarding the Soviet citizen's spiritual life, it was expected that she would freely come to the conclusion that it was simply unnecessary. By requiring an abandonment of religiosity and spirituality, the Secularization Experiment attempted nothing less than to reshape the inner lives of tens of millions of people. Boris Pasternak bitterly remarked, "When I hear people talking of reshaping life, it makes me lose all self-control and I fall into despair. Reshaping life! People who can say that have never understood the least thing about life. They have never felt its breath, its heart — however much they may have seen and done."[2]

The failure of Marxist-Leninists to understand core elements of human nature and human need, as Pasternak indicates, led to an enormous and devastating social experiment unlike any other in human history. In this chapter, I revisit the six basic theoretical assertions presented in chapter 1 to consider what the Secularization Experiment taught us about religiosity and its significance.

SECULARIZATION ASSERTIONS, REVISITED

Assertion 1

Religion is but the false sun which revolves around man
while he is not yet fully self-aware.

—Karl Marx

C. S. Lewis wrote that the promise of religion is like a door "behind which, according to some people, the secret of the universe is waiting for you. Either that's true or it isn't. If it isn't, then what the door really conceals is simply the greatest fraud . . . on record."[3] For much of the nineteenth and twentieth centuries, social science generally supported the idea that there was nothing behind the door and that religion was a colossal fraud waged on the world's population. During this time, debates within psychology and sociology tended to focus on who or what was responsible for this fraud.

In an overview of the philosophy of religion, John Hick outlines six main philosophical proofs of God's existence and then addresses multiple grounds for disbelief.[4] Tellingly, he indicates that "the sociological theory of religion" is one of the primary arguments against the existence of the supernatural. Like Hick, Rodney Stark and Roger Finke see a historical trend of assumed atheism within the social science community; they write that "not only were [early sociologists] the first to use the tools of a developing social science to attack religion, but they tried to make a religion out of their science."[5]

For example, Freud attempted to uncover the "true" psychological basis of religion in his works *Moses and Monotheism* and *Totem and Taboo*. For Freud, religion is essentially a neurosis, instilled by the collective memory of a prehistoric murder of a father by his primitive tribal family, who in turn invented a substitute father figure in the form of a deity. Although Freud's work on religion was certainly innovative, his description of religion's sources remains unsupported by historical evidence or psychological research. Freud's faith that religion is the product of a deep-seated neurosis received acceptance within the psychological community, and religious belief was categorized as a mental illness in the Diagnostic Manual Handbook until very recently. However, current empirical research now finds a strong association between religious belief and physical and mental health,[6] and most psychologists have come to accept religious faith as a natural part of their patients' worldviews.

Like Freud, Marx attributed the origins of religion to something other than the supernatural, but in Marx's view, the origins of religion are social, not psychological. In his work *Theses on Feuerbach*, Marx critically points out that Feuerbach "does not see that the 'religious sentiment' is itself a social product."[7] This idea that religious feelings and sentiments are socially constructed dominated classical social theory and inspired a shared belief that social change would doom religion to the "trash bin" of history. Although the specifics of their measurements and definitions may differ radically, Auguste Comte, Emile Durkheim, Karl Marx, Max Weber, and Talcott Parsons generally agreed that religion declines due to the effects of modernization.[8] Religion was expected to disappear under the strain of scientific advancements and new secular philosophies. A nearly universal consensus concerning the modern decline of religion persisted for most of the twentieth century until a group of researchers, using the United States as a case study, began to seriously question this assumption in the 1980s and 1990s.[9] These researchers point out that the United States is one of the most modernized and technologically advanced countries in the world yet remains one of the most religious by measures of church affiliation, attendance, and religious belief. Their work generated a vigorous and ongoing debate concerning how best to measure religiosity and what theoretical model best explains religious change.[10]

Marxist-Leninists forcefully applied the basic principles of the modernization theory of secularization to create a progressive environment that, in theory, would naturally stifle antiquated religious beliefs. The Soviet Secularization Experiment tested whether education, industrialization, and modernization arouse disbelief. Soviet officials provided secular educations that specifically highlighted the falsity of religion to millions of Soviet citizens, many of whom had no previous exposure to formal schooling. Also, rapid industrialization introduced Soviet farmers and peasants to new wonders in technology, health, and science, revealing the fallacy of many outdated ideas concerning the natural world. The values of education and modernization were central to Soviet culture and provided the rationale for massive and expensive efforts to industrialize and collectivize as well as legitimated the hard labor of average Soviet citizens. In addition, most Soviet scientists and intellectuals were averse to addressing religious issues and generally espoused atheistic attitudes in accord with official ideology. Nevertheless, these educational efforts failed to undermine widespread belief in God.

Instead of demonstrating that science and technology are naturally hostile to religious ideology, the Secularization Experiment teaches us two important lessons concerning the effects of modernization and how social scientists should approach the topic of religion. First, Communist Party leaders discovered no clear causal relationship between modernization and declining religiosity, except that modern society alters the social conditions in which all ideologies exist. Consequently, modernization may affect the popularity of particular religious and political ideologies, but it in no way necessitates the complete abandonment of absolutist or dogmatic forms of belief. The acceptance of technology and scientific knowledge is completely compatible with faith in nonempirical claims and ideological inflexibility. As such, religious concepts are as fit to survive in a modern setting as any political or moral system of belief.

If religion does decline under conditions of modernization, we must ponder the social, economic, and cultural conditions that bring about secularization instead of assuming that individuals are wising up to the fraud of religion. Declines in religious memberships and church attendance in the Soviet Union were the result of social and cultural conditions unrelated to educational and technological advancements. Namely, the Soviet state directly attacked churches, synagogues, and temples, making it difficult for religious groups to recruit members and promote their theological messages. This change in government policy shifted cultural norms and social incentives away from religion. Still, religious repression could not fully dislodge religious faith from the predominantly Orthodox, Catholic, and Muslim cultures of the Soviet Union.

Ironically, the Soviet project promoted an atheist ideology that was no more scientific or empirically supported than traditional religious worldviews. And similar to religious dogmatists, scientific atheists demanded absolute faith and commitment to their ideology without ever considering the weaknesses and inconsistencies of their own ideas. Consequently, devotion to natural science, technological advancement, and industrialization did nothing to advance free discourse and objectivity in social, political, and religious discussions. To further our understanding of positive or negative correlations between religiosity and modernization, we need to explain why certain belief systems are more popular within specific political and economic structures. In the case of the Soviet Union, modernization had no effect on religious belief in the general public. In addition, the atheistic ideology of Soviet elites grew more dogmatic and less scientific as Communist leaders intensified their quest for technology, industrialization, and collectivization.

The Secularization Experiment also warns us against the dangers of relying too heavily on theological assumptions when studying the sociology of religion. Marxist-Leninists were convinced that religion was demonstrably false and consequently failed to comprehend many of the deeply spiritual aspects of religious practice. Their disbelief prevented them from taking religious ideas seriously, causing them to misinterpret theological worldviews as pseudoscientific and religious language as more literal than it was. In one example, Stalin asked an aide to FDR "whether the President, being such an intelligent man, really was religious as he appeared or whether his professions were for political purposes."[11] For Stalin, it was beyond belief that an intelligent person might take religion seriously. On the other hand, social scientists certainly should not commit the opposite error of assuming the validity of religious concepts; this could conversely lead to religious advocacy. Instead, social science must reserve judgment on theological arguments concerning the truth of scriptures sacred to a specific group.

Although theological objectivity is an ideal, one wonders if it is philosophically possible. Political scientist Daniel Levine argues that all scientific inquiries concerning religion are innately atheistic; he explains, "A positivist approach brings the observer close to the position of the 'village atheist' to the extent that it predisposes one to concentrate on the externals of behavior, fitting these into the observer's own categories of analysis with little or no attention to the meaning or significance of action to those involved."[12]

Levine's description of religious research aptly fits the approach of Marxist-Leninists, but it need not be applied to all social scientific studies of religion. In fact, sociologists may pay close attention to the meaning individuals' attach to their beliefs to better understand religious behaviors. In this way, the beliefs themselves are not called into question but are considered honest expressions of an individual's perceptions. As Pitrim Sorokin points out, most of the world believes in "supersensory, metalogical, or transcendental subjects: 'God,' 'the soul,' 'the ultimate reality' . . . and the like. They constitute a substantial portion of sociocultural reality in the form of revealed religions, values, beliefs, transcendental philosophical systems, and the like. One may like or dislike any of these aspects, but no sane person and no sound empirical observer can fail to perceive that all of these aspects are given as data in sociocultural reality."[13]

And as data, religious belief in the Soviet Union proved to be a social reality for millions of Soviet citizens, regardless of their changing social and economic circumstances. By assuming the falsity of religion, Marxist-Leninists seriously misjudged the strength and meaning of religious belief, which offered something personally reassuring beyond the frequent dullness of Soviet life. Although social science cannot judge the truth of religious belief, the Secularization Experiment empirically demonstrated that whether the "sun" of religion is real or false, it certainly is not setting.

Assertion 2

There are rites without gods, and indeed rites from
which gods derive.
> —Emile Durkheim,
> *The Elementary Forms of Religious Life*

Emile Durkheim created a powerful heuristic tool by conceptually splitting the social world into realms of the sacred and the profane. According to Durkheim, societies are united through a shared sense of values and collective ritual activities. These sacred values and rites hold special reverence and help individuals bond around a common purpose while also identifying deviants and outsiders. Although Durkheim noted that religious systems of thought predominantly define the objects, texts, and behaviors that acquire sacred status, his assertion concerning the independence of rites and gods indicates that sacred practices do not require references to the supernatural realm. In fact, Durkheim believed that religious concepts were mainly transposed onto sacred rites after their cultural adoption. Marxist-Leninists similarly viewed religious ritual behaviors as distinct and potentially detachable from their conceptual religious framework. Consequently, Communist Party leaders promoted traditional ritual activities that removed religious symbolism and language from their practice. They felt that they could retain a unified sense of the sacred through rites without gods.

Many classical and contemporary observers of social practices speak of a "civil religion," in which members of a society bond around traditional behaviors and a common reverence for certain moral principles. Most aspects of a civil religion are not overtly religious: They do not directly reference religious concepts or beliefs. Alexis de Tocqueville noted in his visit to the United States in 1831 that the separation of church and state had produced a uniquely American civil religion, in which democratic ideals held a sacred status.[14] In a more contemporary context, Robert Bellah argues that national symbols and "American values" are sacred to the American public. For instance, there are clearly defined norms concerning the handling of the American flag — one should never let it touch the ground, and it should only be disposed of in a ritual ceremony. In 2005 and again in 2006, the U.S. House of Representatives proposed an amendment to the Constitution that reads, "The Congress shall have the power to prohibit the physical *desecration* of the flag of the United States" (italics mine). The overtly religious language of this amendment is probably no mistake, as policy makers seek to invoke deep emotions in their supporters. Bellah also observes that the United States Constitution is considered a sacred moral covenant for many American citizens.[15] These examples are some of the many instances where national symbols, anthems, and documents inspire a shared reverence and sense of the sacred.

Soviet culture created a new set of symbols and values intended to inspire a secular version of sacredness. All of the elements of civil religion described by Bellah in the United States were also present in the Soviet Union. National symbols, anthems, ceremonies, honors, and rituals overwhelmed Soviet culture. Pictures of Lenin and Stalin adorned public buildings and private residences, and propaganda posters filled community spaces in the same way as commercial advertisements have engulfed American culture. Movies, music, and the arts were dedicated to communicating respect and admiration for Soviet life and the values of Communism. The Soviet government also generously offered medals, ribbons, and awards to instill a sense of communal devotion and moral unity. Visitors to the Soviet Union will recall that many individuals proudly wore their medals, which were sometimes indications of military service but could also designate other accomplishments, like bearing a certain number of children.

Although Communist Party leaders consciously attempted to manufacture a new civil religion, their efforts necessarily diverged from common notions of civil religion. Mainly, civil religions are a blending of national and religious symbols and values; in contrast, the Secularization Experiment hoped to detach one from the other. American civil religion is essentially the intersection of nationalism and Protestant Christianity. The American flag attains its sacredness because it represents "one nation *under God*," as the Pledge of Allegiance has repeatedly communicated to generations of American schoolchildren since 1954. And many Americans believe that the United States demands respect not because it is technologically advanced or militarily superior to all other nations but because God has blessed it, making it the "best" country in the world, as most presidential addresses affirm. The sacredness of national identity and civil society in the United States fully depends on a shared religious sensibility. Without God or a religious underpinning, American symbols lose their sacredness. This being the case, what sanctified Soviet symbols, rituals, and identities in the absence of God?

Ironically, Communist Party leaders may have unwittingly relied on God in their attempts to consecrate their values. The Secularization Experiment sought to create a new culture — one that radically changed individual identities, personal motivations, and historical worldviews — but it ultimately produced a society that replicated many of the traditional characteristics of the religious culture Soviet officials hoped to destroy. The asserted divinity of the czarist monarchy was replaced by the asserted inevitability of the Communist autocracy. The Russian idea of Moscow as a third Rome, a place where Christian unity ultimately would be realized, was replaced by the idea that Soviet Communism marked the end of history and the realization of earthly utopia.[16] A morality based on infallible religious authority was replaced by a morality based not on reason, science, and social justice, as was purported, but on the infallible authority of Lenin and Stalin. And finally, traditional churches were replaced by the "church of Communism."

The intent of the atheist campaign of substitution was to rid the world of the supernatural. Instead, the Communist Party simply confused Soviet citizens, many of whom were unable to follow the nuances of the philosophical distinction between worship of God and worship of worldly objects. The mystification of Marxist-Leninist rhetoric became most evident in the rhetorical games of its leaders and their ideological manipulations of common concepts. Stephen Hanson traces how Soviet leaders sought to implement new conceptions of time in which their predictions and goals were not limited to linear rational ideas of time but were conceived of as "time-transcendent."[17] In a review of Soviet newspaper articles, Jeffery Brooks concludes that "the gaps between past, present and future vanished in the press's near mystical account of Soviet life . . . it was an attempt to force past, present, and future into a single magical continuum."[18] Dead heroes were referred to as living in a state of perpetual animation, similar to the ageless corpse of Lenin. Current economic and social projects were spoken of as successes, the historic significance of their outcomes already realized. Although these types of language games are common in modern politics, the vastness of Soviet ideological rhetoric created an atmosphere where human discourse appeared mystically detached from empirical reality.[19] Within the rhetoric of utopianism, Soviet citizens were asked to view their society as a realization of some otherworldly realm.

Soviet rituals were also problematic in that they mimicked religious rites so closely that Lenin, Stalin, and Marx appeared as stand-ins for God. And the religious imagery of the Soviet era often evoked religious sentiments and not antireligious fervor, as indicated by devout Soviet citizens crossing themselves upon seeing Lenin. How could a society supposedly based on materialism create a system of ideological mysticism and sanctified rituals? The answer lies in the emotional ardor and ideological exclusiveness of Russian revolutionaries. Communist distain for religion far exceeded the notion that religious institutions served as tools of political oppression. The very idea of God disgusted Lenin, Stalin, and many revolutionary activists. Their passion to rid the world of the supernatural ironically explains why they were so quick to don the garb of religion. To prevent people from worshiping God, they demanded that the public worship Communism. Of course, the irony of this campaign was lost on Soviet elites. That they consecrated their own beliefs and mimicked the rituals of the "backward" peasants did not strike them as paradoxical.

Perhaps if Communist Party elites could have realized the hypocrisy of the Secularization Experiment, they might have also recognized its terrible inefficiency. Why did Soviet propagandists spend so much time and effort to create a substitute religion when they could have co-opted one much more easily? In many ways, atheist substitutes for religion were a convoluted means to co-opt the tried and true practices of religion. But Marxist-Leninists became so stuck on replacing God that they failed to see that God may be easier to convert than the general public. In other words, the Soviet government was in a better position to manipulate the spokespersons of God — religious leaders and church hierarchies — than change the entire belief system of a population that had absorbed traditional religious worldviews over centuries. Portions of Christian and Islamic doctrines may easily be shown to support communitarian values and forcefully reject the inequalities and injustices of monarchy or the cruel social Darwinism of capitalism. For example, Jesus' Sermon on the Mount is often used by liberation theologians to demonstrate an anticapitalist sentiment within Christianity.

With financial support and reassurance, the Orthodox Church, the Roman Catholic Church, and Muslim leaders may have eventually come to legitimate Communist rule. These religious groups could have incorporated Soviet national symbols and Communist rhetoric into their religious traditions. In turn, the Soviet government could have regulated and suppressed religious minorities to maintain weak religious monopolies throughout the regions of the Soviet Union. Russians would remain Orthodox, Lithuanians would remain Catholic, and Uzbeks would re-

main Muslim, but their religious leaders would urge them to be faithful
followers of the Communist Party. In this way, Communist Party leaders
could have created a new civil religion in which God no longer consecrated the czar but now sanctified the Communist Party, much the same
way that mainstream American Christianity enhances the legitimacy of
the U.S. government.

Of course, it is impossible to know how successful this strategy would
have proved. But the supernatural has been successfully renamed,
repackaged, and resold throughout world history as different political
actors and systems utilize religious symbols and rhetoric to justify their
own political ends. Never before had a government attempted to wipe
the religious slate clean. The Soviet dream of ridding the world of religion was simply too ambitious to be realized overnight. Even though
Communist Party thinkers came to understand that individuals still
needed and demanded rituals and sacred ideals, their attempt to divorce
the sacred from traditional religious worldviews was overly simplistic
and failed to recognize the power of the concept of God to legitimate values and motivate behavior. In attacking God, Communist Party leaders
foolishly alienated a potential ally in their quest for ideological domination. Although there may be rites without gods, as Durkheim posited, the
Secularization Experiment demonstrated that godless rites lack the
authority and influence of religious rituals in a world where religious sentiments are ingrained into the fabric of social life.

Assertion 3

Bishops and archbishops enjoy authority merely as
deputies of the temporal power.
> —Leon Trotsky,
> *The History of the Russian Revolution*

Marxist-Leninists believed, as Trotsky notes, that religious leaders are
wholly dependent on secular forms of power for their authority. In other
words, without the continued support of political and economic elites,
religious authority would simply evaporate. This perspective assumes that
religious institutions and their accompanying theologies provide nothing
more than an ideological justification of existing power relations. Accordingly, powerful individuals or groups most likely find religious doctrines
inoffensive because they favor the status quo and therefore are happy to
foster their persistence. In addition, religious organizations may serve as a

supplementary means to regulate the behavior of a population and extend the control of the power elite. The Secularization Experiment revealed that this assertion concerning the temporal nature of religious authority is only partially correct.

By ending state support for religious groups and enacting new policies of religious regulation, the Soviet state successfully toppled the hierarchy of the Russian Orthodox Church. Left with few resources, the Orthodox Church was unable to retain most of its clergy and severely reduced the number of sermons, services, and church outreaches it performed. This reversal of fortune reveals how the Orthodox Church depended on the czarist regime for its religious dominance in many Slavic lands. Similarly, Soviet rule eliminated the institutional forms of Islam. Within a few decades, the vast network of Islamic schools and courts vanished. Of course, this occurred due to more than just a shift in governmental backing. Instead, these institutions were forcefully shut down, even when they were supported and financed by local communities.

Nevertheless, the ability of religious groups to resist the harsh anti-religious policies of the Soviet Union was dependent on their material and political resources. The Roman Catholic Church retained its independence from the government and its ties to the international church, which enabled it to maintain its institutional hierarchy and religious authority among the Roman Catholic population. Consequently, how dominant religious institutions weathered Soviet repression is mainly explained by differences in their temporal authority as opposed to differences in the devoutness or faith of their members. Trotsky was correct that state and economic power were the primary determinants of these forms of religious dominance.

Nevertheless, Trotsky's perspective and that of other Marxist-Leninists ignore another crucial source of religious authority — religious faith. Small Protestant groups flourished not as a result of their material or political power but due to the commitment of their relatively powerless members. Of course, the political and social authority of these groups remained quite circumscribed and did little to challenge the power of the state. But a basic faith in religious theologies persisted throughout the Soviet Union, even when elites openly discouraged religious indoctrination. And the vitality of religious belief after the fall of the Soviet Union indicates that the religious faith of Soviet citizens did not rely solely on the temporal power of religious institutions. Instead, religious ideas and commitments were instilled in the Soviet population in ways that superseded any political or economic authority. Marxist-Leninists incorrectly assumed that a widespread faith in Communist ideals would naturally follow from the political and economic authority of the Communist Party. Although patterns of belief often obey the demands of temporal authority, as Trotsky notes, sometimes the causal direction is reversed and temporal authority becomes dependent on preexisting patterns of belief. The Soviet project demonstrates, more than anything, that lasting political authority depends as much on ideas as on social and economic power.

The Secularization Experiment is a case study in ideological diffusion and political legitimation. Soviet leaders enjoyed unchallenged control over every aspect of Soviet society up until the fall of the Soviet Union. Few experts predicted the Eastern European revolutions of 1989 that led to the demise of Soviet Communism.[20] Why was this? First, although these revolutions produced major social and political changes, they did not resemble classical revolutions in many key ways. S. N. Eisenstadt points out that these revolutions were predominantly bloodless (except in Romania), with the charismatic and utopian revolutionary elements entirely missing.[21] In addition, most of the events or structural conditions that scholars expect to precede a social revolution were also missing. Daniel Chirot argues that (1) there was no sudden economic crises throughout Eastern Europe, (2) no foreign unrest such as war ignited these revolutions, (3) there was no clear conflict within the ruling elite, and (4) social protesters were not aggressively mobilizing.[22] Based on this summary, Chirot concludes that "most widely accepted sociological models of revolution are of limited help in explaining what happened in Eastern Europe in 1989."[23]

After the revolutions of 1989, theorists naturally set about trying to make sense of these seemingly unique and largely unpredicted events. The result was a myriad of narrative explanations to uncover the causal mechanisms that produced these specific revolutions.[24] Certainly, many scholars stress Soviet Communism's inability to compete with the economic successes of Western capitalism.[25] But most agree that the Communist regimes ultimately fell because they lost their legitimacy. In other words, much of the public simply had no faith in the social system, and their distrust pushed low-level political and economic instability to the point of collapse.

But why did Communist regimes have such trouble generating and maintaining legitimacy? Theories of ideology advanced by Alvin Gouldner and Robert Wuthnow place a high importance on the sources of cultural production.[26] According to these theories, education and mass media produce culture through the dissemination of ideology. In theory, if one had total control of the means of cultural production, one could control the ideology of a population. This perspective can be likened to the general causal model of Marxist-Leninists who exercised expansive power over the sources of cultural production and built a vast ideological monopoly.

The unexpected battle over belief in God embodied the larger struggle to legitimate Soviet rule. If Soviet citizens were not becoming atheists, this failure indicated a major flaw in the Soviet ideological machine. In fact, beliefs about God should have been easier to squash than beliefs about what is economically advantageous or socially just. For instance, arguments about the economic benefits of Communism could be undermined by personal experiences of economic need. And the Communist vision of social justice could be challenged when individuals saw their friends and neighbors unfairly punished by authorities. In contrast, religious beliefs are not empirically confirmed; they are based in faith. Therefore, atheist propaganda should have been very effective because it attacked something that was nonempirical.

In addition, scientific atheism appeared to have every social advantage. The Soviet government successfully suppressed religious activity and subsequently reduced levels of religious capital. And scientific atheism enjoyed a level of state support rare for even religious monopolies. Nevertheless, the most generous estimates of atheistic belief show that less than one-fifth of Soviet citizens were atheists at the height of Communism, and this number dramatically drops to less than 4 percent of the population immediately following the fall of the Soviet Union. On what authority or empirical evidence did Soviet citizens base their persisting religious belief?

Several important circumstances explain why complete control of the sources of cultural production did not successfully instill an atheist ethic among the Soviet population. First, religious belief was not the result of scientific ignorance and therefore could not be dispelled simply through education. Soviet schools were decidedly antireligious, but educators misunderstood religious explanations as misguided quests for scientific understanding. Consequently, they criticized aspects of religion that were largely unimportant to believers.

Second, Soviet ideological messages, symbols, and rituals could not by themselves generate belief. Beyond the incessant distribution of propaganda materials and the introduction of atheist rituals, Soviet propagandists never established any personal connection to their population. It was not enough to simply control the sources of cultural production — Soviet leaders needed to implement their propaganda efficiently and effectively. In their propaganda efforts, they could have learned valuable lessons from successful religious missionaries, who understand the primary importance of social networks and community ties. Successful ideologies are not imposed on a population from above but must inspire the hearts and minds of a people from within their ranks.

Finally, religious worldviews offer something lacking in Soviet Communism — an object of devotion, a God, who purports to care about the individual. Communist ideology focused on saving society while often appearing indifferent to the plight of individual citizens. Soviet citizens were expected to sacrifice their bodies, minds, and souls for some greater good. Simply repeating this message through official channels did little to instill a heartfelt faith in the listener.

All of these factors suggest that individuals think about their beliefs and weigh competing ideological messages against their own experiences and emotions. In the final analysis, economic and political elites can determine the amount of resources dedicated to various forms of religious proselytizing and ideological diffusion, but these resources do not fully predict the success of their efforts. The weak appeal of scientific atheism in Soviet Union indicates that cultural promotion, by itself, is not enough to guarantee a doctrine's popularity. As Stark and Finke note about religious proselytism, "People do not simply succumb to missionary efforts, for conversion not only involves interaction, it quite clearly involves introspection."[27] Introspection, in this case, refers to a process of evaluating one's empirical surroundings as well as one's emotional needs. Although religious authority often depends on earthly power, as Trotsky notes, it does not follow that the ideological conversion of a population can be completely coerced. Instead, temporal power gives advantages to favored belief systems but cannot ensure their adoption.

Assertion 4

Religious or magical behavior or thinking must not be
set apart from the range of everyday purposive conduct,
particularly since even the ends of the religious and
magical actions are predominantly economic.
                    — Max Weber, *Economy and Society*

Max Weber observed that religious individuals and groups behave in ways that are predictable because they tend to be economically rational. Pascal provides us with the most notable explanation of why the rational person is religious. "You must either believe or not believe that God is —

which will you do? A game is going on between you and the nature of things which your day of judgment will bring out heads or tails. If there were an infinity of chances, and only one for God in this wager, still you ought to stake your all on God; for though you surely risk a finite loss by this procedure, any finite loss is reasonable, even a certain one is reasonable, if there is but the possibility of infinite gain."[28] Pascal's argument, popularly known as "Pascal's wager," sounds convincing, but many religious believers found it "vile," to quote William James's reaction.[29] James thought that reducing religious faith to a self-interested calculation was obscene and tarnished the heartfelt humility and integrity of many religious believers. Nevertheless, Pascal insisted that although religious belief may advocate selflessness in this life, it was prudent and rational considering the ultimate payoff may offer in the afterlife.

Although Weber asserted that religious behavior tended to be economically rational in many instances, his perspective was not applied to the systematic study of religion in any rigorous way until fairly recently. In the 1970s, economists Azzi and Ehrenberg demonstrated that the amount of time individuals allotted to religious activities followed predictable economic choice patterns.[30] And the economist Laurence Iannaccone has spent considerable effort calculating why individuals will rationally accept the inherent risk in religious commitment; his work, and additional research from a handful of sociologists, has led to a growing movement to apply rational choice assumptions to the study of religion. The assumption that individuals are self-interested actors is utilized in rational choice research to model a person's thought process. Researchers extrapolate from this model of individual decision making to generate hypotheses concerning societal-level trends.[31] As a form of methodological individualism, rational choice assumptions provide the theoretical framework from which researchers can posit general expectations about large-scale social behavior.[32]

Theorists of religion tend to utilize a broad definition of rational choice, avoiding the idea that individuals are simply interested in material goods. Stark and Finke admit that a strictly economic version of rational choice fails to recognize the nonmaterial goods of religion; they explain that initial attempts to understand the rationality of religion were naive because "too little explicit attention was given to the emotional and expressive components of religion, not sufficient scope was given to the typical elements of religious practice such as ritual, sacrifice, prayer, and the like."[33] Instead, current rational choice theorists assume that religious individuals behave according to a "maximization assumption," or the idea that humans attempt to gain the most at the least cost.[34] This perspective predicts that religious believers will try to find the most efficient and effective means to achieve their goals. Therefore, as Weber asserted, religious behavior should be no different from everyday purposive conduct.

What becomes interesting in predicting the behavior of religious individuals is that their goals are distinctively different from nonreligious individuals. Rational choice theorist Michael Hechter argues that to better model behavioral expectations, we must understand an individual's "immanent" values; these are "ends that are valued for themselves alone, rather than for what they can yield in exchange."[35] Written and espoused religious doctrines provide a way to determine an individual's stated immanent values. For instance, if a person says that she is a devout Christian, then we can expect her to behave in ways consistent with Christian doctrines, even if these behaviors are costly to her. This would show that the individual maintains her Christian ideals regardless of the worldly disadvantages of religious participation and devotion.

The Secularization Experiment dramatically increased the worldly disadvantages of religious expression. Using rational choice assumptions, we can hypothesize about individual-level behavior and reactions of institutions to these changing circumstances. Let's begin with religious institutions. Facing the harsh realities of Soviet antireligious policy, churches and religious groups necessarily selected between strategies of voicing opposition to Soviet rule or proclaiming loyalty to Soviet demands. Religious leaders calculated their best responses to repression. The actual complexity of these calculations is immeasurable, but we can begin with a simple assumption that religious officials placed high value on the survival of their group. Therefore, we would expect all religious leaders to make compromises to secure the perseverance of their religious organization.

As we would expect, many religious leaders sought to compromise and even collaborate with Soviet forces. This was certainly the case with the Russian Orthodox Church. Although Orthodox leaders initially voiced opposition to Soviet rule, they soon compromised with Soviet officials in hopes of gaining government favors. Similarly, Islamic groups throughout Central Asia offered relatively little resistance to Soviet rule. Muslim clerics and leaders calculated the benefits of Soviet Communism and found that they could subsist under repressive policies while enjoying the gains of industrialization, universal health care, and public education. Protestant groups reacted in ways similar to Muslim ones. In general, Protestants worked loyalty for the Soviet regime while covertly continuing their religious practices.

In other cases, churches actively opposed Soviet policies and even became vessels of political opposition to Communist rule. The most dramatic case of religious opposition to Communism occurred in Poland, where the Roman Catholic Church initiated the anti-Communist solidarity movement. Similarly, the Roman Catholic Church in Lithuania consistently attempted to fight Soviet repression any way it could.

Differences in how religious groups reacted to Soviet rule provide us with the opportunity to further theorize about why these differences occurred. Under what circumstances would a religious group oppose Soviet rule? All religious groups naturally opposed the religious repression of the Soviet Union, but only certain groups were in the position to voice their opposition while remaining in tact. Institutional responses to Soviet repression say less about the religious commitment of leaders and more about the resources and organizational structure of the group. The size of a group was an initial determinant of whether it was in the position to voice political opposition. Minority religious groups were simply too small to directly challenge Soviet repression. On the other hand, Soviet authorities found these groups difficult to monitor, and many flourished under the radar of Soviet surveillance. Although majority religious groups had large numbers of members to bolster their potential political power, they found it difficult to hide their activities from authorities. Therefore, majority religious groups were forced to decide how actively they would oppose Soviet restrictions.

Essentially, two institutional factors explain the reaction of majority religious groups to Soviet oppression. First, a group's autonomy from the state before Soviet rule determined its ability to withstand Soviet infiltration. The Russian Orthodox Church simply had no way to oppose Soviet demands because it had formerly been the property of the czarist regime. By default, Soviet officials inherited total control of the church when they took over the government. In contrast, the Roman Catholic Church was largely independent of state control and, therefore, had resources that were unavailable to the Orthodox Church. Second, the institutional structure of the religious group determined its ability to organize any sustained opposition. Islamic groups in regions that were overwhelmingly Muslim lacked the organizational hierarchy to fight Soviet authority. Because they lacked the organizational means to mobilize active oppositions, Islamic elites infiltrated the Communist political system in ways unthinkable to Christian leaders. Whereas the Roman Catholic Church hoped to overcome Soviet rule and the Russian Orthodox Church begrudgingly offered the Soviets its loyalty, Islamic groups became a religious voice that penetrated the Communist Party.

The combination of institutional autonomy and institutional unity within a strict hierarchy allowed the Roman Catholic Church to challenge Soviet authority in ways unthinkable to other majority religious groups. Taken together, these factors show why Roman Catholic leaders were in the best position to voice opposition to Soviet religious repression (see figure 13).

As religious leaders juggled resources and navigated the waters of a new political and ideological world, religious followers similarly considered their options. The Secularization Experiment put the immanent values of religious believers to the ultimate test. By altering incentive structures and societal norms, Communist Party officials forced religious individuals to decide between suffering for their stated beliefs and identities and enjoying social and economic benefits by abandoning their religion. Because the costs of religious affiliation and participation were so high, we would expect many religious believers to publicly disavow their religious identities. As expected, most Soviet citizens opted to relinquish their religious memberships and cease their religious behaviors to avoid punishment and harassment. This outcome reveals that millions of religious believers valued their economic and social livelihoods over their need to publicly practice their religion. Of course, many of these individuals continued religious practices in private. And in the case of Muslims, Islamic doctrines advocated religious secrecy under conditions of repression. Therefore, we cannot assume that drops in religious memberships and practices necessarily indicate a total abandonment of religion.

On the other hand, some religious individuals were certainly church opportunists who left their churches when the going got tough. But after the fall of the Soviet Union, most nonaffiliated individuals expressed religious beliefs and indicated that they were privately loyal to their religious traditions even when they did not outwardly express it.[36] Others actively took up atheist identities that they later disavowed — examples of Communist free riders. Whether religious individuals abandoned their religious institutions out of indifference or fear is difficult to ascertain, but a comparison of religious groups provides some insights.

For the most part, the size, autonomy, and institutional structure of religious groups greatly determined whether their members would remain loyal to them.[37] Protestant groups fared well because they offered members religious goods in the safety of more secluded surroundings. Muslims similarly went underground in attempts to hide from Soviet oppression. Although the success of these religious groups is difficult to ascertain due to their covert nature, the relative vitality of Muslim and Protestant

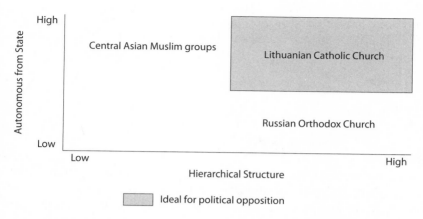

Figure 13. Organizational Components Affecting the Political Influence of Majority Religions.

groups following the fall of the Soviet Union indicates that covert religions were truly popular and offered an alternative to individuals who did not want to directly oppose Soviet rule but wished to maintain their religious commitments. And the Roman Catholic Church retained members due to its institutional autonomy and political strength. In this instance, Roman Catholics rallied behind their church because they felt unified and empowered in their religious identity; in fact, the Polish Catholic Church actually increased its membership during Communist rule.

In general, most religious believers sought self-preservation, attempting to protect themselves by either abandoning their public religious identities or insulating themselves within powerful religious institutions where there was safety in numbers. In contrast, a committed minority of religious believers boldly risked imprisonment and death by publicly maintaining their religious ties and continuing to advocate religious ideas in conditions of ultimate peril. These few individuals demonstrated an attachment and dedication to their religious community that could not be shaken by threats, imprisonment, and even death. The experience of clerics, nuns, and religious devotees in Gulag camps most vividly depicts the hardships that certain individuals were willing to suffer in defense of their faith. Their singular devotion represents an exception to the general pattern and indicates that religious behavior can sometimes exceed rational choice expectations.

To better explain even the most extreme religious behavior, religious theorists have begun to calculate the importance of otherworldly benefits, in ways similar to Pascal's wager. According to these theorists, we need to consider seriously the allure of the next world to understand religious martyrdom and extremism.

Assertion 5

Religion is concerned with the supernatural; everything
else is secondary.
               —Rodney Stark and Roger Finke, *Acts of Faith*

The Secularization Experiment offered the best available test of the largely untestable proposition that humans have a natural religious instinct. The Soviet population showed that widespread religious belief can persist over a seventy-year period, even as religious institutions lose the ability to indoctrinate the young and as political forces actively try to undermine faith in the supernatural. Perhaps this is the result of religious instinct. Both social and natural scientists have posited that a religious sentiment is deeply ingrained in human nature. For instance, Richard Dawkins, along with others, advocates an evolutionary theory of religion, in which religious belief initially served some survival value and consequently got instilled in human psychology.[38] And geneticist Dean Hamer has argued that heredity is partly responsible for whether a person has the "self-transcendence" trait; individuals with this genetic trait feel more connected to the world and are more willing to believe in nonobservable phenomena.[39] In turn, Hamer argues that genetics predict how religious individuals will be. Max Weber also suggests that individuals have differing natural affinities to religious matters, which explains why certain individuals are more devout than others.[40]

Contemporary social theorists talk about specific differences in religiosity measures as based partially on individual religious preferences. Darren Sherkat defines *religious preferences* as "the favored supernatural explanations about the meaning, purpose and origins of life — explanations that cannot be proved nor disproved."[41] As such, some people prefer tightly knit religious groups that construct rigorous guidelines of behavior, while others may prefer religious doctrines that stress individual choice. The source of these preferences is not entirely clear. Whereas the geneticist Dean Hamer suggests that they may be the result of inborn psychological traits, sociologists Darren Sherkat and John Wilson demonstrate that religious preferences can shift as individuals encounter new circumstances and become ensconced in new social networks, suggesting that preferences are adaptable.[42] Most likely, a person's religious

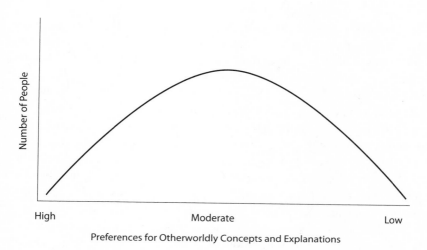

Figure 14. Assumed Normal Curve of Religious Preferences Driving Religious Demand.

preferences are a result of their biological predilections as realized and inspired by interactions with close friends and family. Therefore, one can never theoretically detach the biological or genetic foundations of religious preferences from the social and cultural location of the individual. One's psychological predisposition and social networks work in tandem to produce a distinct religious personality.

At the societal level, Rodney Stark and Roger Finke have argued that religious demand is constant in all cultures.[43] More specifically, they posit that religious demand is an assumed normal distribution of religious preferences (see figure 14). This means that within any population, most individuals are predisposed to be moderately religious, a few individuals will be naturally nonreligious, and a few individuals will be intensely religious. This assumption is very difficult to test within one society, and the concepts of "very religious" and "moderately religious" are difficult to measure cross-culturally. Nevertheless, a few basic facts about religion around the globe suggest that the assumption of a natural distribution of religious preferences is not far-fetched.

First, very few individuals in the world consider themselves atheists or agnostics. And although nontheistic or pantheistic religions still exist, current survey research indicates that belief in monotheism is an omnipresent constant across agrarian, industrial, and postindustrial countries.[44] Because dramatic cultural, economic, and social differences have little impact on belief in God, we can conclude that very general religious worldviews are universally appealing. Second, cross-cultural research on religious regulation indicates that whenever religious freedom is available, multiple religious traditions tend to flourish. Stark and Finke note that "in complex societies, the range of possible religious choices is usually very substantial, but even in preliterate groups, religious factions are common and new religious movements often arise."[45] This indicates that no one religion can fully meet the religious demands of a population. And religious homogeneity only appears to exist when religious diversity is legally and socially repressed.[46] Taken together, the ubiquity of belief in God around the world combined with enormous diversity in religious traditions suggest that a basic demand for a religious worldview is universal, yet no singular religious doctrine can satisfy everyone.

It appears evident that any religious or ideological monopoly will fail to gain universal acceptance among a population that is naturally intellectually and spiritually diverse. Nevertheless, the Soviet campaign to generate an ideological monopoly ignored something that appears to be the singular unifying element of most worldviews — belief in God. For this reason, Soviet propagandists faced even greater obstacles than the average religious monopoly, which at least offers individuals an image of God.

What is it about the idea of God that is so universal and seemingly important? In his analysis of the religious revivals in post-Communist Russia, Andrew Greeley found that belief in a caring God was more predictive of religious participation than whether an individual attended church as a child, was married to religious person, or had a religious experience.[47] This finding demonstrates that the idea of a caring God is one of the most appealing aspects of religion. In our research on religious devotion, my colleague Christopher Bader and I have also found that individuals attend church to the extent that they believe God is a caring and personally engaged being.[48] Our research suggests that individuals are drawn to religion out of a desire for a personal relationship with the supernatural. The idea of a caring God not only presents a picture of the universe as meaningful and ultimately fair but also as loving and concerned with the individual. This key aspect of religion cannot be replicated in secular terms.

Although belief in God appears to motivate individuals differently (at its most extreme, this belief can inspire individuals to risk their lives), there is something universal about its appeal. By killing the idea of God, Communist Party officials abandoned one of the essential objects of human faith. Soviet leaders may have been better served by somehow retaining a conception of God that fit into their ideological and political goals. Instead, Soviet thinkers failed to comprehend the power of the idea of God and misguidedly dismissed supernatural concepts as insignificant when, in fact, this idea can inspire and legitimate a wide variety of political, social, and existential worldviews.

Assertion 6

Market forces constrain churches just as they constrain
secular firms.

> —Adam Smith, *An Inquiry into the Nature and*
> *Causes of the Wealth of Nations*

The fall of Soviet Communism dramatically altered religious markets. Old and new religious ideas openly spread across the vast regions of the former Soviet empire. Foreign missionaries and formerly underground religious groups viewed their future with extreme optimism, believing that they were part of an epic religious reawakening. And religious revivals occurred. Many new religious movements established inroads to the "secularized" population of the Soviet Union, and former Soviet citizens appeared eager to explore new ideas and faiths. Religious membership increased, church attendance swelled, and opinion polls indicated very few individuals were committed atheists or even agnostics.

The most surprising aspect of these religious revivals is the form they took. In the final analysis, old religious monopolies have reestablished some of their former dominance. This is startling because new religious movements are heavily funded by international organizations and very adept at dealing with conversion and proselytizing in modern societies. In contrast, monopoly religious organizations were severely weakened under Communist rule and faced vigorous religious competition. Under these circumstances, one might expect the emergence of a religious market similar to United States', where many religious groups openly compete for religious adherents. Instead, the religious markets of the former Soviet Union look surprisingly similar to those of pre-Communist times.

Market forces constrain churches through legal regulations and restrictions just as they constrain businesses with laws concerning conduct, contracts, and trade. Most modern nations tend to favor particular religious groups in certain ways. This, in turn, insures the ongoing success of these groups. In the former Soviet Union, historically traditional religions are once again reestablishing an intimate relationship with newly forming governments.[49] What predicts how governments will treat a religious group? In the Soviet Union, the atheistic ideology of the Soviet government predicated the repression of all religious groups. In the post-Communist world, newly created governments of the former Soviet Union naturally want to develop a kinder and gentler view of religion. In navigating their religious policies, political actors seek to establish social and institutional ties that will solidify their hold on power. Religious groups offer something attractive to new political leaders — legitimacy. In turn, political elites can offer favored status to loyal religious groups. This relationship explains the emergence of religious monopolies that rely on government support and regulation of religious competition.

Politicians across the former Soviet Union have tended to foster mutually beneficial relationships with religions that enjoyed favored status in pre-Communist times. These religions have a historic connection to national and ethnic identities, and leaders seeking to strengthen a shared national character often invoke the collective memory of past national glory. President Yeltsin very quickly developed ties to the Russian Orthodox Church to not only distance himself from Soviet Communism but also to exhibit his core Russian identity. In a regional analysis of religious freedom throughout the newly created Russian Federation, my colleague Christopher Marsh and I found that local governments that were more efficient and organized tended to enact laws that greatly favor the Russian Orthodox Church.[50] This reveals that the most effective political actors in Russia have similarly pursued a close relationship with the Orthodox Church in hopes of fostering a strong religio-national identity that further legitimates their power.

Similarly, although the regions of Central Asia are predominantly run by former Communist elites, these individuals were quick to remind the public of their Muslim identities. In turn, these political leaders favor Islamic groups that were closely tied to the Communist Party. This has led to unrest and rebellion as outside Muslim groups jockey for political power and religious dominance. Unlike the Russian Orthodox Church in Russia, no single Muslim group can claim exclusive ties to newly emerging national identities. Therefore, established political actors and emerging religious leaders in Central Asia fight over what it means to be Muslim.

Ironically, the most successful aspect of the Secularization Experiment — the separation of church and state — is being undone as churches and states realign to create new religious monopolies. Market forces certainly constrain churches, and the most sophisticated and resourceful political leaders continue to use this basic relationship to their advantage as they seek the support of religious authority.

THE POLITICAL PROS AND CONS OF GOD

In 1937, the Communist Party reaffirmed its basic position on God with this proclamation in a prominent Soviet newspaper: "We repudiate the writings about God and we assert that there was not and there is not any such person. This fact has been established on the basis of scientific data concerning the origin of man as well as the origin of the universe."[51] As we have seen, the Soviet Secularization Experiment was successful in reducing certain aspects of religiosity. But it ultimately failed to stamp out religious faith, and, in fact, it created a series of problems for the Soviet state that may have been avoided altogether had authorities not attacked the idea of God.

Marxist-Leninists clearly understood the importance of religious supply in determining the content and vitality of a population's religiosity. They correctly recognized how most modern governments sustained religious monopolies through state support and religious regulations. They also understood how individuals are constrained in their attitudes by the available ideological options. Consequently, Communist Party elites copied many of the tactics employed by successful religious monopolies to establish their own ideological monopoly.

But why wasn't the new Soviet ideological monopoly able to replace the old religious monopolies? Due to their strong faith that atheism was an observable truth, Soviet leaders misunderstood why many Soviet citizens were religious. By offering modern education and community rituals, Marxist-Leninists believed they could better fulfill the misdirected religious needs of their population. But the Soviet ideological campaign dismissed and ridiculed the idea of God and failed to comprehend how much average Soviet citizens had come to rely on theological conceptions of the world to make sense of their earthly lot.

Although Soviet repression quickly diminished religious activity, it also created a situation in which relatively innocuous expressions of religion, such as praying in one's home, became acts of political rebellion. For this reason, dreams of an atheist society led Soviet officials to wage a futile atheistic campaign with growing material costs and diminishing political returns. The religious reforms of glasnost in the 1980s were evidence of the Soviet regime, for the first time, giving up this never-ending wrestling match with religion — an opponent with little upper-body strength but amazingly resilient legs.

The Soviet Secularization Experiment must be called a failure because its intent was nothing less than the universal acceptance of atheism. Had

Soviet officials set their sights lower, on, say, dramatically reducing church attendance and affiliation, they may have found ways not to alienate religious believers or force them into politically hostile stances. This possibility was considered by some early Bolsheviks, but its potential effectiveness is impossible to predict after the fact. Nevertheless, some comparative examples of modern church-state relationships reaffirm that trying to kill God is a political dead-end. In fact, if one's goal is to reduce expressions of religiosity while also bolstering the legitimacy of one's political regime, then invoking God is a well-established strategy.

Political elites must work within the cultural history they are given. As Marx famously noted, "Men make their own history, but they do not make it just as they please; they do not make it under circumstances chosen by themselves, but under circumstances directly encountered, given and transmitted from the past."[52] In attempting to expunge the idea of God from all discourse and culture, Communist Party leaders encountered one of the most deeply embedded features of pre-Soviet culture. Theological traditions develop over centuries and are perpetuated by complex networks of local organizations and long-standing cultural norms. Unlike Communist Party leaders, most modern political elites know not to mess with these traditions or are active devotees of them. Consequently, political regimes tend to either foster a positive association with popular religious traditions or, at least, indicate that they are not opposed to the ideals and beliefs espoused by them.

Today, political regimes in Western Europe, the United States, and Communist China all grapple with how to approach religion and the idea of God. In each case, the society's religious history guides how political leaders and regimes interact with religious institutions. Their individual successes at invoking God for their political ends provide further evidence of the folly of trying to kill God.

Western Europe

Grace Davies accurately characterized Western Europe as having a religious culture of "believing without belonging."[53] Because many Western Europeans retain nominal religious identities, perhaps her sentiment may be better expressed as "believing without participating." Simply put, Western Europeans believe in God but are unlikely to attend church, pray regularly, or participate in religious rituals. According to the World Values Survey, some of the least religiously active countries in the world are Denmark, Great Britain, Finland, France, Iceland, the Netherlands,

Norway, and Sweden.[54] Despite weekly church attendance rates that hover around 20 percent of their populations, a clear majority in each country expresses faith in God.[55] By measures of religious participation and belief, Western Europeans today look a lot like the Soviet population under Communism — showing few public displays of religiosity but privately holding onto religious faith.

But the political and religious culture of Western Europe is in marked contrast to that of the Soviet Union. Most Western Europeans are free to participate in any religious activity they choose. So why don't they? Rodney Stark and Laurence Iannaccone argue that part of the reason is that over time, Western European countries have developed moderately restricted religious markets that are often dominated by single state churches.[56] As a consequence, individual religious identities in Western Europe tend to be based on ethnicity or nationality and not on any outward expression of religious devotion. The irony of this situation is that instead of producing a very religious society, close ties between church and state often generate a religiously apathetic yet seemingly spiritually content population.

Perhaps this occurs because individuals are not denied religion but also need not work for it. Jose Casanova points out that "the national churches [of Western Europe] remain there as a public good to which [Europeans] have rightful access when it comes time to celebrate the transcendent rites of passage, birth, and death. It is a peculiar situation that explains the lack of demand and the absence of a truly competitive religious market in Europe."[57] Western Europeans can therefore maintain their private spirituality while relying on the public goods supplied by state churches without having to contribute time, money, or effort. Without the support of the state, the onus is on the individual parishioners and clergy to keep their church alive.

From the perspective of political elites, state churches offer some useful benefits. First, political opposition tends not to be religiously motivated because so few in the population are religiously active. Second, state churches provide a unifying cultural and moral focal point in times of crisis and serve as the institutional embodiment of a nation's civil religion. In other words, state churches enhance the concept of a national identity while reducing the extent to which religious issues guide political action.

A key difference between the state churches of Western Europe and the "Church of Communism" developed by Communist Party officials is how each relates to the main theological traditions in its society's cultural history. State churches across Western Europe propagate theological world-views that are rooted in their national history. Conversely, atheist propaganda, symbols, and rituals demeaned all that was historically sacred in pre-Soviet culture. Although Soviet citizens may have been willing to reorganize the institutional structures of their society, they were unwilling or unable to relinquish their inner faiths. The Soviet Secularization Experiment misguidedly assumed that culture and ideology are simply imposed from positions of institutional power, but in reality, political elites must negotiate and compromise with cultural, religious, and ideological traditions if they are ever to successfully cultivate them for their own ends.

The case of Western Europe demonstrates that under the proper cultural and political circumstances, religion can be rendered relatively impotent in political and social life. Soviet leaders inherited cultures with similar characteristics to those of Western Europe — namely, most regions of the Soviet Union contained weak religious monopolies that ascribed religious identities to a majority of their populations. If the Soviet regime could have ideologically co-opted these religious organizations, they might have generated a religious cultural situation similar to many Western European countries, in which religion persists but is not vital to the political or economic issues of the day. Instead, Soviet rule forced religion into a permanent state of political opposition.

The United States

God looms large in American life, in contrast to Western European culture. Americans are some of the most religiously active people in the postindustrial world. They pray more, go to church more, and participate in religious activities more than any population in Western Europe.[58] And the United States has no official state church. In fact, the constitutionally mandated separation of church and state has allowed the religious economy of the United States to become one of the most vibrant and diverse in the world today. Gordon Melton estimates that the United States contains over twenty-one hundred distinct religious groups from a myriad of world religious traditions.[59] Under these circumstances, no single religious organization can claim the status of a national religion.

One might assume that the legal requirements that separate church and state in tandem with high levels of religious pluralism would lead to the diminishing political influence of religion, because no single religious group could effectively guide public policy. But in the United States, over 75 percent of Americans consider themselves Christians, and, of those,

70 percent are Protestants.[60] Consequently, many aspects of American civil religion, such as the sacredness of the flag and other national symbols, along with the ritual aspects of American political institutions, are imbued with references to Protestant Christian culture.[61] In addition, presidential candidates very openly and proudly proclaim their religious devotion and how their faith, usually a brand of traditional Protestantism, influences their behavior. In 2000 and 2004, George W. Bush made much of his miraculous born-again experience and his promise to "recommit [his] life to Jesus Christ."[62] And in 2000, Al Gore also conspicuously announced that he was "a child of the Kingdom and a person of strong faith."[63] The fact that 2004 candidate John Kerry is Roman Catholic may have diminished the import of his claim to faith, although John F. Kennedy demonstrated that it was possible for a non-Protestant Christian to become president. But in general, Americans like their presidents to be committed Protestants who indicate that their religious faith is an important guide for their actions.

Religion has always been central to American politics, and politicians have often touted their faith as a symbol of their integrity and moral respectability. Recent research conducted by myself and my collaborator, Christopher Bader, reveals that religious beliefs and, more specifically, ideas about God are powerful determinants of public opinion in the United States. Specifically, Americans who believe in an engaged and authoritarian God are much more likely to oppose abortion, gay marriage, stem-cell research, physician-assisted suicide, and the legalization of marijuana, regardless of their political party affiliation or religious tradition.[64] Furthermore, we found that the effect of theological beliefs on public opinion is more notable in the United States than across both Eastern and Western Europe.[65] And many Americans reference what they believe God wants as the rationale for their specific political attitudes.[66] As such, beliefs about God play a critical role in determining the political worldview of Americans.

Conservative politicians in the United States have successfully targeted religiously devout Americans by taking up policy issues, such as the criminalization of abortion, that are highly salient to various American religious groups. The "Republicanization" of American Protestantism is a fairly recent phenomenon and marks the successful courting of dominant Evangelical religious groups by the Republican Party. In the 1976 election, most Evangelical Protestants voted for Democratic Party candidate Jimmy Carter, who was an Evangelical Southern Baptist but liberal on social policy issues.[67] By 2000, Evangelical Protestants voted overwhelm-

ingly for George W. Bush, a born-again Christian with conservative attitudes on social policy. In essence, the Republican Party has successfully
convinced many American Protestants that it faithfully represents God in
American politics; in fact, national survey data from 2005 indicates that
nearly all individuals who believe that God favors their political party are
Republicans.[68]

In response to the outreach of the Republican Party, socially conservative religious groups became, as sociologists Regnerus and Smith
argue, more public policy oriented, "constituting a reversal of past generations" of religious conservatives, who mainly withdrew from
American public life.[69] The concomitant public retreat of politically liberal religious activists, such as the religiously based movements that
sparked the American civil rights campaign of the 1960s, may have been
the result of the Democratic Party's general abandonment of overtly religious language. In American politics, the courting of religious sentiments
remains an important aspect in determining a winning political agenda,
and, in recent decades, the Republican Party has most successfully in-
voked God in its political language.

Even in a country that forbids the institutional collaboration of
church and state, religious sentiments continue to play a powerful role in
setting the political agenda and determining election outcomes. Whether
out of sincerity or political calculation, George W. Bush has successfully
drawn connections between his national and international policy preferences and the religious values of the country. With "God on his side,"
Bush has been able to dramatically expand the power of the presidency,
instigate a preemptive war, and get reelected. Although Marxist-Leninists
would certainly shutter at the corporation friendly policies of the Bush
administration, they would most likely marvel at the grassroots support
Bush has generated among millions of working-class Americans simply
because of his religious identity.

Communist China

Communist China has used the Soviet Union as a model for many of its
social, economic, and cultural policies. But China has also learned and
diverged from the example set by the Soviet Union. During the Cultural
Revolution (1966–76), Chinese officials brutally attacked all religious
groups and leaders using tactics comparable to those of Stalin in the
1930s. But before the Cultural Revolution and from 1979 until today,
the Chinese Communist regime officially recognizes a limited number of

religious organizations that are closely monitored by the Communist state. Similar to the Soviet regime, the Chinese government advances scientific atheism as its official ideology. Although current religious regulations are quite repressive in comparison to democratic regimes around the world, China's religious policies most closely resemble those of the Soviet glasnost period.

Although religious growth is difficult to document, there are a number of sources from both in- and outside of China indicating that traditional and Western religions are on the rise. As during the glasnost era in the Soviet Union, partial religious repression can inspire religious innovation and opposition. Chinese scholar Yunfeng Lu argues that China's religious policies have had the unintended consequence of pushing suppressed religious groups to be more innovative, adaptive, and aggressive; his research on the Yiguan Dao sect supports this claim.[70] And a growing literature indicates that Christianity is becoming more popular across mainline China.[71] Although Christianity is an official religion in China, religion scholar Fenggang Yang points out there is a burgeoning underground "grey religious market" in China; this market is similar to that of the catacomb Catholic Church in Lithuanian — an underground extension of a publicly recognized religion.[72] Through this grey market, Yang argues that Christianity and various qigong (breathing) religions have been making inroads to the Chinese population.

The Communist Chinese regime is not only aware of the underground vitality of certain religious movements but is beginning to recognize that outright repression may not be the best way to control unwanted religious activity. In 1990, Communist Party official Chen Yun instigated a new discussion about the compatibility of an atheist state and religious freedom; he warned Chinese president Zemin: "Recently I have looked at some materials concerning the increasingly serious problem of religious infiltration, especially the increasingly rampant practice of using religion as a cloak to carry out counter-revolutionary activities. I feel deeply disturbed. Using religion to win over the masses — especially young people — has always been a favorite trick of both our domestic and foreign class enemies. This is a bitter lesson of several of the communist-led countries that recently lost power. Now it is time for Party Centre to deal vigorously with this matter. We must ensure that it cannot become a destabilizing factor."[73] Realizing that religion had grown into a powerful anti-Communist force across Eastern Europe and within the Soviet Union, the Chinese government began to closely consider the anti-Communist potential of Christian groups and the organizational ability of new qigong groups, such as Falun Gong. Although the Chinese government continues to repress and dismantle religious groups that it views as institutional competition to the state, it has begun to rethink the role of religious faith in Communist society.

In 1993, President Zemin issued several new directives regarding state religious policy. In general, he reasserted that the Chinese government officially recognized a list of traditional religious groups, but more revealingly and innovatively, he indicated that it was the Communist Party's goal to "positively guide religion to be compatible with socialist society"; this meant that the party "must give expression to the political nature of religious work and concretely talk politics in religious affairs."[74] Since this initiative, the Chinese government has continued to tightly control religious activity, with some internationally visible embarrassments involving the repression of Falun Gong demonstrations and its continued problems with popular religious leaders of Tibet. Nevertheless, China persists in trying to innovate its religious policies and urging religious groups to be supportive of the Communist project.

Two developments appear especially important to the future of religion and politics in China. First, certain Chinese scholars and officials have become increasingly interested in how religion can be used to inspire prosocial and economically productive behavior. A visiting journalist to Beijing recounts that an official lecturer at the Chinese Academy of Social Sciences admitted in a public statement that

> one of the things we were asked to look into was what accounted for the success, in fact, the pre-eminence of the West all over the world. We studied everything from the historical, political, economic, and cultural perspective. At first, we thought it was because you had more powerful guns than we had. Then we thought it was because you had the best political system. Next we focused on your economic system. But in the past twenty years, we have realized that the heart of your culture is your religion: Christianity. That is why the West has been so powerful. The Christian moral foundation of social and cultural life was what made possible the emergence of capitalism and then the successful transition to democratic politics. We don't have any doubt about this.[75]

This Weberian theoretical position would never have been expressed publicly in the Soviet Union, which indicates that the Chinese Communist Party has begun to look more seriously at how religion affects society than the Soviet regime ever did. That said, it is unclear what this social science perspective would mean to state policy. China has no strong tradition of Christianity, and it seems impossible that the Chinese government would ever attempt to foster Christian growth in hopes that it could provide a religious cultural basis for its brand of socialism. Nevertheless, Chinese officials have begun to think differently about emerging Christian movements in China and may try to foster the socialistic element in Christian thought instead of forcing Christians into a position of political opposition.

Second, the Chinese government has recently begun to fund certain traditional Confucian practices, ceremonies, and temples. In 2004, the Communist Party held a highly publicized ceremony called the Veneration of Confucius, unveiled a "holy statue" of Confucius, and announced plans to open one hundred Confucius Institutes globally over the next few years.[76] Instead of only advancing atheist substitutes for religion, the Chinese regime now provides Confucian ceremonies, temples, and teachings as public goods. As Anna Xiao Dong Sun notes, "The state is beginning to recognize the importance of identifying Confucianism (or Confucius) as a unifying element in Chinese society. Such a symbol is needed for the representation of a national culture in the global context. . . . The growing number of worshippers at Confucius temples also suggests an increasing need among ordinary people for a religious system that is deeply rooted in Chinese tradition, with long-established customs and rites, such as the blessing of exam-taking students."[77]

This "Confucius strategy" may prove quite effective at limiting religious opposition to Communist rule and appeasing the latent spiritual and ritual needs of the Chinese population for several reasons. First, Confucian beliefs and rituals are traditional to Chinese culture. As such, Chinese Communists can hold onto and be proud of important aspects of their cultural history. In contrast, Soviet citizens were asked to relinquish some of their most sacred customs and were even taught to view them as insidious. Second, the philosophical teachings of Confucius have no clear modern political or social ideology and are mainly concerned with the moral action of the individual. Consequently, the Communist regime currently views these teachings as nonthreatening to their economic and political plans; in fact, the morality of Confucius may serve to motivate diligent and loyal behavior. Finally, Confucius thought has no clear conception of God or a single deity who can approve or disapprove of the political regime. In other words, the Communist Party may be able to undermine modern monotheism by drawing on the nontheistic spiritual traditions of China's past. In the end, the funding of traditional Confucius temples and rituals strategically promotes nonthreatening and nonmobilizing spiritual activities.

These developments demonstrate that Chinese Communists have realized that they must reconcile the dream of atheism with the reality of religious persistence. Whether they will be able to tame religion to their own ends is matter for future consideration. I expect that if the Chinese government can allow and support certain expressions of spirituality, it may succeed where the Soviet Union failed. The result may be a weak religious economy similar to that of Western Europe — where individuals are spiritually content yet religiously apathetic. On the other hand, the history of antagonism between religion and Communism along with the increasing popularity of Christianity might still inspire religious believers in China to discount the official ideology of their state in favor of their religious faiths. If this situation continues to develop, then the tension between religion and Communism will persist until one has disappeared. And if the Soviet Union is any indication, one should not bet against the resiliency of religion.

GOD AND ATHEISM

When asked why, as an atheist, he writes so much about religion, Salmun Rushdie stated that this was quite natural because "atheists are obsessed with God."[78] Marxist-Leninists certainly were. Ironically, their obsession with atheism led them to pay too much attention to God. In the end, they would have been better off leaving God alone and working with the religious culture they were given.

The contemporary social sciences are obsessed with the idea of secularization. The secularization thesis indicates that religion will die out as the world modernizes. But there seems little evidence to support this general hypothesis. Instead, there is lots of evidence to indicate that modern church-state relationships dramatically change over time and alter the composition of religious markets, which, in turn, have dramatic effects on the religiosity of a population. Downward trends in religious affiliations and belief are generally the result of weak religious markets along with the diminishing political import of religious ideas. The Soviet Secularization Experiment set out to weaken religious markets, which it did quite successfully, and diminish the political importance of religion, at which it summarily failed.

The Soviet regime turned religion into a political enemy through its own fixation with destroying the idea of God. For Marxist-Leninists, it was not enough to simply weaken religious markets; they also wanted their citizenry to be convinced atheists. But in this task they had bitten off more than they could chew. First, the idea of God was simply too ubiquitous to erase. The concept of a transcendent God had been used by Russians, Lithuanians, Uzbeks, and other Soviet peoples for centuries to explain their way of life, their conceptions of social justice, their relationships to one another, and their individual purposes and dreams. The historical development of Christianity and Islam throughout the lands that were to become the Soviet Union infused these cultures with the idea of God at every level of social life.

Second, the idea of God was too psychologically ingrained to erase. Ancient symbols of God permeated churches, homes, and public spaces, and God's presence was felt on a daily basis for millions of Soviet citizens. Why the idea of God is so ingrained in the human mind is perhaps a philosophical question that the social sciences can do little to answer. Certainly, the cultural ubiquity of the idea of God explains some of its psychological embeddedness. But in addition to sociological factors, is the idea of a transcendent being instinctual, as some geneticists and biologists currently argue?[79] Does the idea of God best answer certain basic existential questions to which most humans are philosophically inclined? Or, as religious believers purport, does God reveal himself to humans? Although the Soviet Secularization Experiment demonstrated the remarkable extent to which religious belief is ingrained, it is unable to parse out the genetic, philosophical, or mystical sources of religious faith.

Around the world, religious expression is by no means monolithic; it takes numerous forms, and religious commitment varies greatly in its level of intensity. Western Europe, the United States, Communist China, and the Soviet Union all attest to radically differing religious cultures and levels of secularization. But religious faith endures in all of these societies, and the idea of God, in all its multiple forms, is one of most shared beliefs in the entire world.[80] How this belief manifests itself in behavior and commitment is the function of historical, cultural, and political circumstances. Variations in church-state relationships, religious markets, and the historical traditions of a culture best explain current variations in the political and social importance of belief in God.

Even among Marxist-Leninists, the idea of God became an object of fixation, albeit one of manic disgust. By many counts, the Soviet Secularization Experiment crippled organized religion, but the tradition of God, to paraphrase Marx, never ceased to "weigh like a nightmare on the brain of the living" in the Soviet Union.[81] And regardless of whether one considers the idea of God a nightmare or a dream in today's world, God remains a persistent and significant aspect of the human experience.

Notes

INTRODUCTION

1. Richard Dawkins (2006), Samuel Harris (2005), Christopher Hitchens (2007), and Victor Stenger (2007) are a few of the recent best-selling authors who argue passionately that religion is harmful and that atheism is the only rational or scientific response to modernity.

2. Norris and Inglehart's (2004) analysis of religious belief shows that belief in God is very popular around the globe and that there is no statistical differences in belief between agrarian, industrial, and postindustrial societies.

3. Bourdeaux (1981) relates this story of a religious political prisoner as told to him by a Russian clergy member.

4. Conquest 1990 reproduces the prison writings of Nikolai Bukharin.

5. Cantril 1960: 43.

6. As quoted in Freeze 1995: 305.

7. Gregory Freeze (1995: 339) makes a powerful argument that "it was the ritual and especially calendrical reform that galvanized the laity into uncompromising opposition" to the renovationist movement.

8. As quoted in Szczesniak 1959: 49.

9. As quoted in Szczesniak 1959: 191.

10. Patriarch Tikhon died in 1925, leaving a church without its leader. This had severe ramifications for the Russian Orthodox Church for decades to come. See Dickinson 2000b for detailed information concerning Soviet and Russian Orthodox relations in the 1920s.

11. Luukkanen (1994) discusses the motivations and reasons for this change in religious policy in great detail.

12. Peris (1998) provides an extensive look at the League of Militant Atheists and explains the rationale for many of their duties.

13. Binns (1979, 1980) describes the origins of what he calls the Soviet ceremonial system and how it ironically came to undermine its own ideological purposes.

14. Lane 1981: 71.

15. As quoted in Braun 1959: 39.

16. Another unwelcome result of the 1937 census was that it revealed a decline in the population of the Soviet Union, an indication of the demographic damage wrought by Stalin's collectivization project.

17. Young 1997a: 278.

18. See Yakovlev 2002.

19. Ratushinskaya 1987: 51.

20. Dickinson 2000a: 332.

21. Dickinson 2000a: 330.

22. For instance, Orthodox churches in the United States still retain their ethnic identifiers — Russian Orthodox, Armenian Orthodox, and so forth.

23. As quoted in Szczesniak 1959: 66.

24. Dickinson 2000b: 338.

25. Braun 1959: 83.

26. As quoted in Bach 1958: 118.

27. As quoted in Hartfeld 1976: 243.

28. The content of belief under Communist rule is one of the most uncertain topics imaginable. High uncertainty is the result of a systematic restriction of personal expression under Soviet rule. Consequently, Soviet citizens had incentives to hide their real beliefs. Timur Kuran (1995) calls this phenomenon *preference falsification* — "the act of misrepresenting one's genuine want under perceived social pressures." Of course, preference falsification is ubiquitous even in societies where expression is not regulated. Individuals will tend to conceal certain wants or opinions that are socially unpopular. In Soviet society, unpopular opinions were clearly defined and quite broad in their scope. This resulted in a very narrow range of opinions and expressions that were socially acceptable. Therefore, one would expect that many Soviet citizens pretended to support secularization policies and believe official statements about the incompatibility of religion and science in order to avoid social and legal sanctions.

But preference falsification is difficult to prove. Are individuals saying something because they think it is appropriate, or are they expressing their true beliefs? Kuran argues that the best time to uncover instances of preference falsification is when a population radically alters its opinions in response to the lifting of restrictions on expression. Based on this indicator, there is substantial evidence of widespread preference falsification among the Soviet population. Those who defected to the United States often expressed distain for Communism, and after the fall of the Soviet Union, many individuals indicated that they were opposed to the system. Of course, defectors would naturally dislike the country they were leaving, and former Soviet citizens would be foolish to proclaim allegiance to a system that no longer existed.

29. Hartfeld 1976: 248.

30. Kotkin (2001) writes effectively of the general malaise that swept over Soviet society in the final decades. Also, Kowalewski (1980b) argues that during

the Brezhnev era, Communist loyalists began to openly abandon their faith in Marxist-Leninism.

31. Kotkin (2001) argues how perestroika unintentionally and ironically destroyed the dreams of Gorbachev and his followers to create a "true" Communist society.

32. Constructing an accurate picture of life in the Soviet Union is highly problematic. There are good reasons to question even the most basic data sources from the Soviet Union because Soviet leaders purposely circulated misinformation to their own citizens and abroad. For instance, Stalin famously doctored photographs so that the historical record of important events would be altered. Also, Soviet cartographers drew false maps of the Soviet Union so that invading forces or counterrevolutionaries would have trouble locating cities, towns, and landmarks. The result is a confusing array of competing claims about Soviet geography and history. Similarly, Soviet social scientists collected vast amounts of data about the Soviet public, but there is evidence that much of the reported data were falsified to support certain ideological agendas and cover up findings that were embarrassing to leaders. To add to this problem, individuals who opposed the Soviet regime had incentives to falsify or misrepresent life in the Soviet Union to bias opinion against Soviet rule. Therefore, no single source of data accurately captures the reality of Soviet life. While this is theoretically true of any data source, the problem is compounded when information has been systematically skewed to produce an intentionally inaccurate picture of reality.

33. Tucker (1961) and Schumpeter (1943), for instance, have both argued extensively that Marxism is its own religion, with its own eschatology and teleology.

34. Thrower (1992) describes in detail the elements of Soviet Communism that mirror classical and contemporary definitions of civil religion.

35. For instance, Robert Bellah (1975: 33–34) argues that the U.S. Constitution is a part of American civil religion as it is conceived of as a covenant with God.

36. Robbins (1988) explicates a series of research projects in the 1970s and 1980s that reintroduced the idea of brainwashing and the largely inaccurate claim that cults kidnap their members.

37. For instance, Barker (1984) undermined the popular notion that the Moonies kidnapped, confined, or drugged converts and argues that cult recruitment cannot be properly described as "brainwashing."

38. A contemporary example of apparent irrational behavior or religious brainwashing is the recent phenomenon of Muslim suicide bombers. But from the theoretical perspective of rational choice, one could figure out the logic to these extreme acts if one properly understood the social and political circumstances of these activists along with their religious worldview. For instance, blowing oneself up makes some sense if this provides a person with a direct pass into paradise.

39. Filatov (2000: 102) argues, "Russia is still one of the most secularized countries in the world, if not the most secularized."

40. Bourdeaux (2000: 13) maintains that "the revival of all religions. . . . is one of the most interesting, significant, but least-known factors in the recent development of Russian society."

41. As quoted in Walters 2002: 157.
42. Bourdeaux 1981: 31.
43. Bourdeaux 2000: 12.
44. Stark and Finke (2000: 193) most clearly describe this position by finding that "religious demand is very stable over time and that religious change is largely the product of supply-side transformations."
45. Smith 2003: 120.

1. DREAMS OF SECULARIZATION

1. As quoted in Cantril 1960: 27.
2. Martin 1978: 3.
3. See Swatos and Olson 2000 for a detailed look at both sides of the secularization debate.
4. As quoted in Beeson 1982: 94. This quip has also been attributed to other Communist Party elites, so it is unclear whether Yaroslavski coined this particular phrase or was repeating something he heard elsewhere.
5. As quoted in Davidson 1992: 55.
6. Dark and Sussex 1938: 21.
7. Wooten 1992: 16.
8. Comte [1830–42] 1969.
9. Dark and Sussex 1938: 116.
10. Durkheim [1912] 1995: 135.
11. Yaroslavsky 1934.
12. Dark and Sussex 1938: 94.
13. Iannaccone 1990.
14. When referring to hypothetical religious individuals, I will always refer to the individual as a female. This make sense because women tend to more religious than men across cultures. Therefore, it is good to keep in mind that when discussing religious commitment, we are often speaking of women.
15. Yaroslavsky 1934.
16. Hanson (1997: 20) refers to the Soviet conception of time as a complex mixture of "time-denying" and "time-embracing" rhetoric.
17. Stark and Finke 2000: 203.
18. For studies of religious deregulation in Europe, see Stark and Iannaccone 1994; for deregulation in Latin America, see Gill 1998; and for the United States, see Iannaccone, Finke, and Stark 1997.
19. If we assume that human preferences concerning worldviews are diverse, no single religious or political doctrine can naturally attract all members or even the majority of a society unless alternative worldviews are somehow regulated or repressed.
20. Iannaccone 1991.
21. See Warner 1993 for a detailed description of the new theoretical paradigm in the sociology of religion.
22. The religious pluralism hypothesis is most clearly stated and defended in Stark and Finke 2000. This hypothesis has generated a substantial amount of controversy. Generally, the pluralism hypothesis has been used to explain reli-

gious growth in the United States. But Olsen (1999) and Breault (1989) have taken on the pluralism hypothesis in its most sacred territory, namely the United States. They argue that Stark and Finke's analysis of the United States is statistically flawed and that "without these problematic statistical controls, most contemporary and historical analyses of US data reveal a negative association between religious pluralism and church membership" (Olsen 1999: 149).

2. THE ATHEIST CRUSADE

1. Bourdeaux 1965: 124.

2. In the strictest theological sense, "the incorruptibility of remains was neither a canonical requirement for sainthood nor sufficient evidence for canonization; most popular claims of sanctity were rejected by church investigatory commissions. Yet the conviction that the body of a saint does not decay after death continued to be widespread" (Tumarkin 1997: 5).

3. This proclamation appeared in paper *Izvestiya* in January of 1924. As quoted in Thrower 1992: 83.

4. Wynot 2003:19.

5. As quoted in Tumarkin 1997: 166.

6. As quoted in Tumarkin 1997: 175.

7. Gellner 1995.

8. Chirot 1991.

9. McDaniel 1996: 101–102.

10. Marx [1848] 1978: 54.

11. Cantril 1960: 5.

12. Cantril 1960: 5.

13. Conquest 1968: 7.

14. Conquest 1968: 5.

15. *Jugendweihe Guidelines* 1960.

16. Fitzpatrick 1999: 8.

17. Van den Bercken 1989: 123.

18. Yaroslavsky 1934: 59.

19. William Husband (2000: 35) argues, "The advent of a new society was to make the eradication of religion all but automatic. . . . In this belief the party turned out to be greatly mistaken. The Bolsheviks had anticipated post-revolutionary battles involving political parties, classes, nationalities, and interest groups. What they did not foresee was the extent to which competing cultural perceptions and aspirations that emerged around the issue of atheism would bring an important cultural dimension into the equation as well."

20. Durkheim ([1912] 1995: 212) contended that religion is "broader than the idea of gods of spirits and so cannot be defined exclusively in those terms."

21. Robert Bellah and Phillip Hammond famously observed that nationalism or patriotism represents a "civic religion" with its own set of sacred symbols and ceremonies. Nevertheless, Bellah and Hammond (1980: 4) argued that "there is an implicit but quite clear division of function between civil religion and Christianity [in the United States]." Therefore, the concept of a "civil religion" might be more concisely described as the secular part of a system where certain religious

and secular ideologies coexist peacefully to the extent that politicians and secular leaders utilize generic religious language while various religious organizations express feelings of nationalism.

22. Stark and Finke 2000.
23. Beissinger 1988: 127.
24. Yakovlev 2002: 157.
25. Pospielovsky 1987: 1.
26. Yakovlev 2002: 161.
27. Yakovlev 2002: 156.
28. Pospielovsky 1987: 26.
29. Pospielovsky 1987: 65.
30. Fitzpatrick 1999: 27.
31. Yakovlev 2002: 165.
32. Fletcher 1981: 130.
33. Applebaum 2003: 305.
34. Applebaum 2003: 529.
35. Fletcher 1981: 135.
36. Buss 1987: 148.
37. Buss 1987: 151.
38. Van den Bercken 1989: 136.
39. Powell 1975: 41.
40. Buss 1987: 47.
41. Epstein 1995: 181.
42. Yakovlev 2002: 158.
43. Peris 1998: 85.
44. Bourdeaux 1981: 96.
45. Shahrani 1995: 278.
46. Bennigsen and Broxup 1983: 48.
47. Rashid 2001: 47.
48. Keller 2001a: 230.
49. Berlin 1996: 119.
50. Kolarz 1961: 11.
51. Peris 1998: 85.
52. Powell 1975: 47; Bociurkiw 1971: 51.
53. Yaroslavsky 1934: 48.
54. Kolarz 1961: 20.
55. Peris 1998: 94.
56. Van den Bercken 1989: 143.
57. Bourdeaux 1965: 107.
58. Bociurkiw and Strong 1975: 153.
59. Van den Bercken 1989: 138.
60. Vignieri 1965: 227.
61. Vardys 1978: 114.
62. As quoted in Anderson 1944: 93–95.
63. Binns 1979: 594.
64. Binns 1979: 595.
65. Binns (1979: 588) notes that the Orthodox Church never accepted the

new calendar, which put the church "out of step with the ordinary working life and caused confusion over its festival dates."

66. Pospielovsky 1987: 59.

67. Stehle 1965: 76.

68. Binns 1979: 590.

69. Peris 1998: 88.

70. Binns 1979: 590.

71. Lane 1981: 84.

72. Peris 1998: 86.

73. Binns 1979: 598.

74. Binns 1979: 598.

75. Kaariainen 1998: 34.

76. Kolarz 1961: 24.

77. Kotkin 1995: 227.

78. Peris 1998: 93.

79. Dawkins 2006: 278.

80. Stephen Hanson (1997) offers an intriguing look at how Soviet leadership manipulated conceptions of time during the Soviet era. Hanson employs a Weberian theory of social time to show how Soviet institutions were constricted by redefined and reconceptualized ideas of time.

81. Muravchik 2002: 60.

82. Muravchik 2002: 61.

83. Stark and Finke 2000: 142.

84. Carroll 2005.

85. Stark 2001.

86. Stark 2001: 33.

87. Kaariainen 1998: 35.

88. Berlin 1996: 119.

89. Gellner 1995: 1.

90. Šik 1976: 402.

91. Stalin 1940: 54.

92. Lane 1981: 21.

3. SHUTTING OFF RELIGIOUS SUPPLY

1. Applebaum 2003: 244.

2. Bourdeaux 1981: 88.

3. Chaves and Cann 1992; Finke and Stark 1992; Gill 1998; Iannaccone 1991; Stark and Iannaccone 1994; Stark and McCann 1993.

4. Studies of religious deregulation in Europe (Stark and Iannaccone 1994), Latin America (Gill 1998), and the United States (Iannaccone, Finke, and Stark 1997) show that reductions in state regulatory policies will lead to the introduction of new religious doctrines and the growth of minority religions. Based on these findings, Stark and Finke (2000: 284) conclude, "The capacity of a single religious firm to monopolize a religious economy depends upon the degree to which the state uses coercive force to regulate the religious economy."

5. Gill 1998: 68.

6. Iannaccone 2002.

7. Tobias 1956: 12.

8. Dickinson 2000b: 331.

9. For instance, longitudinal changes in religious memberships may be partially due to migration patterns. This is certainly the case for the republics of Central Asia.

10. This seems especially plausible when one considers the weaknesses of monopoly religions. Areas with a very high percentage of population in one religious groups probably also contained a large number of people who were weakly attached to the religion. In other words, it is unlikely that 90 percent of a population will be actively committed to one religion. Therefore, we might expect more substantial drops in religious memberships in regions with more powerful religious monopolies.

11. Bennigsen and Wimbush 1985; Azrael and Payin 1996.

12. McDaniel 1996: 14.

13. Buss 1987: 17.

14. Ramet 1998: 229.

15. Fletcher 1965: 123.

16. Fitzpatrick 1999: 128.

17. Ramet 1998: 230.

18. Davis 1995: 115.

19. Fletcher 1965: 6.

20. Fletcher 1965: 119.

21. Davis 1995: 127.

22. Iannaccone 2002.

23. Iannaccone 2002.

24. Barrett, Kurian, and Johnson 2001.

25. Corley 1996.

26. See Barrett, Kurian, and Johnson 2001.

27. Barrett, Kurian, and Johnson 2001.

28. Helby 1976: 90.

29. Durasoff 1969: 79.

30. Sawatsky 1984.

31. Helby 1976: 109.

32. Barmenkov 1983: 112.

33. Durasoff 1969: 219.

34. This is not to say that some Orthodox clergy and members did not actively resist Communist oppression. But these instances really demonstrate the resolve of individual actors more than the steadfastness of the church institution.

35. Jurgela 1976: 284.

36. Vardys 1978: 125.

37. Jurgela 1976: 293.

38. Tobias 1956; Ramet 1998.

39. Tobias 1956: 308.

40. Bourdeaux 1979: 4.

41. "Only donations by the faithful supported [the Roman Catholic Church], but even these had to decrease as the country was pauperized by the introduction

of the ruble at par value with the litas [the Lithuanian currency], though its actual purchasing power was only 25 percent of the latter" (Vignieri 1965: 217).

42. Bourdeaux 1979: 5.

43. Oleszczuk 1988: 49.

44. *First Book of Demographics for the Republics of the Former Soviet Union* 1992; Remeikis 1980: 128.

45. Remeikis 1980: 128.

46. These numbers can be found in Sipaviciene 1997: 17 and also in Tobias 1956: 301. Germany invaded the Soviet Union approximately a year after the Soviets first occupied Lithuania. Lithuanians took advantage of the wartime weakening of Soviet rule to declare their independence, which was short-lived as Germans reoccupied the region and surprisingly maintained some of the Soviets' anti-Catholic policies (see Bourdeaux 1979: 23–27). The subsequent war and postwar years dramatically altered the ethnic and religious makeup of Lithuania.

47. Sipaviciene 1997: 17.

48. Sipaviciene 1997: 19.

49. Vignieri 1965: 225.

50. Vardys 1978: 114.

51. Remeikis 1980: 123.

52. Solchanyk (1985) argues that while Poland's influence on Lithuanian dissent is difficult to measure, Lithuanian nationals maintained that it was invaluable.

53. The church in Poland was very successful in combating Communism because it enjoyed several advantages that were unavailable to Lithuanian Catholics. First, the historic link between Polish nationalism and Roman Catholicism was greatly strengthened during and immediately following World War II. Simply put, Poland became a "nearly homogeneous Catholic nation through the murder and expulsion of Jews [due to the Nazi invasion] and through ethnic migrations resulting from Stalin's movement of the Polish state westward in the late 1940s." Second, because the Roman Catholic Church in Poland had a long history of coping with and surviving various political systems, it "relied for additional church income on 'voluntary' (that is, customary) donations from parishioners" and not simply a system of state subsidies. In fact, Poland was the only Roman Catholic country in Eastern European without a church tax prior to Communist rule. Under Communism, it continued to be entirely dependent on voluntary contributions from its congregation. Surprisingly, Stehle reported, even "the income of the average priest was more than that of a minister of state" in Poland in the 1960s. Therefore, Polish Communists faced a formidable opponent in the Roman Catholic Church.

54. Bociurkiw and Strong 1975: 215.

55. Johnston 1994: 21.

56. Boiter 1980: 70.

57. Armstrong 2002: 158.

58. Armstrong 2002: 169–70.

59. Ro'I 1984: 79; Rywkin 1982: 70.

60. Rashid 1994: 56. Because Islam was used as an ethnic identifier, the measurement of actual practicing Muslims becomes difficult. In addition, the number

of Muslims in Central Asia and the Soviet Union depends on how researchers define *Muslim,* and census reports differ immensely during the Soviet era, with some reports admitting that their count of Muslims is a rough estimate. The growth of intermarriage following the great in-migration of non-Muslims into Central Asia further complicates matters. By 1967, around 10 percent of marriages in Central Asia were of people with mixed religious backgrounds. Whether offspring from mixed marriages were considered Muslim by researchers is unclear.

61. Brown 2000: 31.

62. Eliade 1985: 77.

63. Brown 2000: 46.

64. "From around 850 . . . power came to be divided between the Sultan, who managed military affairs and enforced law and order, and the ulama who managed social, family and commercial affairs. The religio-political project of the Prophet and early Imams was replaced, among Sunnis and Imami Shi'ites, by political quietism" (Black 2001: 349). Consequently, the ulema often deferred new and pressing political decisions to ruling sultans, leading to a "political quietism" among Islamic clerics. In fact, "the weight of Muslim tradition was on the side of political submission. . . . Caliph Umar, often singled out in the hadith literature as the epitome of early Arab boldness, is related to have admonished, 'If he (the ruler) oppresses you, be patient; if he dispossesses you, be patient.' There are also numerous hadiths of this sort attributed to Muhammad" (Brown 2000: 55).

65. Black 2001: 279.

66. Brown 2000: 49.

67. Conflict between Muslims and czarist Russia occurred on occasion, but their relationship remained relatively peaceful. For the most part, many of the more conservative Islamic leaders showed themselves to be allies of czarist Russia, and in return the czar did not feel threatened by Islamic institutions (Akiner 1996). In part, this relationship stemmed from the fact that imperial Russia rarely infringed on the daily lives of Muslims. Of course, Muslims were subject to attempts by Christian proselytizers to convert them, but they freely maintained Islamic schools and institutions without interference from czarist officials. Occasional conflicts concerned the ubiquitous problem of rising taxes (Wheeler 1969). See also Khalid 2007: 56.

68. Taheri 1989: 142.

69. Wilhelm 1971: 158.

70. Khalid 2007: 41.

71. Badan 2001: 183.

72. Keller 2001a: 318.

73. Bennigsen and Lemercier-Quelquejay 1967: 114.

74. Wilhelm 1971: 258.

75. Trofimov 1995: 15.

76. Wilhelm 1971: 265.

77. D'Encausse 1970: 239.

78. Haghayeghi 1995: 38.

79. D'Encausse 1970: 14.

80. Bethmann 1958: 16.

81. Glenn 1999: 94.

82. Bennigsen and Lemercier-Quelquejay 1967: 145.
83. Brown 2000: 55.
84. Kamp 2006: 231.
85. Northrop 2004: 348; and Kamp 2006: 230.
86. Bennigsen and Lemercier-Quelquejay 1967: 186.
87. Bennigsen and Lemercier-Quelquejay 1967: 194.
88. Glenn 1999: 97
89. Haghayeghi 1995: 38.
90. For an introduction to the Soviet treatment of Jews, see Shaffer 1974; Altshuler 1987; Freedman 1984; Miller 1984; and Schwartz 1951.
91. Altshuler 1987: 10.
92. Altshuler 1987: 56.
93. Schumacher 1977: 52.
94. Shahrani 1995: 276.
95. Bourdeaux 1981: 90.

4. HUNTING FOR RELIGIOUS DEMAND

1. Kolarz 1961: 96.
2. Kolarz 1961: 20.
3. Furman and Kaariainan 2003.
4. Froese and Pfaff 2001.
5. Khalid 2007: 129.
6. Muller 1992.
7. Niyazi 1998: 42; D'Encausse 1970.
8. Rashid 2001: 23.
9. Bennigsen and Lemercier-Quelquejay 1967: 182.
10. Haghayeghi 1995: 80.
11. Nyang 2002: 103.
12. Akiner 1996: 115.
13. Bennigsen 1981: 98.
14. Akiner 1996: 115.
15. Trofimov 1995: 15.
16. Von Stackelberg 1967: 95.
17. Trofimov 1995: 15.
18. Stark 2001: 178.
19. Iannaccone 1990: 229.
20. Iannaccone 1990: 229.
21. Peris 1998: 91.
22. Powell 1975: 80.
23. Binns 1980: 176.
24. Yurchak 2006: 16.
25. Wanner 1998: 165.
26. Wanner 1998: 167.
27. Yurchak 2006: 295.
28. Poliakov 1992: 102.
29. Anderson 1994: 384.

30. Keller 2001b.
31. Poliakov 1992: 107.
32. Poliakov 1992: 107.
33. Glenn 1999: 92.
34. Akiner 1996: 114.
35. Keller 2001a: 328.
36. Bennigsen and Lemercier-Quelquejay 1967: 150.
37. Atheist recruitment occurred despite some formidable obstacles in Central Asia. First, atheist proselytizers encountered something new in the recruitment of Muslim people — they were accustomed to attempts of Christian missionaries to convert them to a new faith. In Eastern Europe, Roman Catholics and Orthodox believers had never really encountered active attempts to convert them to a different faith. These churches enjoyed a monopoly influence over their populations and were assisted by the state in dispelling religious competitors. While Islam was certainly a majority religion in Central Asia, Muslims had encountered Russian missionaries and were familiar with their tactics. Ironically, Christian proselytism had prepared Muslims to view atheists as simply a different breed of foreign missionary. The head of the League of Militant Atheists, Yaroslavsky, was aware of this phenomenon and saw it as a potential problem for atheist recruitment.
38. Wanner 1998: 167.
39. Binns 1980: 183.
40. Binns 1980: 11.
41. Peris 1998.
42. Corley 1996: 11; Fletcher 1981: 211.
43. Pospielovsky 1987: 65.
44. Barrett, Kurian, and Johnson 2001.
45. Pospielovsky 1987: 65.
46. In addition, individuals may have overreported religious memberships and belief prior to Communist rule. Numerous studies of societies containing majority religious groups that are heavily supported by the state show that religious commitment tends to be weak (see Stark and Finke 2000). Prior to Communist rule, most of the regions of the Soviet Union contained a single dominant religious group (usually the Orthodox Church) enjoying strong support from the state. Therefore, the religious commitment of many Soviet citizens may have been quite weak prior to Communism; in turn, some individuals were probably happy to indicate their long-standing disbelief in a new environment where disbelief was encouraged. And later in this chapter, I present data which indicates that church attendance was quite weak in many countries prior to Communism (see figure 2).
47. Pospielovsky 1987: 26.
48. Pospielovsky 1987: 65.
49. Conquest 1990; Yakovlev 2002.
50. Yakovlev 2002: 161.
51. Tismaneff 1942: 97.
52. Luukkanen 1997: 161.
53. Powell 1975: 48.

54. Barmenkov 1983: 131.
55. Barrett, Kurian, and Johnson 1980.
56. Kotkin 1995: 228.
57. Kuran 1995.
58. Greeley 2003: 105.
59. Greeley 2003: 100.
60. Yurchak 2006: 228.
61. I have excluded Chinese citizens from the analysis — with the Chinese included, atheists constitute around 3 percent of the world population. The China case is problematic to any analysis of world religion for two reasons. First, the Chinese government is openly hostile to religious practice, and therefore citizens have major incentives to falsify their preferences. Second, Chinese constitute a major portion of the world population. Therefore, the negative impact of China's antireligious policies greatly biases world population percentages.
62. As quoted in Muravchik 2002: 340.
63. Stark 1996a: 18.
64. Gill and Lundsgaard 2004.
65. Stark and Finke 2000: 135.
66. Peris 1998: 101.
67. Young 1997a: 132.
68. Yaroslavsky 1934: 48.
69. Bourdeaux 1965: 125.
70. Bociurkiw and Strong 1975: 157.
71. Tismaneff 1942: 103.
72. Peris 1998: 175.
73. Van den Bercken 1989: 146.
74. Stark and Finke 2000: 88, italics in original.
75. Fitzpatrick 1999: 8.
76. Eliade [1957] 1987: 206, italics in original.
77. Miner 2003.
78. As quoted in Tismaneanu 1988: 13.
79. Berlin 2004: 143.
80. Conquest 1990: 118.
81. Buruma 2005: 37.
82. Berger 1967.
83. Marx 1959: 263.
84. Berger 1967: 113.
85. Sherkat 1997: 68.
86. Stark 1996b: 144.
87. Mann 1986: 23.
88. Stark and Bainbridge 1997: 162.
89. Stark and Bainbridge 1997: 162.

5. AFTER ATHEISM

1. There is some controversy concerning the extent of the religious revival that has occurred in the former Soviet Union. Certain scholars, such as Michael

Bourdeaux (2000), call the religious growth in Russia an unqualified revival, others like Philip Walters (2002: 157) refer to the religious change as one of "restoration" and "innovation," while Sergei Filatov (2000:102) argues that "the successes of the Orthodox, of Protestantism, Catholicism, Islam and the new religious movements are much more modest than hoped for in the late 1980s."

2. Wimer 1986: 43.

3. Greeley 2003: 108.

4. Berlin 2004: 149.

5. Corley 1996.

6. Filatov 1999: 165.

7. Filatov 1999: 175.

8. Tishkov 1997: 116.

9. Lewis 1999: 96.

10. Finke and Stark 1992; Stark and Bainbridge 1987; Stark and Finke 2000.

11. Kirill 1999: 71.

12. Filatov 1999: 164.

13. Rywkin 1982: 89.

14. Khalid 2007: 104.

15. Khalid 2007: 89.

16. Akiner 1996: 106.

17. Bennigsen and Broxup 1983: 27.

18. Shahrani 1995: 285.

19. Atkin 1995: 250.

20. Badan 2001: 184.

21. As quoted in Pungur 1992: 122.

22. Dunlop 1995: 29.

23. As quoted in Anderson 1994: 184.

24. Anderson 1994; Borowik and Babinski 1997; Bourdeaux 2000; Greeley 1994; Greeley 2003; Ramet 1998; Swatos 1994.

25. The *World Christian Encyclopedia* provides affiliation data for all the world's religions and for all the former states of the Soviet Union. "It does this by setting out summaries of the survey data produced every year by a vast decentralized investigation quietly undertaken by churches and religious workers across the world" (Barrett, Kurian, and Johnson 2000: viii).

26. Bourdeaux 2000; Ramet 1998.

27. Brutal Turkish attacks on Armenia between 1894 and 1915 created an Armenian diaspora of many wealthy patrons and leaders of the Armenian Apostolic Church (Marshall 2000: 58). Although the Armenian Apostolic Church is profoundly tied to Armenian national identity and history, it initially was decimated by the genocidal attacks of the Turks prior to Soviet control. With the fall of Communism, the Armenian Apostolic Church has reestablished itself as the state church of Armenia. The unprecedented religious revival in Armenia reflects the return of a state church that was essentially exiled for the past century.

28. Bruce 1999b: 72.

29. Using the Herfindahl Index (see table 11) to measure religious pluralism is potentially problematic; see Voas, Crockett, and Olsen 2002 for a detailed discussion of methodological problems with the Herfindahl Index. In addition, data

used to produce my pluralism measure does not distinguish between competing branches of Islam; consequently, religious pluralism in Islamic regions may be underreported.

30. The correlation between religious pluralism and religious growth is −0.192. Not only is the finding nonsignificant, it is in the wrong direction.

31. Tishkov 1997: 134.

32. Elliot and Corrado 1997: 338.

33. Catherine Wanner (1998) provides an excellent overview of the reemergence of religious national identities in post-Soviet Ukraine. Zoe Knox (2005) similarly explains how religious national identities developed in post-Soviet Russia.

34. Davis 1995: 222.

35. Anderson 1994: 182.

36. Ellis 1996:124.

37. As quoted in Billington 1999: 55.

38. Billington 1999: 55.

39. Ellis 1996: 148.

40. Pospielovsky 1987: 55.

41. Bourdeaux 1995: 118.

42. Walters 1999: 48.

43. Ro'I 1984: 20.

44. Walters 1999: 31.

45. Witte and Bourdeaux 1999: 12.

46. Broun 1998: 258–59.

47. *Forum 18* 2004.

48. Nevertheless, scholars of religion in Russia have warned, "The Orthodox, for their part, need to recognize that religious pluralism is unavoidable in a free society, and that the renewal of state-enforced Orthodox privilege would only sap its spiritual vitality" (Elliot and Corrado 1997: 357).

49. Knox 2005: 191.

50. Rashid 2001: 45.

51. Atkin 1995: 256.

52. Shahrani 1995: 288.

53. Marshall 2000: 185.

54. Gvosdev 2001: 86.

55. Marshall 2000: 304.

56. Haghayeghi 1995: 71.

57. The lack of political change "has been most noticeable in Turkmenistan, Tajikistan, and Uzbekistan, and less apparent in Kazakhstan and Kyrgyzstan. The root of the problem lies in the fact that contrary to postcolonial governments, the Central Asian independence did not alter, to any significant degree, the republican power structure, leaving in tact a Communist personnel whose authority is being slowly challenged by the very nature of the reforms they are obligated to undertake" (Haghayeghi 1995: 133).

58. Glenn 1999: 131.

59. Rashid 2001: 55.

60. Atkin 1995: 259.

61. Atkin 1995: 253.
62. The correlation between levels of regulation and levels of pluralism for all the countries in my sample is -.671 and significant at the .01 level.
63. The correlation between regulation and the growth of majority religions is strong (.588) and significant at the 0.05 level. This finding is substantial considering the small size of the sample (n = 12). Lithuania has been removed from the analysis due to its extreme exceptionalism. The Lithuanian Roman Catholic is a clear exception to the trend explained above; it was able to recruit a high percentage of the population (19 percent) without any substantial restrictions on religious competitors. That said, the Roman Catholic Church of Lithuania receives some assistance from the new Lithuanian government. "It enjoys the full range of [advantages] found in the traditional Roman Catholic societies of Western Europe: theological seminaries, monastic orders, army chaplains, the right to teach religions in schools, radio and TV studios, and the regular airing of programs and a full range of publications" (Marshall 2000: 205). But while the Lithuanian Roman Catholic Church certainly enjoys these advantages over its religious competitors, official religious laws are more tolerant than in most other former Soviet republics.
64. Kirill 1999: 70.
65. Stark and Iannaccone 1994.

6. THE SOCIAL AND POLITICAL RESILIENCE OF GOD

1. As quoted in Yurchak 2006: 11.
2. Cantril 1960: 99.
3. As quoted in Nicholi 2002: 9.
4. Hick 1983: 31.
5. Stark and Finke 2000: 1.
6. Sherkat and Ellison 1999.
7. Marx [1848] 1978: 145.
8. See Gorski 2000 for a discussion of how classical theorists differed in their explanations of secularization.
9. Stark and Bainbridge 1987; Stark and Iannaccone 1994; Warner 1993.
10. Chaves and Gorski 2001; Olsen 1999; and Stark and Iannaccone 1994.
11. Miner 2003: 318.
12. Levine 1981: 9.
13. Sorokin [1943] 1998: 109–10.
14. De Tocqueville [1832] 1990.
15. Bellah 1975.
16. See McDaniel 1996 for a discussion on the history of the "Russian idea."
17. Hanson 1997.
18. Brooks 2000: 79.
19. Mikhail Epstein (1995) traces the meaning and absurdity of Soviet rhetoric in his book *After the Future*.
20. Timothy Ash is highly regarded for predicting the fall of Communism before the fact, and Randall Collins also claims to have made a similar prediction. See Chirot 1999.

21. Eisenstadt 1999.

22. Chirot 1999.

23. Chirot 1999: 35.

24. These explanations provide both external and internal explanations, with the latter further subdivided into political-economic or cultural explanations. Daniel Chirot (1991) and Janos Kornai (1992) both stress Soviet Communism's inability to compete with the economic successes of Western Capitalism. Shmuel Noah Eisenstadt (1999) views the political oppression of totalitarian regimes as ultimately unsustainable. And Timothy McDaniel (1996) argues that Communism produced a fragmented and morally destitute culture that finally corroded the social structure.

25. Chirot 1999; Kornai 1992.

26. Gouldner 1976; Wuthnow 1989.

27. Stark and Finke 2000: 137.

28. Pascal 1932: 233.

29. James [1897] 1961: 229.

30. Azzi and Ehrenberg 1975.

31. Kiser and Hechter 1991, 1998.

32. Coleman 2000.

33. Stark and Finke 2000: 83.

34. Stark and Finke 2000; Iannaccone 1991.

35. Hechter 1997: 152.

36. Greeley 2003.

37. Albert Hirschman (1970) categorizes three responses to decline in organizations and states: exit, voice, and loyalty. The exit option refers to instances where individuals simply leave the organization or state; the voice option refers to when individuals protest authority; and the loyalty option refers to when individuals remain steadfast to their prior commitments. Within the context of the Secularization Experiment, both religious institutions and religious believers pondered options of exit, voice, and loyalty.

38. Dawkins 2006: 172.

39. Hamer 2005.

40. Weber 1978.

41. Sherkat 2003.

42. Sherkat and Wilson 1995.

43. Stark and Finke 2000.

44. Norris and Inglehart 2004.

45. Stark and Finke 2000: 114.

46. Stark and Bainbridge 1987; Stark and Iannaccone 1994; Warner 1993.

47. Greeley 2003.

48. Froese and Bader 2007.

49. See Knox 2004.

50. Marsh and Froese 2004.

51. McDaniel 1996: 116.

52. Marx [1852] 1998: 15.

53. Davie 1994.

54. Norris and Inglehart 2004.

55. Norris and Inglehart 2004: 90.

56. Stark and Iannaccone 1994. Barro and McCleary (2005) provide a detailed analysis of which countries in Western Europe contain state churches; their analysis supports the general hypotheses of Stark and Iannaccone.

57. Casanova 2006: 16.

58. Norris and Inglehart 2004.

59. Melton 1996.

60. These statistics are based on the 2004 General Social Survey.

61. See Bellah 1975 and Greeley 1972.

62. As quoted in Goldstein 1999.

63. As quoted in Goldstein 1999.

64. Froese and Bader 2007.

65. Froese and Bader 2007.

66. This finding is indicated by a series of qualitative interviews with Americans conducted at Baylor University concerning how their religious beliefs inform their political attitudes. Results will be publishing in a forthcoming book by Froese and Bader.

67. Woodberry 1996.

68. See Bader, Froese, and Mencken, forthcoming.

69. See Regnerus and Smith 1998.

70. Lu 2004.

71. Aikman 2003.

72. Yang 2006.

73. As quoted in Lambert 2001: 124.

74. Lambert 2001: 125.

75. As quoted in Aikman 2003: 5.

76. Sun 2005.

77. Sun 2005: 249–50.

78. Salman Rushdie, in June 23, 2006, interview with Bill Moyers. See transcript at www.pbs.org/moyers/faithandreason/portraits_rushdie.html.

79. Geneticist Dean Hamer in *The God Gene* (2005) argues that many individuals are genetically predisposed to religion.

80. See Norris and Inglehart's (2004) analysis of world beliefs and values.

81. Marx [1852] 1998: 15.

Bibliography

Aikman, David. 2003. *Jesus in Beijing: How Christianity Is Transforming China and Changing the Global Balance of Power.* Washington, D.C.: Regnery Publishing.

Akiner, Shirin. 1996. "Islam, the State and Ethnicity in Central Asia in Historical Perspective." *Religion, State, and Society* 24(2–3): 91–125.

Alaolmolki, Nozar. 2001. *Life After the Soviet Union: The Newly Independent Republics of the Transcaucasus and Central Asia.* New York: State University of New York Press.

Altshuler, Mordechi. 1987. *Soviet Jewry since the Second World War: Population and Social Structure.* New York: Greenwood Press.

Anderson, John. 1994. *Religion, State and Politics in the Soviet Union and Successor States.* Cambridge, England: Cambridge University Press.

Anderson, Paul. 1944. *People, Church and State in Modern Russia.* London: Student Christian Movement Press.

Applebaum, Anne. 2003. *Gulag: A History.* New York: Doubleday.

Armstrong, Karen. 2002. *Islam: A Short History.* New York: Modern Library.

Atkin, Muriel. 1995. "Islam as Faith, Politics and Bogeyman in Tajikistan." In *The Politics of Religion in Russia and the New States of Eurasia,* ed. Michael Bourdeaux. New York: M. E. Sharpe.

Azrael, Jeremy, and Emil Payin. 1996. *Cooperation and Conflict in the Former Soviet Union: Implications for Migration.* Santa Monica, CA: RAND.

Azzi, Corry, and Ronald Ehrenberg. 1975. "Household Allocation of Time and Church Attendance." *Journal of Political Economy* 83(1): 27–55.

Bach, Marcus. 1958. *God and the Soviets.* New York: Growell.

Badan, Phool. 2001. *Dynamics of Political Development in Central Asia.* New Delhi: Lancers' Books.

Bader, Christopher, and P. Froese. 2005. "Images of God: The Effect of Personal

Theologies on Moral Attitudes, Political Affiliation and Religious Behavior."
Interdisciplinary Journal of Religious Research 1(11): 1–43.

Bader, Christopher, P. Froese, and F. Carson Mencken. Forthcoming. "American
Piety 2005: Content, Methods, and Selected Findings from the Baylor Religion Survey." *Journal for the Scientific Study of Religion*.

Barker, Eileen. 1984. *The Making of a Moonie: Brainwashing or Choice?*
Oxford: Basil Blackwell.

Barmenkov, A. 1983. *Freedom of Conscience in the USSR*. Moscow: Progress
Publishers.

Barrett, David, George Kurian, and Todd Johnson. 1980. *World Christian Encyclopedia*. New York: Oxford University Press.

———. 2001. *World Christian Encyclopedia*. 2nd ed. New York: Oxford University Press.

Barro, Robert, and Rachel McCleary. 2005. "Which Countries Have State Religions?" *Quarterly Journal of Economics* (November): 1331–70.

Bax, Ernest. 1972. *The Religion of Socialism*. Freeport, NY: Books for Libraries
Press.

Beeson, Trevor. 1982. *Discretion and Valour: Religious Conditions in Russia
and Eastern Europe*. Philadelphia: Fortress Press.

Beissinger, Mark R. 1988. *Scientific Management, Socialist Discipline and Soviet
Power*. Cambridge, MA: Harvard University Press.

Bellah, Robert. 1975. *The Broken Covenant: American Civil Religion in Time of
Trial*. New York: Seabury.

Bellah, Robert, and Phillip Hammond. 1980. *Varieties of Civil Religion*. San
Francisco: Harper and Row.

Bennigsen, Alexandre. 1981. "Official Islam and Sufi Brotherhoods in the Soviet
Union Today." In *Islam and Power*, ed. Alexander Cudsi and Ali Dessouki.
London: Croom Helm.

Bennigsen, Alexandre, and Marie Broxup. 1983. *Islamic Threat to the Soviet
State*. London: Croom Helm.

Bennigsen, Alexandre, and Chantal Lemercier-Quelquejay. 1967. *Islam in the
Soviet Union*. New York: Praeger Publishers.

Bennigsen, Alexandre, and S. Enders Wimbush. 1985. *Muslims of the Soviet
Empire*. London: C. Hurst and Company.

Berdyaev, Nicolas. [1931] 1966. *The Russian Revolution*. Ann Arbor: University
of Michigan Press.

Berger, Peter. 1967. *The Sacred Canopy*. New York: Doubleday.

———. 1997. "Epistemological Modesty: An Interview with Peter Berger."
Christian Century, October 29, 972–75, 978.

Berlin, Isaiah. 1996. *The Sense of Reality: Studies in Ideas and the History*. London: Pimlico.

———. 2004. *The Soviet Mind: Russian Culture under Communism*. Washington, D.C.: Brookings Institution Press.

Bethmann, Erich. 1958. *The Fate of Muslims under Soviet Rule*. Washington,
D.C.: American Friends of the Middle East.

Billington, James. 1999. "Orthodox Christianity and the Russian Transformation." In *Proselytism and Orthodoxy in Russia,* ed. John Witte and Michael Bourdeaux. New York: Orbis Books.

Binns, Christopher. 1979. "The Changing Face of Power: Revolution and Accommodation in the Development of the Soviet Ceremonial System: Part I." *Man* 14(4): 585–606.

———. 1980. "The Changing Face of Power: Revolution and Accommodation in the Development of the Soviet Ceremonial System: Part II." *Man* 15(1): 170–87.

Black, Antony. 2001. *The History of Islamic Thought: From the Prophet to the Present.* Edinburgh: Edinburgh University Press.

Bociurkiw, Bohdan. 1971. "Religion and Atheism in Soviet Society." In *Aspects of Religion in the Soviet Union,* ed. Richard Marshall. Chicago: University of Chicago Press.

Bociurkiw, Bohdan, and John Strong. 1975. *Religion and Atheism in the USSR and Eastern Europe.* Toronto: University of Toronto Press.

Boiter, Albert. 1980. *Religion in the Soviet Union.* London: Sage Publications.

Borowik, Irena. 1994. "Religion in Post-Communist Countries." In *Politics and Religion in Central and Eastern Europe,* ed. William H. Swatos. London: Praeger.

———. 1997. "Institutional and Private Religion in Poland, 1990–1994." In *New Religious Phenomena in Central and Eastern Europe,* ed. Irena Borowik and Grzegorz Babinski. Krakow: Zaklad Wydawniczy.

Borowik, Irena, and Grzegorz Babinski. 1997. *New Religious Phenomenon in Central and Eastern Europe.* Krakow: Nomos.

Bourdeaux, Michael. 1965. *Opium of the People: The Christian Religion in the USSR.* London: Faber and Faber.

———. 1979. *Land of Crosses: The Struggle for Religious Freedom in Lithuania, 1938–1978.* Devon: Augustine Publishing Company.

———. 1981. *Risen Indeed: Lessons in Faith from the USSR.* New York: St. Vladimir's Seminary Press.

———. 1995. *The Politics of Religion in Russian and the New States of Eurasia.* New York: M. E. Sharpe.

———. 2000. "Religion Revives in All Its Variety: Russia's Regions Today." *Religion, State, & Society* 28(1): 9–21.

Braun, Leopold. 1959. *Religion in Russia: From Lenin to Khrushchev.* Paterson, NJ: St. Anthony Guild Press.

Breault, K. D. 1989. "New Evidence on Religious Pluralism, Urbanism, and Religious Participation." *ASR* 54: 1048–53.

Brooks, Jeffery. 2000. *Thank You, Comrade Stalin! Soviet Public Culture from Revolution to Cold War.* Princeton, NJ: Princeton University Press.

Broun, Janice. 1998. "New Russian Law Puts Religious Freedom at Threat." *The Month,* July, 255–61.

Brown, Carl L. 2000. *Religion and State: The Muslim Approach to Politics.* New York: Columbia University Press.

Bruce, Steve. 1999a. *Choice and Religion.* Oxford: University Press.

———. 1999b. "Modernization, Religious Diversity and Rational Choice in Eastern Europe." *Religion, State, & Society* 27(4): 265–75.

Bryan, Fanny. 1986. "Anti-Islamic Propaganda: Bezbozhnik, 1925–35." *Central Asian Survey* 5 (1): 29–47.

Budd, Susan. 1977. *Varieties of Unbelief*. London: Heinemann Educational Books.

Buruma, Ian. 2005. "The Indiscreet Change of Tyrrany." *New York Review of Books* 52(8): 37.

Buss, Gerald. 1987. *The Bear's Hug: Religious Belief and the Soviet State*. London: Hodder and Stoughton.

Byrnes, Timothy. 2001. *Transnational Catholicism in Postcommunist Europe*. New York: Rowman and Littlefield Publishers.

Camus, Albert. 1956. *The Rebel*. New York: Vintage Books.

Cantril, Hadley. 1960. *Soviet Leaders and Mastery over Man*. Rahway, NJ: Rutgers University Press.

Carroll, Jon. 2005. *San Francisco Chronicle*, April 8.

Casanova, Jose. 2006. "Rethinking Secularization: A Global Comparative Perspective." *Hedgehog Review* 8(1–2): 17–22.

Chaves, M., and David Cann. 1992. "Regulation, Pluralism, and Religious Market Structure: Explaining Religion's Vitality." *Rationality and Society* 4(3): 272–90.

Chaves, Mark, and Phillip Gorski. 2001. "Religious Pluralism and Religious Participation." *Annual Review of Sociology* 27: 261–81.

Chirot, Daniel. 1991. *The Crisis of Leninism and the Decline of the Left*. Seattle: University of Washington Press.

———. 1999. "What Happened in Eastern Europe in 1989?" In *The Revolutions of 1989*, ed. Vladimir Tismaneanu. New York: Routledge.

Chumachenko, Tatiana. 2002. *Church and State in Soviet Russia: Russian Orthodoxy from World War II to the Khrushchev Years*. New York: M. E. Sharpe.

Coleman, James. 2000. *Foundations of Social Theory*. Cambridge: Harvard University Press.

Collins, Randall. 1998. *The Sociology of Philosophies: A Global Theory of Intellectual Change*. Cambridge, MA: Harvard University Press.

Comte, Auguste. [1830–42] 1969. *Cours de philosophie positive*. Brussels: Culture et Civilisation.

Conquest, Robert. 1968. *Religion in the USSR*. New York: Fredrick A. Praeter.

———. 1990. *The Great Terror: A Reassessment*. Oxford: Oxford University Press.

Corley, Felix. 1996. *Religion in the Soviet Union*. London: Macmillan Press.

Dark, Sidney, and R. S. Sussex. 1938. *The War against God*. New York: Abingdon Press.

Davidson, Nicholas. 1992. "Unbelief and Atheism in Italy, 1500–1700." In *Atheism from the Reformation to the Enlightenment*, ed. Michael Hunter and David Wooton. New York: Oxford University Press.

Davie, Grace. 1994. *Religion in Britain since 1945: Believing without Belonging*. Oxford: Blackwell.

Davis, Nathaniel. 1995. *A Long Walk to Church: A Contemporary History of Russian Orthodoxy*. Oxford: Westview Press.

Dawkins, Richard. 2006. *The God Delusion*. New York: Houghton Mifflin Company.

D'Encausse, Helene Carrere. 1970. "Islam in the Soviet Union: Attempts at Modernization." *Religion, State & Society* 7(2): 14–25.

De Tocqueville, Alexis. [1832] 1990. *Democracy in America*. New York: Vintage Books.

Dickinson, Anna. 2000a. "A Marriage of Convenience? Domestic and Foreign Policy Reasons for the 1943 Soviet Church-State 'Condordat.'" *Religion, State and Society* 28(4): 337–46.

———. 2000b. "Quantifying Religious Oppression: Russian Orthodox Church Closures and Repression of Priests, 1917–41." *Religion, State, and Society* 28(4): 327–35.

DiDomizio, Daniel. 1997. "The Czech Catholic Church: Restoration or Renewal?" *Religion in Eastern Europe* 17(1): 12–16.

Dietrich, Christian, and Dieterich Schwabe, eds. 1994. *Freunde und Feinde: Dokumenten zu den Friedensgebeten in Leipzig zwischen 1981 und dem 9. Oktober 1989*. Leipzig: Evangelische Verlags-Anstalt.

Dobbelaere, Karel. 1999. "Towards an Integrated Perspective of the Process Related to the Descriptive Concept of Secularization." *Sociology of Religion* 60(3): 229–48.

Dostoevsky, Fyodor. [1864] 1960. *The Brothers Karamazov*. New York: Dutton & Co.

Dunlop, John. 1995. "The Russian Orthodox Church as an 'Empire-Saving' Institution." In *The Politics of Religion in Russia and the New States of Eurasia*, ed. Michael Bourdeaux. New York: M. E. Sharpe.

Durasoff, Steve. 1969. *The Russian Protestants: Evangelicals in the Soviet Union, 1944–1964*. Rutherford, NJ: Fairleigh Dickinson University Press.

Durkheim, Emile. [1912] 1995. *The Elementary Forms of Religious Life*. New York: Free Press.

Eisenstadt, Shmuel Noah. 1999. "The Breakdown of Communist Regimes." In *The Revolutions of 1989*, ed. Vladimir Tismaneanu. New York: Routledge.

Eliade, Mircea. [1957] 1987. *The Sacred and the Profane: The Nature of Religion*. New York: Harcourt.

———. 1985. *A History of Religious Ideas*. Vol. 3, *From Muhammad to the Age of Reforms*. Chicago: University of Chicago Press.

Elliot, Mark, and Sharyl Corrado. 1997. "The Protestant Missionary Presence in the Former Soviet Union." *Religion, State & Society* 25(4): 333–51.

Ellis, Geoffrey. 1996. *The Other Revolution: Russian Evangelical Awakenings*. Abilene, TX: A. C. U. Press.

Engelhardt, Klaus, Hermann von Loewenich, and Peter Steinacker, eds. 1997. *Fremde Heimat Kirche: Die dritte EKD-Erhebung über Kirchenmitgliedschaft*. Gütersloh, Germany: EKD.

Epstein, Mikhail. 1995. *After the Future*. Amherst: University of Massachusetts Press.

Filatov, Sergei. 1999. "Sects and New Religious Movements in Post-Soviet Union." In *Proselytism and Orthodox in Russia*, ed. John Witte and Michael Bourdeaux. New York: Orbis Books.

———. 2000. "Protestantism in Postsoviet Russia: An Unacknowledged Triumph." *Religion, State, and Society* 28(1): 93–103.

Filatov, Sergei, and Lyudmila Vorontsova. 2000. "Catholic and Anti-Catholic Traditions in Russia." *Religion, State and Society* 28(1): 69–84.

Findeis, Hagen, Detlef Pollack, and Manuel Schilling. 1994. *Die Entzauberung des Politischen: Was ist aus den politisch alternativen Gruppen der DDR geworden: Interviews mit ehemals führenden Vertretern*. Leipzig: Evangelische Verlagsanstalt.

Finke, Roger, and Rodney Stark. 1992. *The Churching of America, 1776–1990*. New Brunswick, NJ: Rutgers University Press.

First Book of Demographics for the Republics of the Former Soviet Union. 1992. Shady Side, MD: New World Demographics.

Fitzpatrick, Sheila. 1999. *Everyday Stalinism: Ordinary Life in Extraordinary Times: Soviet Russia in the 1930s*. New York: Oxford University Press.

Fletcher, William C. 1965. *A Study in Survival: The Church in Russia, 1927–1943*. New York: Macmillan Company.

———. 1981. *Soviet Believers: The Religious Sector of the Population.* Lawrence, KS: Regents Press.

Forest, Jim. 1990. *Religion in the New Russia: The Impact of Perestroika on the Varieties of Religious Life in the Soviet Union*. New York: Crossroads.

Freedman, Theodore. 1984. *Anti-Semitism in the Soviet Union: Its Roots and Consequences*. New York: Freedom Library Press.

Freeze, Gregory. 1995. "Counter-Reformation in Russian Orthodoxy: Popular Response to Religious Innovation." *Slavic Review* 54(2): 305–339.

———. 1996. "Subversive Piety: Religion and Political Crisis in Late Imperial Russia." *Journal of Modern History* 68(2): 308–350.

Froese, P. 2001. "Hungary for Religion: A Supply-Side Interpretation of the Hungarian Religious Revival." *Journal for the Scientific Study of Religion* 40(2): 251–68.

———. 2005. "Explaining a Religious Anomaly: A Historical Analysis of Secularization in Eastern Germany." *Journal for the Scientific Study of Religion* 44(4): 397–422.

Froese, P., and Christopher Bader. 2007. "God in America: Why Theology Is Not Just the Concern of Philosophers." *Journal for the Scientific Study of Religion*.

Froese, P., and Steven Pfaff. 2001. "Replete and Desolate Markets: Poland, East Germany, and the New Religious Paradigm." *Social Forces* 80(2): 481–507.

Furman, Dmitry, and Kimma Kaariainan. 2003. "Religioznaya stabilizatsiya: Otnosheniya k Religii v Sovremennoi Rossii." *Svobodnaya Mysl* 7: 18–32, 1533.

Geertz, Clifford. 1968. *Islam Observed: Religious Development in Morocco and Indonesia*. Chicago: University of Chicago Press.

Gellner, Ernest. 1995. "Marx's Failure and Mohammed's Triumph." *The New Presence*, March.

General Social Survey [computer file]. Www.norc.uchicago.edu/projects/gensoc.asp.

Gill, Anthony. 1998. *Rendering unto Caesar*. Chicago: University of Chicago Press.

————. n.d. "The Political Origins of Religious Liberty: Initial Sketch of a General Theory." Unpublished manuscript.

Gill, Anthony, and Erik Lundsgaard. 2004. "State Welfare Spending and Religiosity: A Cross-National Analysis." *Rationality and Society* 16(4): 399–436.

Glenn, John. 1999. *The Soviet Legacy in Central Asia.* New York: St. Martin's Press.

Goldman, Marshall. 1968. *The Soviet Economy: Myth and Reality.* Englewood Cliffs, NJ: Prentice Hall.

Goldstein, Laurie. 1999. "White House Seekers Wear Faith on Sleeve and Stump." *New York Times,* 31 August, A1, A16.

Gorski, Philip. 2000. "Historicizing the Secularization Debate: Church, State, and Society in Late Medieval and Early Modern Europe, ca. 1300 to 1700." *American Sociological Review* 65(1): 138–67.

Gouldner, Alvin W. 1976. *The Dialetic of Ideology and Technology.* New York: Seabury Press.

Greeley, Andrew. 1972. *The Denominational Society.* Glenview, IL: Scott, Foresman.

————. 1994. "A Religious Revival in Russia?" *Journal for the Scientific Study of Religion* 33(3): 253–73.

————. 2003. *Religion in Europe at the End of the Second Millennium.* London: Transaction Publishers.

Gvosdev, Nikolas. 2001. "Constitutional Doublethink, Managed Pluralism, and Freedom of Religion." *Religion, State & Society* 29(2): 81–90.

Haghayeghi, Mehrdad. 1995. *Islam and Politics in Central Asia.* New York: St. Martin's Press.

Halik, Thomas. 1995. *Vira a Kulture.* Prague: Zvon.

Hamer, Dean. 2005. *The God Gene: How Faith Is Hardwired into Our Genes.* New York: Anchor Press.

Hanson, Stephen E. 1997. *Time and Revolution: Marxism and the Design of Soviet Institutions.* Chapel Hill: University of North Carolina Press.

Harris, Sam. 2005. *The End of Faith: Religion, Terror, and the Future of Reason.* New York: W. W. Norton.

Hartfeld, Hermann. 1976. *Faith Despite the KGB.* Chappaqua, NY: Christian Herald Books.

Hechter, Michael. 1987. *Principles of Group Solidarity.* Berkeley: University of California Press.

————. 1997. "Religion and Rational Choice Theory." In *Rational Choice Theory and Religion: An Assessment,* ed. Lawrence Young. New York: Routledge.

Hecker, Julius. F. 1933. *Religion and Communism: A Study of Religion and Atheism in Soviet Russia.* Chapman & Hall Ltd.: London.

Helby, J. H. 1976. *Protestants in Russia.* Dublin: Cahill and Co.

Hick, John. 1983. *Philosophy of Religion.* Engelwood Cliffs, NJ: Prentice Hall.

Hirschman, Albert. 1970. *Exit, Voice, and Loyalty: Responses to Decline in Firms, Organizations, and States.* Cambridge, MA: Harvard University Press.

Hitchens, Christopher. 2007. *God Is Not Great: How Religion Poisons Everything.* New York: Twelve.

Hoppenbrouwers, Frans. 1998. "Nationalist Tendencies in the Slovak Roman Catholic Church." *Religion in Eastern Europe* 18(6): 24–45.

Hunter, Michael, and David Wooton. 1992. *Atheism from the Reformation to the Enlightenment.* Oxford: Clarendon Press.

Husband, William. 2000. *Godless Communists.* DeKalb: Northern Illinois University Press.

Iannaccone, Laurence R. 1990. "Religious Practice: A Human Capital Approach." *Journal of the Scientific Study of Religion* 29(3): 297–314.

———. 1991. "The Consequences of Religious Market Structure." *Rationality and Society* 3(2): 156–77.

———. 2002. "Looking Backward: A Century of International Religion Statistics." Paper presented at 2002 meetings of the Society for the Scientific Study of Religion, www.economicsofreligion.com, accessed September 2002.

Iannaccone, Laurence R., Roger Finke, and Rodney Stark. 1997. "Deregulating Religion: The Economics of Church and State." *Economic Inquiry* 15: 350–64.

Ilyan, Ivan. 1993. *Sochinenia v dvukh domakh.* Moscow: Medium.

International Social Survey Program [computer file]. 1991. Inter-university Consortium for Political and Social Research.

James, William. [1897] 1961. *The Varieties of Religious Experience: A Study of Human Nature.* New York: Collier.

Johnston, Hank. 1994. "Religio-nationalist Subcultures under Communists: Comparisons from the Baltics, Transcaucasia, and Ukraine." In *Politics and Religion in Central and Eastern Europe,* ed. William Swatos. London: Praeger.

Jugendweihe Guidelines. 1960. Berlin: Zentral Auschuss fur Jugendweihe in der DDR.

Jurgela, Constantine R. 1976. *Lithuania: The Outpost of Freedom.* St. Petersburg, FL: Valkyrie Press.

Kaariainen, Kimmo. 1989. *Discussion on Scientific Atheism as a Soviet Science.* Helsinki: Suomalainen Tiedeakatemia.

———. 1998. *Religion in Russia after the Collapse of Communism.* Lewiston, NY: Edwin Mellen Press.

Kagarlitskii, Boris. 2000. *Restavratsia v Rossii.* Moscow: Editorials URSS.

Kamp, Marianne. 2006. *The New Women in Uzbekistan: Islam, Modernity, and Unveiling under Communism.* Seattle: University of Washington Press.

Kaplan, Karel. 1986. "Church and State in Czechoslovakia from 1948 to 1956: Part I." *Religions in Communist Lands* 14(1): 69–71.

Kazintev, Aleksandr. 2004. *Na Chto My Promeniali SSSR?: Simuliakr, ili Stekolnoe Tsartvo.* Moscow: Auza Eksmo.

Keller, Shoshana. 2001a. "Conversion to the New Faith: Marxism-Leninism and Muslims in the Soviet Empire." In *Of Religion and Empire,* ed. Robert Geraci and Michael Khodarkovsky. Ithaca, NY: Cornell University Press.

———. 2001b. *To Moscow, Not Mecca: The Soviet Campaign against Islam in Central Asia, 1917–1941.* London: Praeger.

Khalid, Adeeb. 2007. *Islam after Communism: Religion and Politics in Central Asia.* Berkeley: University of California Press.

Kirill, Metropolitan of Smolensk and Kaliningrad. 1999. "Gospel and Culture."

In *Proselytism and Orthodox in Russia,* ed. John Witte and Michael Bourdeaux. New York: Orbis Books.

Kiser, Edgar, and Michael Hechter. 1991. "The Role of General Theory in Comparative-Historical Sociology." *AJS* 97(1): 1–30.

———. 1998. "The Debate on Historical Sociology: Rational Choice Theory and Its Critics." *AJS* 104(3): 785–91.

Knox, Zoe. 2004. "Postsoviet Challenges to the Moscow Patriarchate, 1991–2001." *Religion, State, and Society* 32(2): 87–113.

———. 2005. *Russian Society and the Orthodox Church: Religion in Russia after Communism.* New York: Routledge.

Kolarz, Walter. 1961. *Religion in the Soviet Union.* New York: St. Martin's Press.

Kornai, Janos. 1992. *The Socialist System: The Political Economy of Communism.* Princeton, NJ: Princeton University Press.

Kostyrchenko, Gennadi. 1995. *Out of the Red Shadows: Anti-Semitism in Stalin's Russia.* Amherst, NY: Prometheus Books.

Kotkin, Stephen. 1995. *Magnetic Mountain: Stalinism as a Civilization.* Berkeley: University of California Press.

———. 2001. *Armageddon Averted: The Soviet Collapse, 1970–2000.* New York: Oxford University Press.

Kowalewski, David. 1980a. "Protest for Religious Rights in the USSR: Characteristics and Consequences." *Russian Review* 39(4): 426–41.

———. 1980b. "Religious Belief in the Brezhnev Era: Renaissance, Resistance and Realpolitik." *Journal for the Scientific Study of Religion* 19(3): 280–92.

Kraut, Benny. 1979. *From Reform Judaism to Ethical Culture: The Religious Evolution of Felix Adler.* Cincinnati: Hebrew Union College Press.

Kuhn, Thomas. [1962] 1996. *The Structure of Scientific Revolutions.* Chicago: University of Chicago Press.

Kuran, Timur. 1995. *Private Truths, Public Lies: The Social Consequences of Preference Falsification.* Cambridge, MA: Harvard University Press.

Lambert, Tony. 2001. "The Present Religious Policy of the Chinese Communist Party." *Religion, State, and Society* 29(2): 121–29.

Lane, Christel. 1981. *The Rites of Rulers: Ritual in Industrial Society — the Soviet Case.* Cambridge, England: Cambridge University Press.

Lechner, F. J. 1989. "Catholicism and Social Change in the Netherlands: A Case of Radical Secularization?" *Journal for the Scientific Study of Religion* 28(3): 136–47.

Levin, Nora. 1988. *The Jews in the Soviet Union since 1917: Paradox of Survival.* Vols. 1 and 2. New York: New York University Press.

Levine, Daniel. 1981. *Religion and Politics in Latin America: The Catholic Church in Venezuela and Columbia.* Princeton, NJ: Princeton University Press.

Lewis, David. 1999. *After Atheism: Religion and Ethnicity in Russia and Central Asia.* New York: St. Martin's Press.

Lu, Yunfeng. 2004. "The Unintended Consequences of Religious Suppression: Understanding the Growth of Suppressed Religions." Paper presented at the October 22 meeting of the Association for the Study of Religion, Economics, and Culture, Rochester, NY.

Luukkanen, Arto. 1994. *The Party of Unbelief*. Helsinki: SHS.
————. 1997. *The Religious Policy of the Stalinist State*. Helsinki: SHS.
Luxmoore, Jonathan. 1997. "Eastern Europe 1996: A Review of Religious Life in Albania, Bulgaria, Romania, Hungary, Slovakia, the Czech Republic, and Poland." *Religion, State, and Society* 25(1): 89–101.
————. 1999. "The Catholic Church and Communism, 1789–1989." *Religion, State and Society* 27(3–4): 310–329.
Luxmoore, Jonathan, and Jolanta Babiuch. 1992. "Truth Prevails: The Catholic Contribution to Czech Thought and Culture." *Religion, State, and Society* 20(1): 101–17.
Machiavelli, Niccolò. 1984. *The Discourses*. New York: Penguin Classics.
Mann, Michael. 1986. *The Sources of Social Power*. Vol. 1. New York: Cambridge University Press.
Marsh, Christopher, and P. Froese. 2004. "The State of Freedom in Russia: A Regional Analysis of Freedom of Religion, Media, and Markets." *Religion, State, and Society* 32(2): 137–49.
Marshall, Paul. 2000. *Religious Freedom in the World: A Global Report on Freedom and Persecution*. Nashville: Broadman and Holman.
Marshall, Richard. 1971. *Aspects of Religion in the Soviet Union, 1917–1967*. Chicago: University of Chicago Press.
Martin, David. 1969. *The Religious and the Secular*. New York: Schocken Books.
————. 1978. *A General Theory of Secularization*. New York: Harper and Row.
Marx, Karl. [1848] 1978. *The Marx-Engels Reader*. Ed. Robert Tucker. New York: W. W. Norton.
————. [1852] 1998. *The 18th Brumaire of Louis Bonaparte*. New York: International Publishers.
————. 1959. *Marx and Engels: Basic Writings on Politics and Philosophy*. Garden City, NY: Doubleday Anchor Books.
McAdam, Doug. 1982. *Political Process and the Development of Black Insurgency, 1930–1970*. Chicago: University of Chicago Press.
McDaniel, Tim. 1996. *The Agony of the Russian Idea*. Princeton, NJ: Princeton University Press.
McLeod, Hugh. 2000. *Secularization in Western Europe, 1848–1914*. New York: St. Martin's Press.
Meadows, Pam. 1995. "Missionaries to the Former Soviet Union and East Central Europe: The Twenty Largest Sending Agencies." *East-West Church Ministry Report* 3(2): 10.
Melton, J. Gordon. 1996. *Encyclopedia of American Religions*. Detroit: Gale Press.
Miller, Jack. 1984. *Jews in Soviet Culture*. London: Transaction Books.
Miner, Steven Merritt. 2003. *Stalin's Holy War: Religion, Nationalism, and Alliance Politics, 1941–1945*. Chapel Hill: University of North Carolina Press.
Mirsky, Georgiy. 1997. *On Ruins of Europe: Ethnicity and Nationalism in the Former Soviet Union*. London: Greenwood Press.
Morris, Aldon D. 1984. *The Origins of the Civil Rights Movement: Black Communities Organizing for Change*. New York: Free Press.

Muller, Tilmann. 1992. "Secret Priests." *World Press Review* 39(4): 33.

Munting, Roger. 1982. *The Economic Development of the USSR.* London: Croom Helm.

Muravchik, Joshua. 2002. *Heaven on Earth: The Rise and Fall of Socialism.* San Francisco: Encounter Books.

Nelson, Robert. 2001. *Economics as Religion.* University Park: Pennsylvania State University Press.

Nemec, Ludvik, 1955. *Church and State in Czechoslovakia.* New York: Vantage Press.

Nicholi, Armand M. 2002. *The Question of God: C. S. Lewis and Sigmund Freud Debate God, Love, Sex, and the Meaning of Life.* New York: Free Press.

Niyazi, Aziz. 1998. "Islam in Tajikistan: Tradition and Modernity." *Religion, State and Society* 26(1): 39–48.

Norris, Pippa, and Ronald Inglehart. 2004. *Sacred and Secular: Religion and Politics Worldwide.* New York: Cambridge University Press.

North, Douglass. 1981. *Structure and Change in Economic History.* New York: W. W. Norton.

Northrop, Douglas. 2004. *Veiled Empire: Gender and Power in Stalinist Central Asia.* Ithaca, NY: Cornell University Press.

Nove, Alec. 1969. *An Economic History of the USSR.* London: Penguin Press.

Nyang, Sulayman. 2002. "Religion and the Maintenance of Boundaries." In *Islamic Political Ethics,* ed. Sohail Hashmi. Princeton, NJ: Princeton University Press.

Oleszczuk, Thomas. 1988. *Political Justice in the USSR: Dissent and Repression in Lithuania, 1969–1987.* New York: Columbia University Press.

Olsen, Daniel. 1999. "Religious Pluralism and US Church Membership: A Reassessment." *Sociology of Religion* 60(2): 149–73.

Osa, Maryjane. 1989. "Resistance, Persistence, and Change: The Transformation of the Catholic Church in Poland." *Eastern European Politics and Societies* 3(2): 268–99.

———. 1997. "Creating Solidarity: The Religious Foundations of the Polish Social Movement." *East European Politics and Societies* 11(2): 339–66.

Pascal, Blaise. 1932. *Penses.* Trans. F. W. Trotter. London: J. M. Dent & Sons.

Peris, Daniel. 1998. *Storming the Heavens: The Soviet League of the Militant Godless.* Ithaca, NY: Cornell University Press.

Plekhanov, George. [1892] 1992. "Notes to Engels' Ludwig Feuerbach." In *Russian Philosophy,* ed. James Edie, James Scalan, and Mary-Barbara Zeldin. Knoxville: University of Tennessee Press.

Poliakov, Sergei. 1992. *Everyday Islam: Religion and Tradition in Rural Central Asia.* New York: M. E. Sharpe.

Pollack, Detlef. 1994. *Kirche in der Organisationsgesellschaft.* Stuttgart: Kohlhammer.

Pospielovsky, Dimitry. 1984. The *Russian Church under the Soviet Regime, 1917–1982.* Vols. 1 and 2. New York: St. Vladimir's Press.

———. 1987. *A History of Marxist-Leninist Atheism and Soviet Antireligious Policies.* New York: St. Martin's Press.

Powell, David E. 1975. *Antireligious Propaganda in the Soviet Union: A Study of Mass Persuasion*. Cambridge, MA: MIT Press.

Pungur, Joseph. 1992. "Protestantism in Hungary: The Communist Era." In *Protestantism and Politics in Eastern Europe and Russia*, ed. Sabrina Ramet. London: Duke University Press.

Raedts, Peter. 1987. *Richard Rufus of Cornwall and the Tradition of Oxford Theology*. New York: Oxford University Press.

Ramet, Sabrina P. 1986. *Social Currents in Eastern Europe*. Durham, NC: Duke University Press.

———. 1993. *Religious Policy in the Soviet Union*. Cambridge, England: Cambridge University Press.

———. 1998. *Nihil Obstat: Religion, Politics, and Social Change in East-Central Europe and Russia*. Durham, NC: Duke University Press.

Rashid, Ahmed. 1994. *The Resurgence of Central Asia: Islam or Nationalism?* London: Oxford University Press.

———. 2001. "The Fires of Faith in Central Asia." *World Policy Journal* (Spring): 45–55.

Ratushinskaya, Irina. 1987. *Religious Prisoners in the USSR*. Keston, England: Greenfire Books.

Reban, Milan. 1981. "Czechoslovakia." In *The Politics of Ethnicity in Eastern Europe*, ed. George Klein and Milan Reban. New York: Columbia University Press.

Regnerus, Mark, and Christian Smith. 1998. "Selective Deprivation among American Religious Traditions: The Reversal of the Great Reversal." *Social Forces* 76(4): 1347–72.

Remeikis, Thomas. 1980. *Opposition to Soviet Rule in Lithuania, 1945–1980*. Chicago: Institute of Lithuanian Studies Press.

Rhodes, Anthony. 1992. *The Vatican in the Age of the Cold War, 1945–1980*. Wilby, England: Michael Russell Publishing.

Rinaldo, Peter M. 2000. *Atheists, Agnostics, and Deists in America*. New York: DorPete Press.

Robbins, Thomas. 1988. *Cults, Converts, and Charisma*. Beverly Hills, CA: Sage.

Ro'I, Yaacov. 1984. *The USSR and the Muslim World: Issues in Domestic and Foreign Policy*. London: George Allen & Unwin.

Rywkin, Michael. 1982. *Moscow's Muslim Challenge: Soviet Central Asia*. New York: M. E. Sharpe.

Sawatsky, Walter. 1984. "Soviet Evangelicals Today." *Occasional Papers on Religion in Eastern Europe* 4(2): 1–20.

Scherer, John L. 1984. *USSR Facts and Figures Annual*. New York: Academic Press International.

Schumacher, E. F. 1977. *A Guide for the Perplexed*. New York: Harper & Row.

Schumpeter, J. 1943. *Capitalism, Socialism and Democracy*. London: Harper.

Schwartz, Solomon. 1951. *The Jews in the Soviet Union*. Syracuse, NY: Syracuse University Press.

Shaffer, Harry. 1974. *The Soviet Treatment of Jews*. New York: Praeger Publishers.

Shahrani, M. Nazif. 1995. "Islam and the Political Culture of 'Scientific Atheism' in Post-Communist Central Asia: Future Predicaments." In *The Politics of*

Religion in Russia and the New States of Eurasia, ed. Michael Bourdeaux. New York: M. E. Sharpe.

Sherkat, Darren. 1997. "Embedding Religious Choices: Preferences and Social Constraints into Rational Choice Theories of Religious Behavior." In *Rational Choice Theory and Religion: Summary and Assessment,* ed. Lawrence A Young. New York: Routledge.

———. 2003. "Religious Socialization: Sources of Influence and Influences of Agency." In *Handbook of the Sociology of Religion,* ed. Michele Dillon. New York: Cambridge University Press.

Sherkat, Darren, and Christopher G. Ellison. 1999. "Recent Developments and Current Controversies in the Sociology of Religion." *Annual Review of Sociology* 25: 363–94.

Sherkat, Darren, and John Wilson. 1995. "Preferences, Constraints, and Choices in Religious Markets: An Examination of Religious Switching and Apostasy." *Social Forces* 73(3): 993–1026.

Šik, Ota. 1976. *The Third Way: Marxist-Leninist Theory and Modern Industrial Society.* Trans. Marian Sling. London: Wildwood House.

Sipaviciene, Audra. 1997. *International Migration in Lithuania.* Vilnius: Lithuanian Institute of Philosophy and Sociology.

Smith, Adam. [1776] 1965. *An Inquiry into the Nature and Causes of the Wealth of Nations.* New York: Modern Library.

Smith, Christian. 1998. *American Evangelicalism: Embattled and Thriving.* Chicago: University of Chicago Press.

———. 2000. *Christian America? What Evangelicals Really Want.* Berkeley: University of California Press.

———. 2003. *Moral Believing Animals.* New York: Oxford University Press.

Solchanyk, Roman. 1985. "Poland and the Soviet West." In *Soviet Nationalities in Strategic Perspective,* ed. S. Enders Wimbush. New York: St. Martin's Press.

Sorokin, Pitirim. [1943] 1998. *On the Practice of Sociology.* Ed. Barry V. Johnson. Chicago: University of Chicago Press.

Stalin, Joseph. 1940. *Stalin's "Kampf": Joseph Stalin's Credo.* Edited by M. R. Warner. New York: Soskin & Company.

Stark, Rodney. 1996a. *The Rise of Christianity: A Sociologists Reconsiders History.* Princeton, NJ: Princeton University Press.

———. 1996b. "Why Religious Movements Succeed or Fail: A Revised General Model." *Journal of Contemporary Religion* 11(2): 133–46.

———. 2000. "Secularization R.I.P." In *The Secularization Debate,* ed. William Swatos and Daniel Olson. New York: Rowman & Littlefield Publishers.

———. 2001. *One True God: Historical Consequences of Monotheism.* Princeton, NJ: Princeton University Press.

Stark, Rodney, and William Bainbridge. 1987. *A Theory of Religion.* New York: Peter Lang.

Stark, Rodney, and William Bainbridge. 1997. *Religion, Deviance, and Social Control.* New York: Routledge.

Stark, Rodney, and Roger Finke. 2000. *Acts of Faith.* Berkeley: University of California Press.

Stark, Rodney, and Laurence R. Iannaccone. 1994. "A Supply-Side Reinterpretation of the 'Secularization' of Europe." *Journal for the Scientific Study of Religion* 33(3): 230–52.

Stark, Rodney, and James C. McCann. 1993. "Market Forces and Catholic Commitment: Exploring the New Paradigm." *Journal for the Scientific Study of Religion* 32(2): 111–24.

Stehle, Hansjakob. 1965. *The Independent Satellite: Society and Politics in Poland since 1945*. London: Pall Mall Press.

Stenger, Victor. 2007. *God: The Failed Hypothesis. How Science Shows That God Does Not Exist*. New York: Prometheus Books.

Sun, Anna Xiao Dong. 2005. "The Fate of Confucianism as a Religion in Socialist China: Controversies and Paradoxes." In *State, Market and Religions in Chinese Societies*, ed. Fenggang Yang and Joseph Tamney. Boston: Brill.

Swatos, William. 1994. *Politics and Religion in Central and Eastern Europe*. London: Praeger.

Swatos, William, and Daniel Olson. 2000. *The Secularization Debate*. Lanham, MD: Rowman & Littlefield Publishers.

Szczesniak, Boleslaw. 1959. *The Russian Revolution and Religion: A Collection of Documents Concerning the Suppression of Religion by the Communists, 1917–1925*. South Bend: University of Notre Dame Press.

Taheri, Amir. 1989. *Crescent in a Red Sky: The Future of Islam in the Soviet Union*. London: Hutchinson & Co.

Thrower, James. 1983. *Marxist-Leninist "Scientific-Atheism" and the Study of Religion and Atheism in the USSR*. Berlin: Mouton Publishers.

———. 1992. *Marxism-Leninism as the Civil Religion of Soviet Society: God's Commissar*. Lewiston, NY: E. Mellen Press.

Tishkov, Valerii A. 1997. *Ethnicity, Nationalism and Conflict in and after the Soviet Union: A Mind Aflame*. London: Sage.

Tismaneanu, Vladimir. 1988. *The Crisis of Marxist Ideology in Eastern Europe*. New York: Routledge.

Tismaneff, N. S. 1942. *Religion in Soviet Russia, 1917–1942*. New York: Sheed & Ward.

Tobias, Robert. 1956. *Communitst-Christian Encounter in East Europe*. Indianapolis: School of Religion Press.

Tomka, Miklos. 1995. "The Changing Social Role of Religion in Eastern and Central Europe: Religion's Revival and Its Contradictions." *Social Compass* 42(1): 17–26.

Trapl, Milos. *Political Catholicism and the Czechoslovak People's Party in Czechoslovakia, 1918–1938*. New York: Columbia University Press.

Trofimov, Dmitry. 1995. *Islam in the Political Culture of the Former Soviet Union: Central Asia and Azerbaijan*. Hamburg: University of Hamburg.

Trotsky, Leon. 1961. *The History of the Russian Revolution*. Trans. Max Eastman. Ann Arbor: University of Michigan Press.

Tucker, Robert. 1961. *Philosophy and the Myth in the Thought of Karl Marx*. Cambridge, England: Cambridge University Press.

Tumarkin, Nina. 1997. *Lenin Lives! The Lenin Cult in Soviet Russia*. Cambridge, MA: Harvard University Press.

Tuzmuhamedov, R. 1973. *How the National Question Was Solved in the Soviet Central Asia (A Reply to Falsifiers)*. Moscow: Progress Publishers.

Van den Bercken, William. 1989. *Ideology and Atheism in the Soviet Union*. New York: Mounton de Gruyter.

Vardys, V. Stanley. 1978. *The Catholic Church, Dissent and Nationality in Soviet Lithuania*. New York: Columbia University Press.

Vignieri, Vittorio. 1965. "Soviet Policy toward Religion in Lithuania: The Case of Roman Catholicism." In *Lithuania under the Soviets: Portrait of a Nation, 1940–65*, ed. V. Stanley Vardys. New York: Frederick A. Praeger.

Voas, David, Alasdair Crockett, and Daniel Olson. 2002. "Religious Pluralism and Participation: Why Previous Research Is Wrong." *American Sociological Review* 67(2): 212–30.

Von Stackelberg, Georg. 1967. "The Tenacity of Islam in Soviet Central Asia." In *Religion and the Search for New Ideals in the USSR*, ed. William Fletcher and Anthony Strover. New York: Praeger.

Wallace, Anthony. 1966. *Religion: An Anthropological View*. New York: Random House.

Walters, Philip. 1999. " The Russian Orthodox Church and Foreign Christianity." In *Proselytism and Orthodoxy in Russia*, ed. John Witte and Michael Bourdeaux. New York: Orbis Books.

———. 2002. "The Encyclopedia of Religious Life in Russia Today: A Landmark Research Project." *Religion, State, and Society* 30(2): 155–60.

Wanner, Catherine. 1998. *Burden of Dreams: History and Identity in Post-Soviet Ukraine*. University Park: Pennsylvania State University Press.

Warner, R. Stephen. 1993. "Work in the Progress toward a New Paradigm for the Sociological Study of Religion in the United States." *American Journal of Sociology* 98(5): 1044–93.

Weber, Max. 1978. *Economy and Society*. Edited by Guenther Roth and Claus Wittich. Berkeley: University of California Press.

Wheeler, Geoffrey. 1969. "National and Religious Consciousness in Soviet Islam." In *Religion and the Soviet State: A Dilemma of Power*, ed. Max Hayward and William Fletcher. New York: Praeger Publishers.

White, Stephen, et al. 2000. "Religion and Political Action in Postcommunist Europe." *Political Studies* 48: 681–705.

Wilhelm, Bernhard. 1971. "Moslems in the Soviet Union, 1948–1954." In *Aspects of Religion in the Soviet Union*, ed. Richard Marshall. Chicago: University of Chicago Press.

Wimbush, S. Enders. 1985. *Soviet Nationalities in Strategic Perspective*. New York: St. Martin's Press.

Wimer, Alice. 1986. "Some Observations on the Hungarian Reformed Church." *Occasional Papers on Religion in Eastern Europe* 6(4): 40–44.

Witte, John, and Michael Bourdeaux. 1999. *Proselytism and Orthodox in Russia*. New York: Orbis Books.

Wittgenstein, Ludwig. 1961. *Tractatus Logico-Philosophicus*. Trans. D. F. Pears and B. F. McGuinness. London: Routledge & Kegan Paul.

Woodberry, Robert D. 1996. "Evangelicals and Politics: Surveying a Contemporary Mason-Dixon Line." Paper presented at the American Sociological Association conference, August 24, 1996, New York.

Wooten, David. 1992. "New Histories in Atheism." In *Atheism from the Reformation to the Enlightenment,* ed. Michael Hunter and David Wooton. Oxford: Clarendon Press.

World Values Survey [computer file]. 1981–84, 1990–93, and 1995–97. Ronald Inglehart et al., producers. Inter-university Consortium for Political and Social Research.

Wuthnow, Robert. 1987. *Meaning and the Moral Order: Explorations in Cultural Analysis.* Berkeley: University of California Press.

————. 1989. *Communities of Discourse: Ideology and Social Structure in the Reformation, the Enlightenment, and European Socialism.* Cambridge, MA: Harvard University Press.

Wynot, Jennifer. 2003. "Russian Orthodox Monasteries Response to the Relics Exposing Campaign, 1917–1922." *Religion in Eastern Europe* 23(1): 24–38.

Yakovlev, Alexander N. 2002. *A Century of Violence in Soviet Russia.* Trans. Anthony Austin. New Haven, CT: Yale University Press.

Yang, Fenggang. 2006. "The Red, Black, and Grey Markets of Religion in China." *Sociological Quarterly* 47: 93–122.

Yaroslavsky, E. 1934. *Religion in the U.S.S.R.* New York: International Publishers.

Yoder, Jennifer A. 1999. *From East Germans to Germans?* Durham, NC: Duke University Press.

Young, Glennys. 1997a. *Power and the Sacred in Revolutionary Russia: Religious Activists in the Village.* University Park: Pennsylvania State University Press.

Young, Lawrence. 1997b. *Rational Choice Theory and Religion: Summary and Assessment.* New York: Routledge.

Yurchak, Alexei. 2006. *Everything Was Forever, until It Was No More.* Princeton, NJ: Princeton University Press.

Zaehner, R. C. 1986. *The Concise Encyclopedia of Living Faiths.* London: Hutchinson.

Zwick, Peter. 1983. *National Communism.* Boulder: Westview Press.

Zygmunt, Joseph. 2000. "When Prophecies Fail." In *Expecting Armageddon: Essential Readings in Failed Prophecy,* ed. Jon Stone. New York: Routledge.

Index

Note: Italicized page numbers indicate tables and figures.

Text:	10/13 Sabon
Display:	Sabon
Indexer:	Margie Towery
Illustrator:	Bill Nelson
Compositor:	BookMatters, Berkeley
Printer and binder:	Sheridan Books, Inc.